HOPE AND THE LONGING FOR UTOPIA

Hope and the Longing for Utopia

Futures and Illusions in Theology and Narrative

Edited by
DANIEL BOSCALJON

☙PICKWICK *Publications* • Eugene, Oregon

HOPE AND THE LONGING FOR UTOPIA
Futures and Illusions in Theology and Narrative

Copyright © 2014 Wipf and Stock Publishers. All rights reserved. Except for brief quotations in critical publications or reviews, no part of this book may be reproduced in any manner without prior written permission from the publisher. Write: Permissions. Wipf and Stock Publishers, 199 W. 8th Ave., Suite 3, Eugene, OR 97401.

Pickwick Publications
An Imprint of Wipf and Stock Publishers
199 W. 8th Ave., Suite 3
Eugene, OR 97401

www.wipfandstock.com

ISBN 13: 978-1-62032-933-7

Cataloguing-in-Publication Data

Hope and the longing for utopia : futures and illusions in theology and narrative / edited by Daniel Boscaljon

xx + 240 p. ; 23 cm. Includes bibliographical references.

ISBN 13: 978-1-62032-933-7

1. Utopias. 2. Utopias—Philosophy. 3. Utopias—Religion. 4. Utopias—Literature. 5. Paradise. I. Boscaljon, Daniel. II. Title.

BL540 B65 2014

Manufactured in the U.S.A.

To David Jasper,
for his support of Theology and Literature at Iowa
and around the world.

There is no religion either in Saint Thomas More's Utopia. *Nothing would be gained by replacing one religion with another. Being neither religious nor secular, More's utopia lies beyond such cleavage. It does not replace one holier-than-thou ideology of the good life and its final vocabulary with another, perhaps softer but equally noxious, ideological version of a similarly final solution. In other words, no island is merely an island, exclusively governed by so-called fundamentalists or by self-styled secularists. Utopia is a challenge to both. Horrifying both of them, it stands or falls as though it were "One nation under God." This phrase is as secular as it is religious. Besides establishing no religion, it warns the nation against the imperialistic pretense of one ultimate and final nation.*

Gabriel Vahanian
Praise of the Secular

Contents

Biographical Information for Contributors | ix
Introduction: The Value of Cultivating Longing in a Secularized World | xiii
—Daniel Boscaljon

Part 1: Relating Hope and Utopia

1 Utopia and Narrative: Theology between the Boundaries of Overhumanization and Hypertheism | 3
 —Verna Ehret

2 Hope, Hatred, and the Ambiguities of Utopic Longing | 23
 —Diana Fritz Cates

3 What Means *Utopia* to Us? Reconsidering More's Message | 41
 — Marybeth Baggett

4 Desiring Utopian Subjects: Collectivity and Its Discontents | 58
 —Holly White

Part 2: Historical and Literary Utopian Visions

5 John Calvin, Geneva, and Godly Patriarchs: Hope and Reality in the Creation of a Christian Utopia | 81
 —Ezra L. Plank

6 Fruit, Fossils, Footprints: Cathecting Utopia in the Work of Miyazawa Kenji | 96
 —Melissa Anne-Marie Curley

7 Walter Kerr's Utopia of Re-Creation | 119
 —Benjamin K. Hunnicutt

8 Reframed Hope: Transcendent Technology and Spiraling Subjectivity in Dystopian Cinema | 137
 —Everett Hamner

Part 3: The Hope for Atheism as a Religious Utopia

9 Who We Are Is God's Dying: The Real Presence of God's Absence in Bonhoeffer's Prison Poems | 157
—Steven Schroeder

10 TechnoTopia: The Convergence of Art and Technology in the Twentieth Century and Beyond | 180
— J. Sage Elwell

11 The Coming Community: Agamben, Benjamin, and the Hope for a Materialist-Messianic Redemption of the Present | 194
—W. David Hall

12 No-Places for Sacred Communities: Hope and the Failure of *Fight Club* | 218
—Daniel Boscaljon

Biographical Information for Contributors

Marybeth Baggett is Assistant Professor of English at Liberty University in Lynchburg, VA. Her research and teaching interests include literary theory, contemporary American literature, science fiction, and dystopian literature, with particular concern for the works of Kurt Vonnegut. Recent presentations cover topics such as humor as hope in Vonnegut's *Player Piano*, the function of grace as salve for political division in Marilynne Robinson's *Gilead*, and the usefulness of Lacan's gaze as a means of understanding Nella Larsen's *Quicksand*. An essay version of this Larsen presentation appears in the Fall 2012 issue of *The Griot*.

Daniel Boscaljon has a doctoral degree in Religious Studies with an emphasis in secularism and theology, and a doctoral degree in English with an emphasis in nineteenth-century American Literature. His interdisciplinary work in both fields explores the liminal margins of human experience, particularly the value of humility and uncertainty. He is the author of *Vigilant Faith: Passionate Agnosticism in a Secular World* (University of Virginia Press, 2013) and editor of *Resisting the Place of Belonging* (Ashgate, 2013).

Diana Fritz Cates is Professor and Chair of the Department of Religious Studies at The University of Iowa. Her research and teaching focus on religious studies, religious ethics, and moral psychology. She is the author of many publications that concern matters of virtue, vice, care, and emotion, including *Choosing to Feel: Virtue, Friendship, and Compassion for Friends* (Georgetown University Press, 1997) and *Aquinas on the Emotions: A Religious-Ethical Inquiry* (Georgetown University Press, 2009).

Melissa Anne-Marie Curley is Assistant Professor of Japanese religion at the University of Iowa. Her research focuses on modern Japanese Buddhism, particularly the interaction of sectarian Pure Land thought and Kyoto School philosophy. Recent publications include "Shinshū Studies and the Legacy of Liberal Thought," in *The Social Dimension of Shin Buddhism*, ed. Ugo Dessì (Brill, 2010) and "Zen-boy Ikkyū," in *Little Buddhas* (Oxford, 2013).

Verna Marina Ehret is an Associate Professor of Religious Studies at Mercyhurst University in Erie, Pennsylvania. Her primary fields of study are philosophical and constructive theology. She has given a number of presentations on redemption and globalization, and her current research focuses on religion, humanism, narrative, and globalization.

J. Sage Elwell is Associate Professor of Religion, Art, and Visual Culture at Texas Christian University. He is author of *Crisis of Transcendence: A Theology of Digital Art and Culture* (Rowman and Littlefield, 2011) and also publishes and presents in the areas of suffering and embodiment, the aesthetics of atrocity, religion and film, and atheism and the arts. He also works as an artist in digital media, photography, and book art.

W. David Hall is Associate Professor of Religion and Philosophy at Centre College. He is editor of and contributor to *Paul Ricoeur and Contemporary Moral Thought* and author of *Paul Ricoeur and the Poetic Imperative*. He has published broadly in the areas of phenomenology, philosophical theology, rhetoric and philosophy, and political philosophy.

Everett Hamner is Associate Professor of English at Western Illinois University—Quad Cities. His essays may be found in *American Literature*, *Science Fiction Studies*, *Modern Fiction Studies*, and *Religion and Literature*. His primary research and teaching interests are in relationships between contemporary fiction and film, global religions and postsecular theory, and intersections of science, technology, and culture.

Benjamin K. Hunnicutt has been a professor of Leisure Studies at The University of Iowa since 1975. He is the author of *Kellogg's Six-Hour Day*; *Work Without End: Abandoning Shorter Hours for the Right to Work*; and *Free Time: The Forgotten American Dream* (Temple Press, 2013). In addition to working as a consultant to unions and businesses interested in shorter work hours and the potential of leisure to improve the community and workplace, Hunnicutt has written for *The Wall Street Journal* and appeared in a variety of nationally and internationally broadcast television and radio programs.

Ezra L. Plank received his PhD from the Department of Religious Studies at The University of Iowa. His dissertation, entitled *Creating Perfect Families: The French Reformed Church and Family Formation, 1559–1685*, examined the zealous program of early modern French Reformed Churches to create domestic microcosms of the larger church, changing nuclear families into spiritual communities. His historical research relies heavily on the use of church discipline records to gain insights into how common people understood, co-opted, and accepted/contested theological ideas.

Steven Schroeder earned his PhD in Ethics and Society from the University of Chicago in 1982. He is the co-founder, with composer Clarice Assad, of the Virtual Artists Collective (vacpoetry.org) that has published fifty collections of poetry since it began in 2004. From 2002–2009 he taught philosophy, poetry, and peace studies at Shenzhen University in China. He currently teaches at the University of Chicago in Asian Classics and the Basic Program of Liberal Education for Adults. His most recent poetry collections are *Turn* and (with Debby Sou Vai Keng) *a guest giving way like ice melting: thirteen ways of looking at laozi*. *Four Truths*, a collection of three short stories and a drama in verse (with paintings by Debby Sou Vai Keng) was published by Wipf & Stock in 2011. A new poetry collaboration with David Breeden, *Raging for the Exit*, was published by Wipf & Stock in 2012.

Holly White is a PhD candidate in the Religion Department at Syracuse University in Syracuse, New York. Her dissertation research analyzes the roles of desire and transcendence in the anti-foundationalist philosophies of Luce Irigaray and Gilles Deleuze. She has taught courses at Syracuse and at Ithaca College on the topics of Utopia, modernity and Western religion, and world religions.

Introduction

The Value of Cultivating Longing in a Secularized World

—*Daniel Boscaljon*

With the blessings of technology, we have infused the twenty-first-century world with matters of the moment: we have acquired a taste for what occurs *now* and no longer have the patience to suffer our dreams to come to fruition. Marketers create a craving for consumption, convenience, and certainty: they frame digital technologies as tools whose use is restricted to temporarily satiating such demands. Eliminating the arduous temporal gap that more ephemeral goods demand, our world provides a series of superficial goods whose certain attainment encourages us to sacrifice the search for that which would provide more authentic fulfillment. Because distractions are available at the swipe of a finger or touch of a button, our scale of time has been reduced, shriveling into the infinitesimal quantities that only our technology could measure: we have learned to become irate when a message that would have taken weeks to deliver requires more than three minutes to process. Our frenzied expectations, gratified for a price that we contentedly pay, keep our attentions fixated on *now*. Problematically, our tendency to sacrifice what is uncertain (the concrete symbols of hope, the specific system of utopia) for that which is easily and often instantly available has diminished our awareness of *longing* as an important human capacity—as well as the attendant virtues of patience, fortitude and perseverance.

    This collection of essays explores possible modes of resisting this trend, once again expanding the potential of the future to incorporate those distant goods capable of reminding us that humans once could long wistfully toward what remained uncertain. Building from definitions of hope and utopia and continuing through historical and contemporary appropriations of these subjects, the collection ends by evoking potential hopes for the continuing work of theology in a secular future. Corporately, the collection demonstrates the continued relevance of religion and theology in a future that even technology cannot entirely disenchant. Spanning a variety of different historical times, cultural mediums and theoretical backgrounds, these essays disclose how we regain access to longing and rekindle our desire for a good future through embracing our frailty and humility with a courage capable of defeating the resigned stance of reductionists.

The prosthetic reach of technology, which instantly offers a set of digitally rendered possibilities, constructs a realm of artificial omnipotence in which we seem anything but frail, humble or finite. Indeed, the convenience and allure of this instantaneous digital world successfully distracts us from understanding the horror induced by a lack of future: we repress our anxieties and mediate them through cultural artifacts that testify to the trauma caused by dwelling in worlds with foreshortened futures. Building on worries sparked with the Cold War threat of immanent annihilation, these post-apocalyptic works feature characters with no hopes for futures. Ranging from *The Terminator* to *The Walking Dead*, such works emphasize a fated and known end of existence that they bleakly insist is inevitable. Perhaps the most resonant example of brute hopelessness is Cormac McCarthy's 2006 novel *The Road*, which introduces readers to a world that is dying, an ashen world of darkness and silence where the remaining humans can do little more than delay their own deaths. This vision of a futureless end shows that hopes in progress were illusion: it induced evisceration, not culmination. Religious beliefs are similarly negated: all attempts to wrestle meaning from the ashes of human pain proved illusory instead of prophetic. Suffering brought nothing more than the delay of death and the need to endure more suffering. McCarthy offers no reason for the appearance of this world, and the protagonist's attempts to make meaning out of the situation falter, stillborn, through a vaguely summoned insistence that he is one of the "good" guys. Offering a secularized wasteland of unrelenting ashen decay, McCarthy forces readers to face the horrors of making choices in a space where the end truly is imminent. The meaninglessness of this end works to deprive readers of understanding any reason for continuation, and even if one sympathizes with the father's desire to provide for his son, why the son would continue to live remains unanswered.

Our unthinking emphasis on *now* and forgetfulness concerning the future causes two serious problems. First, a pernicious cycle develops as we find that trivial goods adequately distract us from deeper sorrows, although successfully inducing our inattention leads us to neglect the work of *repairing* the world in ways that permit healing. This situation comes with excellent economic advantages: misery makes money, as any one distraction occurs with diminishing returns. Unable to wait, we purchase goods we cannot afford in order to gain the moment of forgetfulness capable of displacing our worry. The distractions become increasingly ill-suited to long-term sustenance, and we remain starved for a world filled with compassion instead of suffering—this, in turn, encourages us to once again indulge in what is certain and capable of quickly attending to our desire for distraction. Corporations calculate the economic advantages of these types of goods, things that all-too-often are purchased on credit, and the cycle continues.

A second problem with losing longing emerges when we lose sight of the viability of goods that would require that work of longing, the willingness to desire temporally distant goods beyond our capacity to grasp with certainty. These goods emerge at individual and communal levels—fulfillment, authenticity, security, companionship—that require, as Freud recognized in *Civilization and its Discontents*, a willingness to defer our drive toward pleasure and the decision to sublimate our passions toward attaining more permanent and lofty ends. We forget the magic of uncertainty, the pleasure of surprise, the charm of the unexpected; we relinquish our grasp on the slow process of change by making the same kinds of demands in the same sorts of ways—or, perhaps more often, we simply resign ourselves to accepting the world as it is. Ignoring how we could work to creatively transform the world, we manage to forget that we are culpable for the world's being as it is.

Worse, perhaps, than losing access to the ends toward which our longing would move us is forgetting our capacity for longing altogether. If we become primarily attuned to what is easy and available, our sensitivity to what is distant or arduous will atrophy: our awareness of goods would become restricted to merchandise available for purchase. Longing requires that we balance a positive desire to attain a distant good with a respect for its distance. To desire to long after something curtails our movements toward it: we desire, but delay seeking gratification. We allow our longing to build, allow it to reveal to us our depths, accept the gifts of patience and fortitude that it bestows. We gain an increased awareness of our temporal trajectories, becoming more familiar with our orientation toward a particular goal. Through longing, we gain access to our ability to relate to that which is not consumed, toward that which remains distant and distinct from us, and thereby we maintain our appetite for the fascinating, the mysterious and the tremendous.

A symptom of dwelling in a world without a future, a world that we increasingly embrace, emerges when hope and longing are anchored to an inaccessible past. Although future hopes remain arduous and uncertain, our inability to truly inhabit our memories fills those who fixate there with despair. Additionally, nostalgia causes us to neglect both the good available in potential futures and the suffering manifest in our actual presents. McCarthy's world, like that created in *The Walking Dead* series, is a world without meaning, without hope, without society, without good. Persevering through a dying world is underscored as tragic instead of foolish, but the potency of the book reflects back to us the chilling actualization of our current choices.

Acknowledging the dangers that attend the diminution of our capacity for longing, this book offers a series of essays contemplating the value of two conceptual objects that require longing: hope and utopia. The most robust treatments of hope have emerged in the Christian theological tradition, while utopia is a predominantly secular concept developed atheistically. Hope is also a nonreligious capacity to endure suffering for uncertain ends, and the secular ideal of utopia has inspired religious sects to embody the best possibly future. Both conceptions embrace a positive sense of the future that introduces *longing* within the human heart.

Hope is occasionally confused with faith, but they differ relative to their preference of objects: while objects of faith tend to largely be conceptual and anchored in the present (I believe in X (now)), objects of hope tend to be concrete and anchored in the future. The most authentic objects of faith are non-falsifiable, and assist individuals in each moment by integrating the finite and the infinite; contrariwise, objects of hope are either fulfilled or disappointed at some future point. One's hopes either come to fruition in an occurrent future or are revealed as mere illusions. Objects of an illusory hope—a losing lottery ticket, a get-well-soon card for someone who did not, invitations to a cancelled wedding—quickly become objects that represent despair, pointing out the folly of desiring a concrete indication of what is yet to come.

Like hopes, utopias produce a sense of displacement—often these are temporal, inviting us to dwell within their fictional confines. Hopes emerge through symbols that connect, concretely, the imperfect present and a preferred future: they form bridges of specific possibilities that we wish to see come to fruition. Remaining oriented toward hope prevents us from slipping into despair, which encourages us to want to transform a hope into a certainty, to will it to become a concrete and certain future—problematically, of course, this ignores the fragility of hope, its audacious tendency to inspire us to greatness that ends up, nonetheless, falling short of our desired goal. Like all symbols, however, they persist in a quiet anticipation of becoming activated by someone inspired to embrace its specific possibility.

Unlike hope, which is symbolic, utopias tend to be narrative in their structuration: they disclose an arc that bridges to the audience's present, inviting an integration toward the potential future suggested. An odd form of narrative, however, this arc closes at its end, presenting a perfected world without need for change. This quality of utopia allows it to function as a symbol, albeit one with a narrative foundation, and induces our longing in a similar way—the future is given as something we can grasp as a certainty. Utopias are presented as though they have always already happened—all that is lacking is our participation within them. Moreover, utopias are frequently set up as objectival in their unwavering permanence: having already actualized perfection, inhabitants of a utopic community find change to be threatening. Individuals who are trapped in a world of uncertainty and disappointment are comforted by the allure of a dependable world, one where one's values are permanently rendered and threats to happiness have been abolished. The allure of a utopic narrative arc, in other words, is its beatific conclusion—the unveilation of an absolute system in which all flaws have been fixed. Providing an end to history, utopias undermine the dynamic quality of narrative, driving it into a quiescence that humans find safe and comforting. The best utopic narratives move us to an extent that we are conscripted into concretizing them in our surrounding world: we actively seek to transform a potential future into a reality, forging the narrative into a symbol.

The essays in this volume largely involve interdisciplinary engagements with narrative and theology, which is especially important as utopic visions primarily emerge in terms of narratives, offering stories depicting a place or time distant from contemporary society that attempts to persuade an audience of what must be done to eliminate what the author views as problematic. The tension inherent in the genre is that its very perfection frequently leads to a fear of change, and a conservative drive toward stasis. The unspoken implication underlying many versions of utopia is that, even if perfect, this society's perfection would be limited to its one, ideal, timeless moment. Nonetheless, the dream of seeing one's values enshrined permanently, certainly, pushes us to displace our doubts and embrace this potential future as though it were certain. Teasing apart the theological and philosophical underpinnings of utopian thinking in general, examining particular historical and literary examples of utopia, and gesturing toward the promise of atheistic utopias that discard the fundamentalism of the New Atheists, this collection introduces new possibilities for humans to dwell peacefully and justly with each other. Together, the chapters contribute toward a revitalized sense of the potentiality of utopic thinking, one that grounds its hopes in an embrace of human fragility, failure and imperfection instead of striving for an unrealistic and unrealizable mode of certainty. Put otherwise, these essays direct readers to understand how the value of both hope and utopia most appropriately rest in creating a sense of longing or expectation capable of encouraging our best efforts for the greatest good.

The diversity of materials analyzed and theorists described in this collection testifies to the universal importance of this discussion, and also offers readers a sense of how questions of hope and utopia permeate popular culture and critical thought. The best utopic visions are ambiguous, if not ironic: they direct our attention to the possibility of an accessible good and simultaneously show the impossibility of its enactment. Often, utopic narratives warn that concretizing the depicted society into human communities requires a disciplinary system that undermines the tenets that had initially induced our longing. Most importantly, the wide variety illuminates how a set of problems transcends particular historical and cultural contexts in ways that suggest why the question of hope and utopia remains universal. Utopia shows us that the good place that we desire is the no-place of sheer potentiality—the unreal, the uncertain, the unknown. Engineering our longing, utopias offer a narrative trajectory that instructs us concerning how to acquire the absolute best possibilities.

Part I offers a set of essays that illuminate ways to connect hope and utopia, introducing many of the major tensions developed throughout the remainder of the book. Each of these essays explores the tension located in the importance of emphasizing *longing*—a desire that remains importantly unmet. Verna Ehret's opening essay provides a backdrop for the volume: she discusses the importance of secularism in the twenty-first century before using "utopia" to diagnose the error of religious and atheist fundamentalisms, and concludes by advocating the use of transcontextual narratives capable of embracing continual transformation and renewal, ultimately concluding that utopia summons us to journeys, not destinations. In the second essay, Diana Fritz Cates argues for the value of utopic longing through a Thomistic moral psychology. She warns, however, that there is a risk inherent in hope: hope can give way to hatred if we take our eyes off the distant good for which we long and focus on the obstacles that stand in our way. The third essay provides a rereading of More's *Utopia*; in it, Marybeth Baggett reminds readers that the founding text of the genre featured far more ambiguities than what is currently remembered as More summons his reader to balance an ethical hermeneutic with a sense of social responsibility. Finally, Holly White's "Desiring Utopian Subjects: Collectivity and its Discontents" describes how utopic visions provide humans with a powerful reminder of a desire for collectivity, an embrace of collective (not individual) potentialities that challenge our resigned embrace of the status quo, which dialectically emerges as an individual hope. Theoretically oriented, these essays provide the helpful task of defining hope and utopia as important topics to think today.

Moving through a wide array of historical and cultural examples, the essays in Part II concretize the tensions connecting hope and utopia. The variety of examples illuminate the commonalities that bind questions of hope and utopia together, as each concrete existence shows how an actualized utopia inevitably disappoints. Ezra Plank shows how this lesson infected the hopes of Calvin's Geneva, especially at the micro-communal level of the family. Melissa Anne-Marie Curley demonstrates this through a reading of Kenji's Japanese literature, showing how Buddhist utopias emerge most hopefully in visions of tension and potentiality—not in a fascist actuality. Benjamin Hunnicutt's discussion of Walter Kerr discloses the way that utopic visions influence everyday life, especially in terms of the split between labor and leisure. Finally, Everett Hamner's discussion of science fiction shows how the fears of an actualized "utopia" emerge in the technologically driven plots of sci-fi cinema that are increasingly postsecular in their appropriation of religion. Ultimately, these essays show the value of utopic longings—and the importance of the "good place" remaining a place toward which we strive but do not attain.

Part III concludes with sustained meditations on the question of the connection of atheism and theology as understood through a lens of hope and utopia. Building on the assessments of how utopic visions have proven fallible in the past, these chapters attempt to integrate a constructive view of how atheism might ground communities in the future—or what guidelines, at the very least, an atheistic community would need to keep in mind. Steven Schroeder opens this section with a lyrical, beautiful discussion of how atheism emerges through Christian theology, gently invoking how hope and community appear in the prison poems of Dietrich Bonhoeffer. J. Sage Elwell takes an opposed approach, diagnosing the drive toward a technological atheism as missing the truth of human fragility. David Hall's discussion of the importance of Benjamin in Agamben's thinking discloses the theological depths of the most secularized political communities. Finally, Daniel Boscaljon weaves these strands together by discussing ways that *Fight Club* reveals potentialities for postsecular, atheistic gatherings caused by works of determinate negation—small pools of nothingness.

The thinking behind these chapters largely originated in response to a conference on "Futures and Illusions" held at the University of Iowa in August 2012, sponsored primarily by the Department of Religious Studies, and indicate one dimension of the conversation deserving of more widespread attention. Overall, our hope in publishing this collection was to indicate the importance of living malleably, open to changes and transitions, in ways that both respond to the past and attempt to construct authentic and appropriate foundations for the future. Recognizing that utopian spaces are best preserved as inspirations for our longing instead of spaces that can be actualized in the world allows us to retain a space for hope that does not threaten to marginalize the hopes of those whose values differ from our own.

Part 1

Relating Hope and Utopia

1

Utopia and Narrative

Theology between the Boundaries of Overhumanization and Hypertheism

—*Verna Ehret*

INTRODUCTION

Religion is the deeply human enterprise of evaluating and interpreting self and others based on what concerns one ultimately. Religion simultaneously gives one an image of whom one is meant to be and of a society that promotes this realization in and for others. In other words, religion puts forth a utopic image—the image of a complete human life in relation to culture, society, and civilization as a whole. It is the work of the theologian to engage the changing narratives of religion in order to promote religion's capacity to work continuously toward this utopic vision of human flourishing. But religion is fraught with dangers. Religion is expressed in narrative, and the way the narratives of religion are constructed can either promote or diminish human flourishing. The projected utopias found in thinking that represents trends of overhumanization and "hypertheism" ultimately create or desire exclusive utopias that hinder the flourishing of others.

Building the narrative of religion is a constant and dangerous process. Within a spectrum of voices today, only the most extreme seem to drive the public discussion of religion and human flourishing. David Klemm and William Schweiker express these extremes as based in "hypertheism," which reifies religious narratives of transcendence, or "overhumanization," which seeks to eliminate religious narratives and replace transcendence with the immanence of humanism. Arguably, both positions seek utopia, but from standpoints that are not only mutually exclusive but also insufficient on their own. The overhumanization narrative destroys the religious narrative by seeing religion or the quest for transcendence as a residual quality of undeveloped minds, or at times a threat to life itself. The hypertheistic narrative can focus so much on transcendence and the realization of a particular teleology that it becomes idolatrous and empty, lacking connection to the world. While this tension is daunting, mediation may be possible. Through a modification of Freud's understanding of religion as wish-fulfillment, one can separate the illusory quality of hypertheism, which becomes a kind of idolatry, from the quest for meaning. Utopia, as the always before us but never achieved goal of religion, can mediate between the loss of transcendence and the illusory attachment to knowledge of it.

I argue, then, that there is a theological benefit to using the language of utopia in the analysis of religion. Utopia both reveals some of the pitfalls of overhumanization and hypertheism and demonstrates the benefit of the deconstructive approach found in John D. Caputo's work. Deconstruction need not be the destruction of religion through overhumanization against hypertheism, but rather can be the rethinking of the relationship between transcendence and immanence in religious narratives that allow individuals and communities to live *toward* utopia.

Though our understanding of it may have changed due to postmodern critiques, narrative continues to be the way we both express and understand ourselves as relational beings. While some narratives are transcendental, pointing toward a clear goal that is other-worldly, others are grounded in the immanence of human being in the world, concerned with how we live in and for this world rather than for some other world. How we tell our narrative in relation to other narratives indicates as much to others about who we are as what we actually say about ourselves. It is through narrative that we engage the world and shape the future we project, transcendental or not. That future is a utopic ideal toward which we strive. While some might argue that not all projected futures are utopic, I argue that in unfolding the narrative of our lives we express the quest for utopia because we seek to achieve our best possible selves and our best possible lives. While the image of utopia in a transcendental narrative may differ from ones in immanent narratives, both seek a best possible future. But we can be deceived by and be deceptive in these narratives. The challenge we face is how to navigate this quilt of narratives that can overlap and conflict.[1] The function of the

---

1. See Berger, *Sacred Canopy*.

theologian, then, is to assist in the constant deconstruction and reconstruction of the narratives of religion in an ever-changing world.

The current climate regarding religion seems to be defined by a radical divide between the "hypertheists" who think their particular religious narrative of transcendence holds all of life's answers and find any disagreement to be a threat to their present and future, and the "overhumanizers" who turn to humanism as a replacement for any sense of transcendence, seeing religion as an antiquated and even dangerous tool of oppression.[2] In the unfolding of religious narratives these two extremes leave a vast chasm in the middle, filled with people trying to figure out how to navigate the space between. On the one hand, the idolatrous attachment to a particular religious narrative can become a weapon used against others, seriously diminishing the capacity of the other to flourish. On the other hand, the complete rejection of religion denies its power to help people in fact flourish. Theology is faced with the challenge of speaking to the people between these extremes, to re-imagine religion as utopic wish-fulfillment in terms of living a full human life as a goal toward which one strives.

No single correct narrative of human flourishing exists. While some narratives approach flourishing through a relationship to transcendence, others have rejected confessional forms of religious narratives and view the rise of secularism as offering a more successful approach to human flourishing. Charles Taylor, in his analysis of the rise of secularism, points out that secularism is the move from self-transcendence to immanence, the choice to reject self-transcendence in favor of an extreme and exclusive humanism. Taylor argues that secularism is not simply the loss of something, but involves the attempt to regulate or remove religion from the public square in order to realize the fullness of human life through the basic moral principle of human flourishing. The problematic uses of religion to limit human flourishing seem to be answered by secularism that rejects transcendence in favor of immanence through humanism.[3]

However, the move to secularism does entail a diminution of religion; also, as Taylor points out repeatedly in his text, it introduces a loss of meaning.[4] Taylor notes a desire to eradicate the need for transcendence in the move toward secularism and humanism. However, this need remains. Taylor's modern secularist lives in a tension of humanism and a longing for something religion has provided. Among other things, the modern debate about the fullness of human life and our ethical predicament includes ideas

---

2. Klemm and Schweiker, *Religion and the Human Future*, 13–16.
3. Taylor, *A Secular Age*, 13–15.
4. Ibid., 592–93.

that some things motivate us toward an understanding of fullness, while other things bar the path. Secularism need not be an aggressive stance: as Taylor notes, it often is a reluctant move resigned to accepting seeming scientific refutations of faith. Our reluctant embrace of secularism means that we recognize that something significant to human life has been lost. Taylor says,

> Each side thus turns around and makes the accusation of unrealizable utopia to the other. Nonbelievers scoff at the Christian parousia as a pipe-dream. But as long as Enlighteners keep alive hopes of their own harmony, they will find Christians (and lots of others) warning them against unreal Utopianism. We have to consider two dimensions of Utopia, which correspond to the two facets of modern moral/ethical consciousness we have been examining here: not just the harmony between body and spirit, or bodily desire and our highest aspirations; but also the harmony between all human beings so harmonized, which brings in our attachment to the ethic of universal rights and well-being.[5]

Taylor does not reject utopian visions, but rather argues there seem to be competing ways of approaching utopia—and that ultimately both are necessary. As Taylor explains it, the notion that science or an exclusive humanism can cultivate full human lives requires an incomplete vision of human fulfillment that leaves people acutely aware of a loss of meaning. Thus the modern person lives in the tension between belief and unbelief. And this tension is the starting point of a re-imagining of utopia, not as single paths to follow or goals to achieve but as a productive tension that leads to living differently in the world.

In order to move through this narrative world, the concepts of illusion, wish-fulfillment, hope, and utopia are extremely useful tools. Illusion, using Freud as a starting point for this term, refers to an imagined truth that may or may not be verifiable.[6] Not initially equivalent to delusion, the illusion of religion is the longing for a perfect future seen as one where one is cared for by a loving and powerful father. Freud claims this is wish-fulfillment, referring to the fulfillment of the longings of our heart.[7] But while Freud identified religion as wish-fulfillment to show its weakness and uselessness in modern civilization,[8] I will reimagine the capacity for wish-fulfillment to think about what religion offers to humanity. Although illusion and

---

5. Ibid., 616.
6. Freud, *Future of an Illusion*, 39.
7. Ibid., 38–40.
8. Ibid., 49–50.

wish-fulfillment are often united to show the idolatrous tendencies of confessional religion, Tillich has shown that they can be separated. Wish-fulfillment can be the hopeful longing for a future one projects. This future is utopic in that it is the quest for our best possible future. I follow Caputo in understanding utopia as a journey that continually drives us forward, rather than a destination. Utopia that is realized ceases to be utopia.

WHAT UTOPIA REVEALS ABOUT OVERHUMANIZATION

Overhumanization arises when human dependence on transcendence is seen as a threat to the progress and flourishing of individuals. In the modern period, this overhumanization emerges in a turn to humanism where what is sought is a utopic vision of the capacity for each person to flourish as a human being. This is achieved not through transcendence, but rather through analysis of and respect for humanity as it is without transcendence. The vision is utopic as a hope for realizing what human beings can achieve as human beings, and the realization of this goal requires letting go of our attachment to transcendence, which in the position of overhumanization hinders the development of human beings in isolation and civilizations in cooperation with each other. This move toward overhumanization can be seen in a great number of modern thinkers, but is particularly usefully described through the work of Sigmund Freud.

When Freud argued in *The Future of an Illusion* that religion was an illusion, he was pointing to the danger of religion. Freud describes the danger of religion as keeping humanity intellectually under-developed, in a child-like state of seeking care rather than facing the realities of an uncaring universe.[9] In the contemporary context, the danger can be described as doctrinal inflexibility, though this is not Freud's exact language. In the analysis of this doctrinal inflexibility what one finds is a claim to certainty that is not available to finite human understanding. Such a reliance on certainty, for a human being to claim he or she *knows* exactly what it means to live a full human life and is *the example* of that based on his or her declarations of *belief* alone, is seen as the height of hubris.

As described earlier by Taylor, this analysis of religion has contributed to tension between competing notions of utopia. Freud represents one extreme, but also provides tools to analyze both forms of utopia. In *The Future of an Illusion, Civilization and Its Discontents*, and other works, Freud explores the nature and role of religion in the formation and continuation

9. Ibid., 66–68.

of civilization. Put most basically, without civilization human existence is constantly threatened by other people and by nature itself. Coming together in civilization requires human beings to restrain certain instinctual drives for self-fulfillment at the expense of everyone else, and what one receives in return is protection from all that threatens human life. A narrative is created that gives order, meaning, and purpose—even *telos*—to human life. Freud says,

> [Civilization] includes on the one hand all the knowledge and capacity that men have acquired in order to control the forces of nature and extract its wealth for the satisfaction of human needs, and on the other hand, all the regulations necessary in order to adjust the relations of men to one another and especially the distribution of the available wealth.[10]

He presents us with an image of humanity as selfish, greedy, and appetite driven and thus needing compensation for the privations and frustrations of those appetites incurred by being members of society.[11] Civilization has created social norms of behavior in order to allow us to live together and therefore fend off a universe that does not care about us. When Freud goes on to say that, "Among these instinctual wishes are those of incest, cannibalism, and lust for killing,"[12] one hears the specter of Hobbes telling us that human life in the state of nature is "solitary, nasty, brutish, and short."[13] Confessional religion is used to make promises to people in order to compensate them for their woes in a multitude of ways. In describing the rise of religion, Freud describes the rise of religious narratives as a wish-fulfillment that is the illusory hope for a utopic future where the terrifying qualities of reality can be brought under our control and will at some point no longer threaten us at all. What Freud proposes is an alternative utopic vision of the capacity for human beings to grow up and be in charge of themselves rather than relying on a transcendent power and fulfillment.

Freud proposes this alternative vision because he believes religion does more than simply cause us to restrain our destructive drives and give hope for utopic futures. For Freud, this function of religion was initially useful, but has become deeply problematic. Belief is given the status of truth, and thus the utopia one seeks is seen as realizable in some future. The narratives of all religions (as Freud defines them) are driven by this utopic vision that is illusion and, as illusion, is also idolatrous. The utopic quest has become

10. Ibid., 6.
11. Ibid., 6–7.
12. Ibid., 13.
13. Hobbes, *Leviathan*, 100.

dangerous in holding tightly to a single vision of the present and future for which Freud sees no warrant. Religion, as Freud sees it, originated in order to compensate us for restraining those drives. But when drives are inadequately compensated or are too aggressively restrained, they emerge as neuroses—pathological wish-fulfillment.[14] In Freud's understanding of religion, all of religion seems to have become pathological wish-fulfillment.

Freud identifies his alternative utopic vision in *The Future of an Illusion*. He claims religion has run its course and can no longer properly compensate humanity for what we sacrifice in order to maintain civilization. While useful for what Eliade would describe in *The Sacred and the Profane* as archaic human beings,[15] religion for Freud now holds us in a childlike state, unable to grow up and properly address the world around us. In other words, religion stunts and poisons us. In wrestling with how to liberate people from the damaging illusion of religion, Freud recognizes this quest for care has made human beings helpless, keeping us in a childlike state that will require careful education of the children to remove. The fundamental problem of religion he identifies is that religions cause weakness when the longing for utopia they produce becomes a belief that this utopia can be achieved, and Freud recognizes that such a utopia is unachievable because it is false.[16] In its place, Freud promotes reason as the capacity for human beings to take responsibility for ourselves and move beyond the restrictions placed upon us by religion. Reason opens up possibilities for flourishing through our most basic human capacity.[17]

Freud's claim is supported by the intellectual history of the rise of secularism described by Charles Taylor in *A Secular Age*. Taylor carefully takes the reader through the transformation of society from a strong collectivism where transcendence, teleology, and religion as belief in God are simply given to us, to a society without the capacity to choose otherwise.[18] As indicated previously, the rise of secularism and humanism opens up a choice to accept or reject a vision of utopia dependent upon transcendence. A utopia defined by immanence becomes a way to replace transcendent utopias.[19] This is the trajectory for which Freud hoped; however, something was lost in the transformation and more of the religious was retained than Freud expected.

14. Freud, *Future of an Illusion*, 55–56.
15. Eliade, *The Sacred and the Profane*.
16. Freud, *Future of an Illusion*, 65–69.
17. Ibid., 69.
18. Taylor, *A Secular Age*, 590–91.
19. Ibid., 600–605.

Transcendence, as well as a sense of meaning, is lost in narratives of overhumanization. Religion as a quest for transcendence remains because of this desire for meaning. The utopic vision put forth by Freud where humanity is freed from bondage to the illusion of religion is another kind of wish-fulfillment as illusory or idolatrous as that of hypertheism. In *Civilization and Its Discontents*, Freud tells the story of a friend who describes for him the transforming power of a religious feeling in language reminiscent of Schleiermacher.[20] Freud is dismissive of such a notion, but Charles Taylor argues that the move to humanistic immanence has left those making that move with a feeling of emptiness and meaninglessness. Interestingly, Taylor's book is published in 2007, but it is precisely this emptiness and meaninglessness that Tillich identified as the risk of overhumanization in *The Courage to Be*, published in 1952.

For Tillich, emptiness and meaninglessness were the primary causes of suffering in our time, and Taylor claims that they still are, 60 years later. There is, then, something missing in Freud's analysis of religion. People cling to religion as a meaning giving source of a utopic vision of living a full human life and living well in society. For Taylor, humans are currently forced to find a way to live in this tension, where belief in transcendence is no longer a communal birthright, but is an individual choice. And that tension is deeply troubling.[21] Arguably, this very tension between belief and the rational, transcendence and immanence, highlights the very notion of wish-fulfillment with which Freud began and goes to the heart of the struggle to identify the nature and value of religion in the contemporary world.

Perhaps wish-fulfillment of a certain kind is exactly what religion is. Perhaps religion is not simply childish fantasies and self-projection but rather, as Tillich points out, the *possibility* of fulfilling one's deepest desires to live well as a human being, the longing for reunion with that which makes one whole. Religion can give one a sense of oneself, one's possibilities to be, toward which one can work. Achieving perfection may be fantasy, but working toward it can be a way of living well in the world. Freud may have had a good premise, but his argument is incomplete and therefore the conclusion is flawed. Tillich fears fanaticism in religion as well, and religion that is *illusion* is utterly problematic. But for Tillich, what makes religion idolatrous, or in Freud's language an illusion, is that one takes the finite manifestations of religiosity and gives them ultimate status, holding a single understanding as true against all others as falsehoods.[22] That action can lead to problematic

20. Freud, *Civilization and Its Discontents*, 8–9.
21. Taylor, *A Secular Age*, 616–17.
22. Tillich, *Dynamics*, 142.

utopian visions in both hypertheism and overhumanization. Recognizing the limitations of our humanity opens possibilities for continual improvement by constant evaluation of ourselves in light of what drives us to be better than we are.

How one thinks about religion matters, even for those who do not see themselves as religious, because it shapes one's person and one's relationship to others. Every day people call on religion to guide them through their lives. Religion, as connection with transcendence (however one might describe it), speaks to people in a way that science or humanism alone cannot. It addresses a deep need within people—a longing for wholeness beyond mere biology—and thus one feels incomplete without having some sense of religion. There is more to life than what can be tested. Feeling matters, a point that is noted carefully by Charles Taylor near the end of his tome.[23] The loss of religion involves the loss of the transcendent in favor of the immanent, and comes with a sense of meaninglessness. Taylor, at the end of his analysis, begins a turn back to a kind of immanent transcendence that embraces this tension as the retrieval of meaning without the naiveté of earlier ages.[24] The challenge to Taylor's vision is the constant threat of hypertheism in religion.

WHAT UTOPIA REVEALS ABOUT HYPERTHEISM

The contemporary public square presents us with a multitude of examples for the way religious narratives become hypertheistic, allowing their utopian visions to become the pathological wish-fulfillment Freud feared as the narratives become weapons against others. It becomes a pathological need for the immediate realization of the fulfillment of one's own wishes, laying out a narrative of domination of the world in order to bring about one's own vision of the utopian future for which one hopes. This weaponizes a religious narrative, not only in the unfolding of the narrative, but in the utopic vision itself. Some utopic visions require the destruction of human flourishing as others might see it. The bifurcation between overhumanization that sees religion as that which poisons society and hypertheism that wants to use religion to bend all world-views to one's own validates Freud's assessment of religion as dangerous.

If signs of overhumanization arise in narratives that deride religion throughout culture, signs of hypertheism emerge as particular narratives that undermine the voices of the many in order to enforce the vision of the

---

23. Taylor, *A Secular Age*, 711–27.
24. Ibid., 726.

few. Scholars of religion, for example, have been blamed for the great ills of society, as enemies of true religion and enemies of the true lovers of religion. In this climate, those who take a critical and reflective role in understanding religion are described as the source of great evil in the world. The *National Catholic Reporter*, for example, has been filled with discussions of the Catholic Church as an embattled organization, again due to a hypertheism that holds to certain beliefs as tests of the pious. An August 17, 2012 report, "US Bishops Quietly Adopt Protocols for Theological Investigations" discusses the surprise of many American Catholic theologians over new procedures for investigating theologians that would seem to limit theologians' ability to respond to charges of non-adherence to church doctrine.[25] The Congregation on the Doctrine of the Faith oversees the work of all active Catholic theologians and can challenge their work. Capuchin Fr. Thomas Weinandy, executive director of the Secretariate for Doctrine, has been particularly vocal on ways US theologians deviate from official church doctrine. In a recent address to the Academy of Catholic Theology, Weinandy claimed theologians can be a "curse and affliction upon the church."[26] Moreover, women religious within the church have been under heavy scrutiny by the church hierarchy because they do not fall in line with what is seen as the primary religious issues of our time, homosexuality and abortion. Women religious such as Margaret Farley, a Sister of Mercy, and Elizabeth Johnson, a Sister of St. Joseph, who are also scholars of religion, have been sharply criticized as promoting positions in their recent books that fail to uphold, or, worse, even challenge church doctrine. According to the National Catholic Reporter, Weinandy has been extremely vocal in critiquing Catholic Theologians for undermining the church.

> "Much of what passes for contemporary Catholic theology," he said, "often is not founded upon an assent of faith in the divine deposit of revelation as proclaimed in the sacred scriptures and developed within the living doctrinal and moral tradition of the church." Instead, he said, much Catholic theology has become "an attempt by reason to pass judgment on the content of the faith as if it were of human origin," with theologians as "judges who stand above the faith and arbitrate what is to be believed and what is not." . . . Yet today, he said, "the church is experiencing not a debate among legitimate schools of theological thought, but a radical divide over the central tenets of the Catholic faith and the church's fundamental moral tradition. This is not simply

---

25. McElwee, "US Bishops Quietly Adopt."
26. Allen, "Bishops' Staffer on Doctrine."

an expression of a plurality of Catholic theologies," Weinandy said, "but the very disintegration of the Catholic faith itself."[27]

Weinandy is clearly no fan of Freud and the move from belief to reason. His concern is a narrative of traditional doctrine as he sees it and threats to it from alternative voices. He sees alternative narratives of the unfolding of the Catholic tradition in a socially and culturally diverse world as the destruction of faith at the hands of scholars whenever current church teaching is challenged. It is a symptom of hypertheism when the Catholic intellectual tradition becomes the adherence to the positions of the Vatican without question.

The major organization of women religious in the United States has faced severe criticism by the Vatican in recent years for having the wrong concerns. Their work continues to be with the poor and disenfranchised of society with very little attention paid to homosexuality and abortion. Their fight to refocus the church on its tradition of social justice and advocacy on behalf of the neglected of society puts them at odds with the Vatican, and reminds one of earlier fights of liberation theologians against the church's support of tyrants and neglect of the poor. A specific image of the future is projected within traditional circles, and hypertheists fear that too much thinking and critique will destroy that projected future, which relies on very specific beliefs that must go unchallenged.

Many Catholic theologians in the United States today are increasingly concerned that their ability to engage the tradition intellectually will be seen as being in opposition to the Vatican Congregation on the Doctrine of the Faith rather than open engagement with an ever evolving tradition. This concern has been heightened by the creation of a receivership of the Leadership Conference of Women Religious in April 2012.[28] The power of a single narrative framework that leads to a monistic utopic vision of the good perpetuates an illusory ideal of religion as consolation for a world that is not entirely in one's control and a vision of the future that might not be the one for which one has been hoping. There is a utopian vision that drives voices of hypertheism, and it is a vision that is specific, unquestioned, and from which one dare not diverge because then one thwarts God's plan for humanity. Hypertheism becomes, in Freud's terms, a pathological wish-fulfillment. It is an illusory utopia, projecting a future dependent on a level of certainty humanity cannot have about transcendence. Hypertheists claim to know the mind of God, and while they do not all even agree with each

---

27. Ibid.
28. Zagano, "The Vatican and the LCWR."

other regarding what the mind of God is, they will defend their positions as an absolute truth. Challenging that truth destroys the future.

Religion can be used to manipulate people into giving up everything they have, even their lives and the lives of others, for the sake of an ideal. Mark Juergensmeyer and Reza Aslan have carefully tracked the rise of religious nationalism in the last fifty years. Their evaluations show the power of religion to manipulate minds and hearts with great destructive force.[29] One risk of religion is fanaticism, people using religion as a way to take control in the name of a protective and demanding Father in the effort to control a universe that does not care about humanity. Rather than religion pointing toward that which is of ultimate concern, the focus becomes right belief, the idolatry of belief over the heart of religion. And in these idolatrous forms, religion is justly criticized as a tool of oppression of the many by the few.[30] This type of belief encourages many contemporary humanists and secularists to follow Freud in thinking that one realizes one's adulthood by embracing the little god *logos* and casting off the shackles of belief in a god that is a projection of one's own delusional wishes.[31]

It would seem the answer to these issues is simply to write off religion as an antiquated notion that holds back progress, poisons people's minds against their neighbors, and is destructive to a genuinely civil society. These critics ask, with Freud, if religion simply causes too many problems for it to be useful any longer. If this is religion, then religion does not promote the flourishing of individuals and society. It does not promote civil society. It promotes conformity to a single vision, a single narrative of the ideal human life that will bring fulfillment, and those who deviate, for whatever reason, do so at their own peril. From this understanding, theologians and activists who challenge a single understanding of doctrine imperil the entire world.

Hypertheism is not new in religion. What has arisen over time is the willingness and capacity to challenge such thinking through the rise of secularism and the mass recognition of the capacity for choice, seen particularly in the modern and postmodern turn. The extremism of hypertheism is met with a counter-force of secularism and overhumanization. In responding to this divide, the theologian seeks a way of reframing the narratives of religion in order to reach the often neglected middle, those who find value in both extremes.

---

29. Juergensmeyer, *Terror in the Mind of God*; Aslan, *How to Win a Cosmic War*.
30. Freud, *Future of an Illusion*, 55–57.
31. Ibid., 68–69.

TRANS-CONTEXTUAL UTOPIC NARRATIVES

Doctrinal stances in confessional forms of religion put forth a vision of a transcendental utopia toward which one strives, and, in laying out a path, present one with hope for the realization of that utopia in the fullness of time. The utopia of hypertheism is a wish-fulfillment made possible by simply declaring something to be the case, but in this case it asserts an illusory wish-fulfillment. The illusion-utopia tension is not the exclusive domain of confessional religion. It exists in exclusive secularism as well, in the very attempt to remove religion's influence on society by claiming religion cannot defend itself against the truth and verifiability of science and the power of human reason.[32] This rationalist exclusivity claims to have the sole path to truth and that all truth is subject to the scientific method.[33]

Freud's understanding of religion as wish-fulfillment is incomplete when he simply equates it with illusion, but he does provide a starting point for analysis of the contemporary condition of religion in light of human flourishing. The move beyond the limitations of the extreme perspectives on religion requires pushing beyond Freud to what I have elsewhere called trans-contextual narratives, narratives that are not limited to a single point of view but can mediate between extremes.

Finding the place of religion in a modern world is difficult, but if religion is a deeply human enterprise, then it cannot be found simply in ideas. It must be found in living. Theologians and philosophers locate religion in the concern with suffering and justice. Living a full human life requires not living simply for oneself, but also in community with others. Religion, then, can be seen as the drive toward utopic civilization, a longing that continually moves humanity forward in the work of ethics. In retelling the narrative of religion in this way, the narrative of religion is trans-contextual. It lives in the tension of human life and is constantly in motion, re-evaluated rather than reified in a single context.

One comes to understand oneself in the reflection of one's own being seen in what concerns one ultimately. Religion, according to Paul Tillich, is not a simple set of beliefs, rituals, or rigid moral guidelines: it is a process, not a destination. Religion as the union of faith and belief—as described by Tillich—drives people to reach their full human potential and provides the means to do that through a centering principle or understanding of who one is.[34] Despite his efforts to purge religion from civilization, Freud offers

32. See for example Dawkins, *The God Delusion* or the American Atheists at http://atheists.org.
33. Tillich, *Dynamics*, 92–98.
34. Ibid., 122–29.

avenues for reflecting on the meaning and value of religion in contemporary society. By challenging the pitfalls of religion, the wish to explore one's full humanity is realized as religion, providing one with a sacred center to one's life around which life can be built.

The details of religion, the beliefs, may be open for discussion and tremendous variation. But the heart of religion as desire for connection with that which centers a person is a human drive to realize one's potential. In the *Phaedrus*, Plato (in the voice of Socrates) refers to this longing as divine madness, erotic love that is longing for that which elevates the human soul.[35] This erotic love as desire for reunion unfolds in human relationships with others when those relationships are lived well. Good relationships will support and drive one to elevate oneself to be the best example of a person one can be. Carried forward to Eliade, this longing is for the sacred that breaks up the profane world and gives a focal point to life—gives it meaning.[36] All of these voices lead to Tillich's claim that religion is the centered act of the whole personality. In religion, faith as a state of being grasped by an ultimate concern is united with belief, the concrete expression of faith. They are inseparable, but not interchangeable. The experience of the sacred centers a person, gives a sense of wholeness, but because finitude makes beliefs limited expressions of ultimate concern, beliefs are subject to doubt, challenge, and error. If religion centers a person, the loss of the expression of religion through beliefs threatens the loss of oneself.[37] One can be destroyed by that or, with Socrates, perpetually desire and seek the Good that centers each person.[38]

So the question that people face in the contemporary world as they confront religious narratives is not simply the perennial question of what one means when one says religion, but also what function religion serves for humans and humanity. The question of the nature and function of religion is a perennial question because the context of human experience is constantly in flux. Given this analysis of wish-fulfillment, what Tillich, Eliade, and Plato provide is a foundation for re-imagining religious narrative in each new generation. The narratives of exclusivity in both the overhumanizing and hypertheistic forms that are examples of idolatrous religion can be challenged. The narratives exist, as Taylor pointed out, because of the transformations of human thinking and engagement in the world: the tensions between belief and unbelief, transcendence and immanence, and the desire

---

35. Plato, *Phaedrus*, 60.
36. Eliade, *Sacred and the Profane*, 21.
37. Tillich, *Dynamics*, 115–22.
38. Plato, *Symposium*, 27–31.

for a reasoned life that is also meaningful.[39] More than one narrative works in the human understanding of self and other and the relationship of religion to civilization. The *illusion* of religion is that there is only one narrative. Instead of a single narrative of religion, we need a trans-contextual narrative that is a process of engaging with difference rather than a singular vision.

The trans-contextual narrative lives in the tension of the hypertheists and overhumanizers because the trans-contextual narrative is the narrative of constant transformation. The trans-contextual narrative of utopia posits that utopia is not a place or a goal but a process, not a destination but a journey. That journey is seen in a narrative of religion that is as much doing as it is thinking, and John D. Caputo offers a helpful articulation of an alternative understanding of religion and utopia.

Caputo is famous for his radical hermeneutics and deconstruction. For many, Caputo's deconstruction invites the loss of transcendence, the loss of foundation, the loss of *telos*, the loss of utopia, and the loss of religion. But Caputo's deconstruction is not simply the breaking down of absolutist or exclusivist thinking; instead, Caputo offers a way of re-narrating religion as a trans-contextual narrative, embracing the tension of life in the doing of justice. Trans-contextual narratives may jar some thinkers on the extremes, but it is not the rejection of points of view. Instead, these narratives embrace multiplicity and recognize that multiplicity requires rejecting simple answers and conflict-free domains of truth. These narratives see that the tensions of multiplicity are not threats, but opportunities to bridge between the conflicting needs of individuals and cultures. They offer a utopian vision because they project a hope for the future of humanity, who we might be as individuals and, more importantly, in relation to each other. We are our best selves when we seek continually to improve our relations with each other rather than assuming we have achieved them. The utopian vision here is not a goal to be achieved but a path to be walked. In a Caputo-style utopia people would continually work toward the improvement of life rather than reaching a certain point in the goal and imagining it to be fulfilled without realizing the ever-changing reality of human life. That work would come from a myriad of narratives flowing together rather than a single narrative with a singular goal. The vision drives one forward through the activity of justice rather than the singularity of doctrinal correctness or rational rejection of transcendence.

In his little book, *What Would Jesus Deconstruct: The Good News of Post-modernism for the Church*, Caputo constructively lives in the tension described by Taylor. Built around the 1896 *In His Steps: What Would Jesus*

---

39. Taylor, *A Secular Age*, 429–32.

Do by Charles Sheldon, Caputo unfolds a narrative of the role of religion in contemporary society that challenges the exclusivisms of doctrinal correctness and atheistic humanisms. The deconstruction of which Caputo speaks is the breaking down of barriers in order to build up what I have called a trans-contextual narrative. Caputo says,

> Mark C. Taylor once famously described deconstruction as the hermeneutics of the death of God. But in the view I am advancing here, deconstruction is treated as the hermeneutics of the *kingdom* of God, as an interpretive style that helps get at the prophetic spirit of Jesus—who was a surprising and sometime strident outsider, who took a stand with the "other"—and thereby helps us get a fix on Sheldon's sometimes slippery question. In my view, a deconstruction is good news because it delivers the shock of the other to the forces of the same, the shock of the good (the "ought") to the forces of being ("what is"), which is also why I think it bears good news to the church.[40]

The most radical claim made by this radical hermeneutic is that doctrinal absolutism as it stands today would consider even Jesus a heretic. The deconstruction Caputo puts forth uses the example of Jesus given in scripture to challenge doctrinal absolutes wherever they may be found in order to hear dissenting voices who also seek to flourish through their own experiences in the world.

Caputo is concerned with those excluded by doctrinal correctness. In that sense, he would seem to side with the extreme critics of religion and exclusive humanism as described by Taylor. But Caputo does not reject transcendence; rather, the good news of post-modernism he offers the church is that transcendence *is*— but one cannot give in to the hubris of thinking one knows *what* it is. The church is not the kingdom of God.[41] The vision of utopia Caputo presents, then, constantly moves toward inclusion of the outcast and the marginalized—not by making everyone the same, but rather by accepting them as they come. Caputo says,

> There are, after all, two ways to be on the way: the first, in which one knows the way and the task is to get there (which certainly can be hard enough), and the second, in which one must, like an explorer, find the way. In the latter and, I am inclined to think, more postmodern situation, one is always a little lost, where being lost and being on the way, far from excluding each other,

---

40. Caputo, *What Would Jesus Deconstruct?*, 26–27.
41. Ibid., 35, 131.

mutually imply each other. That is what I mean by giving the spiritual journey some postmodern teeth.[42]

This is the wish-fulfillment of contemporary religion. It is a utopian hope that requires illusion-breaking for both religious and secular minds. However, conceiving of religion as a kind of mediation and bridge building is tremendously difficult. It still presents itself as a truth among falsehoods, and risks self-deception. The answer to this ideological quandary of how to live in the tension of multiple perspectives (identified clearly by Kathryn Tanner[43]) is difficult to achieve without self-deception. Caputo puts forth a position that itself could be deconstructed.

But Caputo works against the notion of infinite deconstruction in order to present something positive. Deconstruction is not simply breaking-down; it is radical reinterpretation within the conditions of multiplicity. Reinterpretation opens the possibility of the impossible: the undeconstructible that is ever beyond human grasp is the impossible utopia toward which we act, though it is never reached.[44] Religion cannot hold steadfast to doctrines that do not speak to human experience, as though a text written nearly 2000 years ago was written for contemporary people and has only one interpretation. The New Testament itself contains multiple voices and multiple visions of Jesus, and Caputo's form of postmodern deconstruction recognizes that multiplicity. Employing the language of utopia reveals the possibilities of deconstruction.

The idea of being lost and still moving toward something is at the heart of this utopian vision. Utopia itself is lost the moment one thinks one has found it. As Caputo points out, "The great dignity of being human lies in pursuing goals for which there is no guarantee of success and even, at a certain point, no hope for success. But being 'religious people,' by which I mean people who dream of things that have never been and ask 'why not?' we still pursue them."[45] This is the alternative to Freud's form of wish-fulfillment. Freud equated wish-fulfillment with illusion. He saw confessional religion as the desire for a particular end that could not be verified but could limit human potential for growth. The transformation of wish-fulfillment is the claim that as human beings we do wish for something, and that something drives our actions. We seek a source of meaning that motivates us and is, therefore, a wish that reflects the deepest longings of our hearts. But the fulfillment of the wish is not a concrete belief; rather, it is the continual

42. Ibid., 39.
43. Tanner, *Theories of Culture*.
44. Caputo, *What Would Jesus Deconstruct?*, 68.
45. Ibid., 50.

hope that a quest for justice brings us ever closer to flourishing as human beings. This is not because the final goal has been achieved, but because there is cooperation between humans that recognizes the validity of different expressions of the goal. The more that difference is embraced, the more it will be possible to live well with each other. Religion is desire and longing, as Plato pointed out, but it need not be the desire for the known. Caputo claims that religion is the passion for the impossible. The path of deconstruction is, according to Caputo, driven by being called by that which is undeconstructible, and beyond us.

Throughout the text Caputo discusses major issues facing religion today and around which, as seen in contemporary culture, the illusion of religion is built—power, violence, homosexuality, abortion. Like Tillich before him, Caputo claims that, "Orthodoxy is idolatry if it means holding the 'correct' opinions about God—'fundamentalism' is the most extreme and salient example of such idolatry—but not if it means holding faith in the right way, that is, not holding at all but being held by God, in love and service."[46] The notion of love and service makes space for a relationship between transcendence and immanence. The utopic ideal expressed here is a trans-contextual narrative because both love and service can be expressed in a multitude of ways and motivated by very different narratives as they are brought together in dialogue.

One often has the feeling with Caputo that he has said much and yet said nothing at the same time. But there is more to his claims than what appears at first glance. When discussing doing justice, Caputo is not saying one does not have an ideology at work—there is always an ideology at work when one thinks one is being just. Rather, he claims that ideology cannot be static. By placing the emphasis on *doing* justice rather than *knowing* what it is, Caputo makes justice possible. As he describes it, if one says one has achieved justice by what one did, then the utopia one projected has also been achieved. But the world is ever-changing, and a claim to knowing and doing justice is the hubris that one knows what one cannot. Claiming to have achieved justice is based in illusion, idolatry, and the loss of motivating utopia. The wish for utopia cannot be fulfilled because, as Caputo explains, then one stops being just. Rather, one must think of justice in terms of Plato's notion of *eros* because the desire for justice keeps one moving toward it. Ideology appears as a benchmark, a tool to evaluate the current situation, but the trans-contextual narrative of religion argues that religion unfolds in the work one does toward human fulfillment and flourishing. Therefore the benchmark can be continually re-evaluated. Caputo's discussion opens

46. Ibid., 131.

up the possibility for a re-evaluation of wish-fulfillment. Through analysis of his work one can see how a utopic vision drives religion toward what is ever before us, always out of reach, always moving forward in the tensions of life. The moment one stops and rests in an absolute, the possibility of utopia disappears because it is not a place to be found: it is a motivating goal that drives us to keep improving ourselves and the world around us.

The notion of religion as wish-fulfillment has a non-pathological form in hope and utopia where hope is the recognition of the already and not yet of human transformation toward one's best self and best societies. Utopia is the journey, not the destination, which constantly drives humanity toward improvement. As finite beings, people lack perfect understanding. People function from within a perspective shaped by time and place. Awareness of the limitations of human perspective is why utopia perpetually drives us forward.

BIBLIOGRAPHY

Allen, John L., Jr. "Bishops' Staffer on Doctrine Rips Theologians As 'Curse.'" *National Catholic Reporter Online*, August 16, 2011. http://ncronline.org/news/people/bishops-staffer-doctrine-rips-theologians-curse#.UDTr3VJRAUc.email.
Aslan, Reza. *How to Win a Cosmic War: God, Globalization, and the End of the War on Terror*. New York: Random House, 2009.
Berger, Peter. *Sacred Canopy: Elements of a Sociological Theory of Religion*. New York: Anchor, 1967.
Caputo, John D. *What Would Jesus Deconstruct? The Good News of Post-modernism for the Church*. Grand Rapids: Baker Academic, 2007.
Dawkins, Richard. *The God Delusion*. New York: Mariner, 2008.
Eliade, Mircea. *The Sacred and the Profane: The Nature of Religion*. Translated by Willard R. Trask. Orlando: Harcourt, 1987.
Freud, Sigmund. *Civilization and Its Discontents*. New York: Martino, 2010.
———. *The Future of an Illusion*. Translated by James Strachey. New York: Norton, 1961.
Hobbes, Thomas. *Leviathan*. New York: Macmillan, 1962.
Juergensmeyer, Mark. *Terror in the Mind of God: The Global Rise of Religious Violence*. Berkley: University of California Press, 2003.
Klemm, David E., and William Schweiker. *Religion and the Human Future: An Essay on Theological Humanism*. Oxford: Wiley-Blackwell, 2008.
McElwee, Joshua J. "US Bishops Quietly Adopt Protocols for Theological Investigations." *National Cathohlic Reporter Online*, August 17, 2012. http://ncronline.org/news/us-bishops-quietly-adopt-protocols-theological-investigations.
Plato. *Symposium and Phaedrus*. Translated by Bejamin Jowett. New York: Dover, 1993.
Tanner, Kathryn. *Theories of Culture: A New Agenda for Theology*. Minneapolis: Fortress, 1997.
Taylor, Charles. *A Secular Age*. Cambridge, MA: Belknap, 2007.
Tillich, Paul. *The Courage to Be*. New Haven: Yale University Press, 1952.

———. *Dynamics of Faith*. New York: Perennial Classics, 1957.
Zagano, Phyllis. "The Vatican and the LCWR." *National Catholic Reporter Online*, April 25, 2012. http://ncronline.org/blogs/just-catholic/vatican-and-lcwr.

2

Hope, Hatred, and the Ambiguities of Utopic Longing

— *Diana Fritz Cates*

At the beginning of the *Nicomachean Ethics*, Aristotle asks his students to identify the highest good for humans, the content of *eudaimonia* or human flourishing. "Surely," he says, "knowledge of this good is . . . of great importance for the conduct of our lives, and if, like archers, we have a target [at which to aim], we are more likely to hit the right mark."[1] What would it be like for a human being to enjoy the realization of his or her full potential? What would it be like for *all* humans to thrive, not only individually, but also in relation to each other, on every level of social organization, from the interpersonal to the (now) global, as mediated by digital technologies? The future comes into being partly through the choices humans make, and we make our best choices, ethically speaking, when we have a working conception of the good in mind.

People often disagree about what makes for a good society, even when they focus on societies of limited scope. For example, many Americans disagree about what a good or ideal American society would look like. Some Americans hope for a social order that, if realized, would tear painfully at what other Americans value greatly. At the same time, other Americans hope for changes that, if brought about, would crush the aspirations of the first group. When people perceive that the ideals and passions of others are opposed to their own, they can feel threatened. They can become defensive

---

1. Aristotle, *Nicomachean Ethics* 1094a23.

and even aggressive. It can seem that, if anything is worth fighting for, it is the way of life that we judge to be best for ourselves, our kin, and future generations. But our opponents are motivated by the same thought.

Idealistic visions can inspire hope and constructive action. They can also ignite hatred and violence. Making use of a Thomistic moral psychology, this chapter explores some of the ambiguities of utopic longing.[2] First, it presents a conceptual analysis of hope, focusing on the hope that can be aroused by a social ideal. Second, it calls attention to the role that the perception of evil can play in the generation of hope. Third, it presents a conceptual and ethical analysis of hatred, which is commonly evoked by the perception of evil. Hatred and its excesses are an ever-present risk of hope. People who strive to bring about social change, on any scale, do well to recognize this.[3]

HOPE

If we wish to explore the dynamics of hope, we must begin by defining it. In a Thomistic perspective, hope (*spes*) can refer to several things. It can refer to an emotion. It can refer to a motion of the will. It can and often does refer to a combination of both. Hope can refer to a moral virtue, that is, to a *habit* of emotion and/or volition that is cultivated, over time, through the use of right practical reason. It can refer also to a theological virtue, to a habit or motion of the will that operates in light of faith, where faith is thought to take people beyond the limits of reason.

Consider hope, first, as an emotion. An emotion (*passio*) is a way of being moved by an object (say, a situation) that we apprehend, via our sensory powers, as bearing on our happiness or the happiness of someone who is important to us.[4] The emotion of hope can be defined as a body-

---

2. Moral psychology concerns the conceptual and ethical analysis of mental states that are quite common to humans and tend to follow common patterns. Moral psychology analyzes such states especially as they relate to moral agency and the formation of moral character.

3. The following is a constructive account that has its basis in a study of Aquinas's theology, anthropology, ethics, and moral psychology, with a focus on the *Summa Theologiae*, *De veritate* (*Disputed Questions on Truth*), and *De malo* (*Disputed Questions on Evil*). More extensive textual documentation can be found in Cates, *Aquinas on the Emotions*.

4. Thomas Aquinas, *Summa Theologiae* (hereafter *ST*) I-II 23.2, 22.3. From a Thomistic viewpoint, our sensory powers include both external and internal senses. Our internal senses include a "common sense" (by which impressions of various kinds are integrated into unified experiences), imagination, an "estimative sense" (by which humans are able to apprehend simple properties such as usefulness, friendliness, or

resonant or felt mode of tending toward a future possibility that we regard as desirable, but not easily attained or guaranteed. In hope, we are aware of challenges, but are not undone by them. We rise to the occasion. We become high-spirited.[5]

A utopia is usually conceived as a perfect society, and most of us would agree that attaining society-wide perfection, according to any description, is impossible for humans. Limits of knowledge and imagination, partial perspectives, self-interested biases, the consequences of previous, poor choices, and so on, predictably condition our interactions. For those of us who acknowledge such limits, it might seem problematic to refer to hope in relation to utopia, for we hope only in what we regard as possible. Yet one function of a utopic vision can be to orient people toward *some* aspects of an ideal society, toward an *approximation* to the ideal, or simply toward the idea of something *better*. I treat utopic longing as a longing for a society that improves significantly on the social forms that people have encountered to date—a society that allows more people to enjoy satisfying lives, and causes fewer people (and other sentient beings) to suffer unnecessarily. I treat it as a form of hope.

As an emotion, hope can pull us in different directions. Inasmuch as we have an attractive possibility in view—for example, a society full of kind and cooperative humans—we are drawn toward that possibility emotionally, and we anticipate the pleasure of uniting with it. However, inasmuch as we are confronted by difficulties—for example, opponents who strike us as mean and uncooperative—we also feel disturbed. If our happy goal seems nonetheless possible to attain, albeit with great effort, we might become energized, even excited, depending on how attractive the goal is and how much we enjoy a challenge. If instead we sense that our goal has become impossible, due to the strength of our opposition and to our own relative weakness, or we sense that it is no longer worth the effort, then we are likely to withdraw. We might suffer the loss of hope and let that be the end of it. We might experience renewed hope as we fantasize about other approaches or a somewhat different goal. We might refocus on our opponents and how much they bother us. Hope—like everything else—is subject to change. It can give way to sorrow, despair, hatred, and so on, depending on the aspects of a situation that grip our attention the most.[6] Generally speaking, hope involves having our attention held primarily by an attractive possibility. In

---

danger), and memory (*ST* I 78.4).

5. *ST* I-II 23.1, 40.1.
6. *ST* I-II 25.1.

hope, we have the impression that yes, we face challenges, but *yes, we can* overcome them and attain what we desire.

If we imagine overcoming an obstacle and attaining a desired goal, and if having this image in mind causes our heart rate to increase or gives us a spurt of energy, then we experience hope as an emotion.[7] Ordinarily, when we entertain a sensory image, our higher intellectual powers become engaged as well. That is, we think about the situation, we project possibilities, we formulate a plan, we make choices, and so on. We do such things because we care about the quality of our lives and the lives of our loved-ones. From a Thomistic viewpoint, if we are motivated by thoughts or reasons, and not simply by sensory impressions, then we experience hope also as a motion of the will (*motus voluntatis*).[8] Hope is usually a mode of passively being moved while, at the same time, deliberately moving ourselves. It is a way of orienting ourselves toward an object that we both sense and judge intellectually to be valuable—not easy to attain, but also not out of the question.

Aquinas characterizes hope also as a virtue or habit of character.[9] He focuses on hope as a *theological* virtue that is made possible by the aid of a mysterious higher power, but his account of virtue allows us to think of hope also as a *moral* virtue. The latter is a good habit that is acquired by choosing repeatedly to tend toward (what we correctly regard as) temporal human happiness or its constituents, despite the obstacles that stand in our way. As a habit of *emotion*, hope disposes us to be drawn, in appropriate ways, toward future possibilities that we sense will be pleasing or beneficial, but difficult to attain. As a habit of *volition*, hope disposes us to move ourselves toward the realization of possibilities that we judge, by the power of our intellect, to be consistent with happiness and the common good, but not easily secured. The moral virtue of hope makes us prone to experience the right kind and amount of emotion and volition whenever we consider finite possibilities that we regard as appealing and worthwhile, but also uncertain.[10]

Aquinas characterizes hope as a *theological* virtue.[11] Theological hope is a habit that is acquired, not by making reasonable choices in light of an ideal of temporal human happiness, but by encountering a power of unlimited goodness. Theological hope is gained by opening oneself to this power, consenting to it as the ultimate source of one's being and fulfillment, and

---

7. *ST* I-II 22.1.

8. *ST* I-II 9.1

9. *ST* II-II 17.1.

10. *ST* I-II 50.3, 50.5, 58.1, 62.2.

11. *ST* II-II 17.5. For further discussion of theological hope, presented in a more traditional Thomistic vein, see Pieper, *Faith, Hope, Love*, 87–138.

reaching out toward a closer relationship to it, relying on it all the while.[12] In Aquinas's words, the object of theological hope is "eternal happiness as being possible to attain by the assistance of God."[13] Theological hope lifts the self above the limits of its own resources, but it is something that establishes itself *within* the self. It becomes a virtue *of* the self. As a virtue, theological hope is relatively stable, but it is not necessarily established once and for all. It can be lost. It can also be regained. It can—indeed, it must—be cultivated.

A person who cultivates theological hope is oriented, by her own will and by what she regards as a power greater than herself, toward a perfective engagement *with* this power. She trusts that this engagement will bring her to a "good place" (*eu topos*), even if she will not be able to enter that place fully until she transcends the limits of temporal life. If a person tries to imagine, by means of her interior senses, what this engagement or place will be like (if she pictures, for example, a tropical paradise or a family reunion), then she will experience hope as an emotion.[14] But inasmuch as what moves her is an object of her intellect (for example, the idea of perfect goodness) and the power of her will (for example, the desire to be perfected by goodness), she will experience hope also as a motion of the will.[15] A person who possesses the virtue of theological hope is oriented primarily by gift and by intention, and secondarily by imaginative longing, toward a more intimate union with the fount of all goodness—a union that she judges to be desirable, but unfathomable . . . meaningful, but strictly speaking incomprehensible.

With respect to the temporal world, a person of theological hope will do more than wait for it to end. She will envision a society that reflects, as much as possible, the goodness at the heart of reality.[16] From a Thomistic viewpoint, she will desire a society in which the dignity of persons is honored—a society that promotes, in a balanced and sustainable way, the exercise of the capabilities that are most definitive of persons' full and pleasant functioning. She will know that humans are in need of restraint, but her priority will be to encourage the realization of potential. In striving for a better society, she will keep the idea of the *highest* good (for all) in mind.[17] This good presents itself to her as a distant possibility, in this life and the

12. *ST* I-II 62.3; II-II 17.2.
13. *ST* II-II 18.2.
14. *ST* I 81.2, including *ad* 2.
15. *ST* II-II 18.1, including *ad* 1.
16. For a Thomistic account of "how Christian hope builds up the temporal human good" (119), see Doyle, *Promise of Christian Humanism*.
17. *ST* I-II 92.1, including *ad* 3.

next. She willingly tends toward it, but without knowing, exactly, what "it" is.

The theological virtue of hope could be constructed to fit religious perspectives other than Christian ones. It could function within some agnostic worldviews, where there is an openness to the idea of cosmic purposefulness, an appreciation of the order and beauty of the natural world, or a curiosity about what holds everything together, but where a person does not find it meaningful to relate in a *personal* way to the purported source of order, beauty, or creativity. Constructing religious hope in cross-traditional perspective is not, however, our present task.

A PROBLEM WITH HOPE

Hope in *some* form is essential for human life. If we have hope, whether it concerns our earthly existence only, or another mode of existence as well, we will be disinclined to let the difficulties of life defeat us. If we hope in a better society, we will resist becoming bitter and misanthropic when, year after year, many of the changes that we desire elude us, and many situations seem to get worse.

Hope inclines us toward what we regard as promising. However, what some of us regard as promising when we look to the future, others regard as menacing. When we hope to bring about positive social change, we attach ourselves to possibilities that at least some of our fellow humans will resist. It is often the anticipation of opposition that evokes hope in the first place. If our goal were easy, we would not *have* to hope for it; we could simply reach out for it and effortlessly attain it. The experience of being in the presence of something high, distant, or uncertain, or something that otherwise complicates the ease of life, is inherent in hope.[18]

One could say that the perception of *evil* is inherent in hope. In a Thomistic framework, evil signifies broadly what is bad, unsuitable, or undesirable. It signifies a relative absence of goodness, a failure of actualization, a cause of diminishment, or an experience of unwanted pain.[19] Evil, like good, is a matter of degree. It is also, to an extent, a matter of perspective. What is good for one person or group can be, in certain respects, evil for another person or group. In addition, what is good for one party, in one respect, can be evil for the same party, in some other respect. By the same token, what is evil for one party can be reconceived, by that party, in a more

---

18. *ST* I-II 23.2.

19. See the first question of *The De Malo of Thomas Aquinas*. See also McCabe, *God Matters*, chapter 3.

positive light. For example, people sometimes choose to interpret painful things that happen to them as opportunities for growth.

The *hope* of one person or group can be regarded as evil by others, and vice versa. For example, from a Marxist perspective, a Christian's hope in a happy afterlife is an opiate, and opiates are evil because they keep people from facing the truth and contributing to genuine social progress. From a Christian perspective, a Marxist's hope in the abolition of religion is evil because it motivates social policies that cut people off from an aspect of their humanity, which they must cultivate if they are to thrive.

If we regard the hopes of others as evil because these hopes aim at something that, in our judgment, is incongruent with human well-being—and if other people regard our hopes in the same way—then we are all in a bind. Our interlocking negative judgments and irritations could make it difficult for us to live and work together. The answer to such a difficulty cannot be to stop thinking in terms of good and evil altogether. We cannot stop judging some situations to be pleasant and desirable and others to be painful and undesirable—not without becoming insensible. We cannot stop judging certain things to be better for humans than other things—not without ceasing to care about real humans and their suffering. We can, however, become aware of the way in which the gain of one thing generally implies the loss of something else. We can resist the temptation to think of good and evil as settled opposites. We can practice empathy and generosity of mind as we consider how situations look from other points of view. We can become humbler about our own, usually mixed motives.

Perceptions of good and evil *can* be instructive.[20] They can make us aware of how much various things matter to us. They can motivate choices that preserve our well-being and the well-being of others. They can provide us with opportunities to think critically about our loves and aspirations. They can challenge us to confront our insecurities. But if we are emotionally or volitionally inflexible, and we are relatively opaque to ourselves, we will be tempted to perceive evils as absolute, located in people other than ourselves, and having nothing important to teach us about ourselves.

HATRED

It is instructive to consider hope in relation to hatred, even though these attitudes are not typically paired by philosophers. Like hope, hatred has several dimensions. Arguably, some of them are less problematic than others, and some are more subject to choice than others, so it is worth teasing them

---

20. *ST* I-II 24.3, including *ad* 1.

apart, even if they generally occur at the same time, as aspects of a single experience.

Hatred, like hope, can refer to an emotion. According to a Thomistic moral psychology, the emotion of hatred is a painful *dissonance* that we experience when we apprehend something via our sensory powers as being unsuitable for us or for someone who is part of us.[21] Hatred is the contrary of love, where the emotion of love is a pleasing *resonance* that we experience when we apprehend something as being suitable for us or for someone who is close to us.[22] Understood in this way, hatred is always caused, in part, by love: we hate a given object because it seems to be destructive of what we love or regard as lovable.[23] In a Thomistic scheme, *every* emotion is caused partly by love—by our love for ourselves and for those whose good we associate with our own. The objects that move us are those that (we sense) have the potential to affect our happiness, for good or for ill.[24]

In light of evolutionary science, the emotion of hatred appears to be natural to humans, as it is to other sentient beings. Specifically, if we did not ordinarily feel uncomfortable when we confront objects that are capable of harming us and, in some cases, are *inclined* to harm us, such as extremely cold temperatures or aggressors who seek to invade our territory and consume our limited resources, we would not be here at all. Our species would have gone extinct long ago, or "we" would constitute a different species. Hatred, understood as an object-oriented, internal disturbance, can hold life-saving information. However, we can be wrong about what diminishes us. We can feel disturbed by something that is not, in fact, harmful to us.[25] We can also be morally wrong about the sorts of interference with our pleasure that justify us in causing others pain. We can be morally wrong in judging our comfort to be more important than others,' simply because it is ours.

As soon as we feel uncomfortable in relation to something that strikes us as evil, we have the ability—and the responsibility, as conditions allow—to examine the way we feel.[26] Once we bring our intellectual powers to bear on the situation and on our reaction to it, it is possible for us to be motivated, in part, by educated judgments. We can use the power of reason not only to

---

21. *ST* I-II 29.1. Readers are asked to set aside, for the moment, their assumptions about what hatred is (what the term refers to), and consider what might be gained by thinking of it in the following way.

22. *ST* I-II 26.1.

23. *ST* I-II 29.2.

24. For an analysis of love, which is prerequisite to an adequate analysis of hatred, see Cates, "Love," 1–30.

25. *ST* I-II 29.1 *ad* 2.

26. *ST* I-II 24.1, 30.3, 59.2; I 81.3.

restrain our behavior, if need be, but also to alter how we feel. We can affirm that our hatred is appropriate and consent to it, such that we continue to feel uncomfortable, but our uncomfortableness is qualified somewhat by a pleasing impression that we are emotionally on target. We can judge that our hatred is inappropriate, withhold our consent from it, and direct our attention to a different facet of the object or a different object that we regard as lovable, such that our love increases and our hatred dissipates. We can reject as bad the hatred that we currently feel, but in a way that ironically generates a strong attachment to that hatred, such that it takes *longer* to dissipate. And so on. Reason is not utterly free in relation to emotion, but neither is it simply emotion's slave—at least, not in people who have a measure of virtue.

As noted previously, when we are motivated by thoughts and reasons concerning goodness, our will is engaged. Whereas the emotion of hatred, in a Thomistic perspective, is the experience of being disturbed by a sensory image or impression, the volition of hatred is more intellectual and agent-active. It is the experience of *dissenting* deliberately to an object that we judge to be contrary to human well-being.[27] It is an interior act by which we fortify ourselves mentally in relation to something that is poised to diminish us or others whom we love. Hatred, like hope, usually operates as an emotion and a volition at the same time. A sensory object that makes us feel uneasy causes us to think about what is important to us, and our thoughts lead us to reject a particular object as evil: thus, emotion gives rise to volition. Or we judge an object of our intellect to be incompatible with human flourishing and we therefore reject it. We think of this object in terms of related sensory images, and these images cause us to feel uncomfortable: thus volition gives rise to emotion.

AVERSION, ANGER, HOSTILITY, MALEVOLENCE, CALLOUSNESS

According to a Thomistic moral psychology, hatred is best understood, not only in relation to love, but also in relation to other interior motions. These other motions are often conflated with hatred and with each other, but it is important not to conflate them.

First, consider aversion.[28] Aversion can refer to an emotion, a motion of the will, or both. Construed as an emotion, aversion refers to a mode of

---

27. *ST* I-II 29.1. This is implied also by an analysis of love as both an emotion and a motion of the will.

28. *ST* I-II 23.2. Aquinas needs the concept of aversion (*fuga*), and he needs to keep it distinct from hatred, if he is to have coherent theory of the emotions, as they operate

being repelled by something that is painful or appears, on a sensory level, to be harmful. As a motion of the will, aversion refers to a mode of turning away from something mentally that we judge to be destructive of human well-being. Relative to these forms of aversion, hatred connotes two things: it connotes an emotional *dissonance* that can, but does not necessarily, give rise to a feeling of being repelled by something. It connotes also a volitional *dissent* that can, but does not necessarily, give rise to an intellectually-informed desire to avert a perceived evil for the sake of some good. Hatred is not the same thing as aversion, but it is a common cause of aversion. We often desire to avoid objects that disturb us and that we reject as contrary to genuine happiness.

Some people think of hatred less as a matter of being averse, and more as a matter of being hostile.[29] The Merriam-Webster Dictionary reflects both perspectives, defining "hate" as "intense hostility and aversion."[30] By conjoining aversion and hostility, this definition occludes the fact that these interior motions orient us in different directions: aversion is a movement away from, while hostility is typically a movement toward or facing, an apparent evil. Nonetheless, the pairing is suggestive. It hints further at some of the complexity of hatred.

Hostility is best characterized as an emotion, which might or might not be expressed in outward behavior. Like the emotion of aversion, hostility can be thought of as a way of being moved by an object that we perceive, on a sensory level, to be painful or harmful. But unlike aversion, hostility is a way of tending *toward* an object in order to fend it off, disable it, dominate it, or the like. It is helpful to distinguish hostility from malevolence, even though the two are often experienced at the same time. The latter is best characterized as a motion of the will. Like the volition of aversion, malevolence can be thought of as a way of moving ourselves in relation to an object that we think of as contrary to goodness. But unlike aversion, it is a way of tending *toward* the prospect of stopping that object, injuring it, or seeing it do poorly.[31]

Hostility and malevolence sometimes take the more specific form of anger. Anger is best understood as an emotion that is caused by a painful

---

in relation to the will. See Cates, *Aquinas on the Emotions*, chapter 6.

29. Aquinas does not distinguish carefully enough between hatred as an emotion and hatred as a motion of the will, or between hatred as the contrary of love and hatred as the contrary of desire, but these distinctions are crucial to the development of an ethic of hatred. See *ST* I-II 29.4, 46.2, 46.6.

30. Merriam-Webster Dictionary, "Hate," http://www.merriam-webster.com/dictionary/hate?show=0&t=1338228785.

31. *ST* I-II 78.3.

impression that we have been intentionally or thoughtlessly slighted by someone who ought to respect us.[32] (By extension, we can be angry with an inanimate object, such as a missing set of keys, which has failed to be duly amenable to us.) Anger includes a desire to denounce the slight and avenge ourselves. Our hope, in desiring vengeance, is to cause our offender pain, against his will, in order to force him to take us—and what he has done to us—seriously.[33] Our further aim, which is often implicit, is to re-establish an appropriate balance of power and regard between us. (In the case of a mere thing, our hope is to make it subject to our desire.) The more anger goes beyond a basic sense of having been treated unfairly, which is a feeling that can be experienced by many animals, and it incorporates higher-level judgments about human dignity and justice, the more it becomes a motion of the will, as well as an emotion.[34]

HOPE IN A SOCIAL IDEAL

Having mapped, in outline, some of the conceptual territory of hatred and related states of mind, we can return to the hope in a social ideal. Suppose our desire for social change is opposed by people who want something very different for the world. Suppose we are offended by (what feels like) their refusal to take us seriously. We are frustrated by (what appears to be) their unwillingness to listen to us, their lack of empathy, and their failure to care about things that ought (we believe) to be important to everyone. We want to defeat their opposition in such a way that we get them to change their hearts and minds. Our overarching purpose is to promote the best conditions for widespread human flourishing. We have reason to believe that our efforts will eventually benefit our opponents as well. In that case, we are most likely in the realm of anger.

Again, suppose we feel disturbed by our opponents because we perceive that they are keeping us from attaining our ideal. We want to defeat their opposition, but we are not inclined to put much time and effort into changing their attitudes. They have proven themselves (in our opinion) to be beyond reason or lacking in good sense. What we want, in effect, is to force them into submission. We might wish to do away with them altogether, sensing that the world would be a better place if they were not in it. If our opponents remain ignorant of the superiority of our vision, and unwilling to join our ranks, then we have no interest in dealing with them as free and

32. *ST* I-II 46.1, 47.1, 47.2.
33. *ST* I-II 46.6.
34. *ST* I-II 46.4, 46.5.

dignified persons. In that case, we are occupied with forms of hostility and malevolence that are in principle distinguishable from anger.

Many people, in diverse cultures, find it easy to admit that they feel anger, for one can almost always interpret a hurtful situation *as* a situation in which one has been treated unfairly. Many people feel justified in the desire to put an offender in his place—after all, the other needs to know his place and behave himself in that place if he is to be a full member of society. Most people are more reluctant to admit that they feel hostile (except in the defense of the innocent) or malevolent (except perhaps toward unambiguous evils) because these interior motions so often tend toward destructiveness, and this destructiveness does not appear to serve a larger ethical purpose, such as justice. There is a lot of room in situations of conflict for faulty interpretation, and the temptation to self-deception can be strong.

Notice that anger, hostility, and malevolence all typically involve a desire to cause someone pain. An angry person desires to cause someone pain because he thinks the pain is deserved. Moreover, the pain will alert the offender to the seriousness of what she has done, which is important to the rebuilding of mutual regard. A hostile person desires to cause pain mainly because he thinks this pain will slow his opponent down or cause her to back off—or (in more malicious cases) it will cause his victim to feel weak and dependent. The hostile person might seek the latter reaction because it brings him pleasure or relief from the pain of his own life. A malevolent person desires to cause pain mainly because he believes the other person is evil and, for that reason, ought to suffer—or (in more malicious cases) the malevolent person simply wishes the other evil, without caring to justify himself.

Hatred, by contrast, is *not* a desire to cause pain. It is not a desire at all, in a Thomistic scheme. It is merely a feeling of being uncomfortable with and hardening ourselves in relation to some aspect of a situation that we regard (rightly or wrongly) as unsuitable. Hatred *can* give rise to subsequent desires. It can give rise to anger *if* the evil that we suffer takes the form of a slight, and the respect of others or the acknowledgment of our human dignity really matters to us. Hatred can cause hostility *if* we sense that hurting someone could make us feel better or more in control. It can cause malevolence *if* we judge that someone is evil and undeserving of a good and pleasant life.

Hatred can give rise to any of these desires, but it does not necessarily do so. Often, hatred simply dissipates. Situations change, and we move on to other concerns. In addition, sometimes hatred is experienced more in the mode of coldness and callousness than in the mode of steamy preoccupation. Some people disturb us, and we become cold and distant toward them, but beyond this we do not care enough to give them our attention. We might not care enough to turn toward them mentally and wish them ill. At the same time, we would not be upset if things were to go badly for them.

ETHICS OF HATRED AND UTOPIC LONGING

In a Thomistic ethical perspective, most emotions and related motions of the will can be appropriate to a situation or inappropriate. They can be justifiable in some respects while being unjustifiable in others. Hatred, in particular, can be suitable or unsuitable. It is morally problematic to hate the wrong object (for example, something that is not in fact harmful), for the wrong reason, in the wrong respect, too intensely (or too weakly), for too long (or too briefly), too indiscriminately (without recognition of the object's concomitant goodness), and so forth.[35] Often the emotion of hatred arises spontaneously, in response to a sensory stimulus, before we have time to think. The point is not to hold persons accountable for initial emotional reactions over which they have no control. Rather, the point is to hold ourselves accountable for the implicit or explicit choices that we make, in light of ethical ideals, to invest in, to withdraw our energy from, or to redirect our initial interior motions.[36]

In a Thomistic perspective, it can be permissible to hate a trait, attitude, behavior, or the like, which we judge *correctly* to be contrary to human well-being. That is, it can be permissible to feel uncomfortable with, and to choose to limit our felt vulnerability (for a time) in relation to, something *in the respect* and *to the degree* that it is evil or hurtful to humans and to other beings whose good we include in our own.[37] However, it is never permissible to hate a person or group of persons as such. What this means, in part, is that it is not permissible to hate a person's existence, such that we are poised, in a subsequent moment, to wish that the person were dead or had never been born. Existence, especially the existence of a person, is essentially good, whatever the person might have made of his or her life so far. The thought of why this person—or any person, for that matter—exists,

35. Aristotle, *Nicomachean Ethics* 1106b16–24.
36. *ST* I-II 24.1.
37. *ST* I-II 29.5.

and what he or she is capable of contributing to the world, under varying conditions, ought to elicit wonder, rather than disdain.

In the same vein, it is never permissible to hate all that a person is or has become. No human being is utterly without redeeming qualities. To the extent that a person has even the *slightest* possibility of realizing *some* potential for goodness, our recognition of this fact must condition the way we experience whatever hatred we might feel. When we fail to admit the possibility of goodness in another, and we choose instead to perceive only what is lacking, we diminish our own moral goodness. We do best as humans, and we are likely to be most satisfied with our complicated lives, if we readily resonate with—and choose to affirm—objects that are, in some respects, poised to please us in ways that are consistent with human well-being.

When Aquinas speaks of hatred as a *habit* of emotion and volition, he usually implies that it is a *bad* habit. It is a vice, rather than a virtue. A disposition to e*xcessive* hatred, or a disposition to hate persons or groups of persons as such, is a common cause of unjustified hostility and malevolence. But hatred is not by definition excessive, nor does it necessarily give rise to unjustified hostility and malevolence. A person *could* be disposed to undergo *appropriate* emotion and volition in response to perceived evils. That is to say, hatred (in our specific sense) *could* name a moral virtue. However, a virtuous response to a hurtful situation would never be one of hatred alone. And it would never be one in which hatred so commands our awareness that we lose the ability freely to detach ourselves from our hatred—or at least begin the process—out of a concern for goodness.

Every evil refers implicitly to something good, such as the fact that the object in question exists at all, that it has potential to actualize, that it sustains the life of something else, that it plays some other role in the larger scheme of things, and so on. An evil can be understood and addressed well only in relation to the good that it diminishes, or from which it detracts. In theory, it is *possible* to exercise a virtuous hatred toward particular aspects of others, but only inasmuch as we experience our dissonance and dissent in the context of virtuous love—only inasmuch as we are, at the same time, well-disposed to be pleased by and to affirm what is good in others and ourselves. In the absence of virtuous love, hatred loses its point as a protector of what we value. It is simply an experience of feeling disturbed by and rejecting what strikes us as negative. By itself, hatred cannot put a person in a flourishing state.

If hatred could, in principle, take the form of a moral virtue, in a context of virtuous love, could it also, like hope, take the form of a *theological* virtue? More precisely, could hatred name a habit that orients humans well in relation to other humans, where the good of humans is viewed against the horizon of the *highest* good?[38] Some Christians (among others) hold that God exhibits hatred. The highest power of the universe hates certain people, especially those who unrepentantly do things that are contrary to God's will. Some Christians hold that their love for God and their hope for redemption *require* that they imitate God and thus hate the people whom God hates. What could it mean, however, to say that God hates people? It could mean that perfect goodness as such does not originate, sustain, attract, or unite with people in the specific manner and to the precise extent that they lack goodness. People who have their origin and end in the source of all goodness, but also live in a world of confusion and misdirection, suffer for their own and each other's unloving choices.

Some religious believers imply more than this when they say that God hates certain people. They imply that God is an all-powerful, personal being who, like them, experiences dissonance, dissent, aversion, hostility, malevolence, anger, and the like (where many of the mental states that we have distinguished are blended together). In holding that God undergoes these sorts of painful responses, people imply that God is vulnerable to being injured by humans who do bad things. God responds to threats and harms by becoming unsettled, putting up defenses, or going on the attack. This thesis contradicts the widely-held notion that God is all-powerful. It suggests that God's power must continually vie with human power. It also suggests that God is one being among others, albeit a superior being, rather than the power of being itself. Anthropomorphic images of a hate-full and fearsome God are often used to justify the hatred of enemies. However, such views of God and the imitation of God cannot withstand scrutiny.

Unlike God, as traditionally conceived, humans *are* vulnerable to other humans. The *emotion* of hatred can alert us to the fact that we stand in relation to something that is capable of hurting us or other people whom we love. The *volition* of hatred can be a mode of protecting ourselves and others, and refusing to tolerate behaviors that cause unnecessary suffering. In principle, it is appropriate periodically to be disturbed by and to reject such evils as bigotry or rape or child abuse or everyday meanness, which we judge correctly to be contrary to human well-being. But the challenge is to conceive evil always in relation to good—to feel pained and resistant toward hurtful things always in light of the goodness that they oppose and which we love.

With respect to people in our communities who hope for a future society that we regard as morally problematic, it can be appropriate to hate the

---

38. Aquinas refers to these virtues more specifically as "infused" moral virtues. See *ST* I-II 63.3.

prospect of that society, just as it can be appropriate to hate the resistance that people pose to our efforts to improve the human condition. The key is to experience such hatred in light of a general ideal of "a good society that is enjoyed by all," which evokes our consent and our sensory resonance, but which we remain reluctant to define in too much detail.

With respect to our opponents, it is important to presume that they, like everyone else, possess notable goodness. Virtue requires that we consistently look for this goodness, take pleasure in it, and affirm it mentally, even as we feel whatever else we feel—if not at the same moment, then in a workable oscillation. If other people pose a danger to us or to the people whom we love, it is appropriate to register this danger and steel ourselves against it. But our next task is to move ourselves, as soon as feasible, to a more subtle and flexible response, reminding ourselves that persons and situations have many facets, and moral agents have the power to examine one facet, then another, and then another, in an effort to attain a reasonably balanced view of what is happening.

Some people are prone to react to the initial stirrings of hatred by being consumed by their hatred. They become obsessed with a perceived evil, and they lose the ability to advance themselves to other considerations. Inasmuch as hatred is a natural response, in a person with a healthy brain, we probably cannot avoid feeling disturbed in some way by the presence of something that strikes us as hurtful. Moreover, in a Thomistic perspective, hatred is a necessary cost of love, within the temporal realm, and a life without love is not worthy of a human being, nor does it lead to flourishing communities. However, Aquinas would have us strive to become more capable of experiencing dissonance and dissent in relation to a particular feature of a situation, without losing touch with other features of the situation, and other situations that warrant openness and affirmation. If we are to thrive in each other's company, we must presume that it is generally possible for us and for others to register the presence of a hurtful object, while remaining capable of evoking alternative perspectives and motives, as needed, to keep ourselves from becoming overly-preoccupied by what appears to be negative.

Ought we to indulge in utopic longing, individually or as members of a group, when other people in our extended communities regard our social ideal as anything but ideal—when these other people are disposed to hate that for which we hope, and even to hate our hope, and we, in turn, are prone to hate the fact that they hate the things that are dear to us? The question is: are we and others emotionally and volitionally capable of managing our response to a perceived evil, such that we keep our initial hatred from becoming excessive and yielding malicious forms of hostility, malevolence, and anger? If we love goodness, we will appropriately hate what is contrary to goodness. Yet we will realize, all along, that the people or groups who oppose us are not defined simply by their opposition to us. They do not exist only for or against us, but in their own right. Both they—and we—are capable of much goodness. Moreover, we are all capable of changing in surprising ways. Indeed, each of us is continually changing. Developing our full human potential requires cultivating habits that reflect an awareness of this fact. It is possible to bring ourselves to love the presumed goodness and potential for goodness of even our strongest opponents, in a manner that reliably qualifies our hatred, as our hatred rises and falls.

It is good to think of the ideal society as a situation in which humans (among other beings) thrive individually, interpersonally, and communally, within the constraints of finitude. Beyond this, it is wise to regard the more specific content of the ideal as somewhat of an open question. (The question ought not to be regarded as *completely* open; there is a range of reasonable views concerning what is good for humans, but it is not the case that anything and everything is consistent with human well-being.) Our opponents are persons who have reasons for embracing the conception of the good that they currently embrace—reasons that they could probably articulate to us, if we were to ask well-formed questions. Close listening can inspire us to reformulate our ideal in ways that are experienced by others as more congenial to their way of thinking.

A utopic ideal can function as a reminder to consider and care about the good for humans, in a way that self-consciously orients us toward an end that we love, but cannot fully comprehend. It can, in principle, expose the limits of any settled view of things. It can continually bring people back to simple moral practices that hold the worst forms of cruelty and callousness at bay. Utopic longing poses moral risks inasmuch as we lack the mental wherewithal to project our ideal while also, at the same time, recognizing that our perspectives and judgments—like those of others—are limited. Yet we have little choice but to cultivate the kind of character that allows us—and hopefully encourages others—to both take and minimize this risk. Doing well as humans requires that we be ever hopeful of the possibility of goodness, especially of the reduction of pointless suffering, while learning to deal with ineliminable features of our animal nature, including our tendency to find certain things in our environment disturbing.

BIBLIOGRAPHY

Aquinas, Thomas. *The De Malo of Thomas Aquinas*. Edited by Brian Davies. Oxford: Oxford University Press, 2001.

———. *Summa Theologiae*. Edited by Petri Caramello. Rome: Marietti, 1950.

Aristotle. *Nicomachean Ethics*. Translated by Terence Irwin. Indianapolis: Hackett, 1985.

Cates, Diana Fritz. *Aquinas on the Emotions: A Religious-Ethical Inquiry*. Washington, DC: Georgetown University Press, 2009.

———. "Love: A Thomistic Analysis." *Journal of Moral Theology* 1/2 (2012) 1–30.

Doyle, Dominic F. *The Promise of Christian Humanism: Thomas Aquinas on Hope*. New York: Crossroad, 2011.

McCabe, Herbert. *God Matters*. New York: Continuum, 1987.

Pieper, Josef. *Faith, Hope, Love*. San Francisco: Ignatius, 1997.

3

What Means *Utopia* to Us?
Reconsidering More's Message

—Marybeth Baggett

UTOPIAN LITERARY HISTORY

Almost five centuries after Thomas More's publication of *Utopia*, the insights of that work have all but disappeared beneath the mountain of fiction, criticism, and theory that has been built up around it. In many ways, the popular and critical reception of More's text epitomizes the prediction about the written word Plato offers in the *Phaedrus*.[1] It has lost the protection of its author, and the many translations, adaptations, and appropriations of More's material make difficult authentic engagement with his work. Yet, in light of More's contemporary influence, his historical reputation, and his contribution to the popularization of humanism, *Utopia* deserves a reading untainted by the filter of the writing that follows in its wake, for such derivative work ultimately departs and detracts from More's project.

    Utopia's very title mobilizes in a contemporary reader's mind at least the popular understanding of the term,[2] a place of perfect order and perfect

---

    1. Plato, *Phaedrus*, 70.
    2. The *OED* offers two primary definitions of the term—one based on More's text and its literary derivatives (1.a "An imaginary island, depicted by Sir Thomas More as enjoying a perfect social, legal, and political system" and 1.b. "Any imaginary, indefinitely-remote region, country, or locality") and a second based on its popular interpretation (2.a. "A place, state, or condition ideally perfect in respect of politics,

happiness that satisfies all inhabitants and satiates their minds and their bodies. Yet the popular usage of the term "utopia" has only a passing resemblance to the contents of More's book, which does include blueprints for an apparently perfect society but which also contextualizes those blueprints within a conversation that challenges the advisability of implementing those plans. Thus, as I will argue below, More's text requires and teaches a careful hermeneutic that encourages personal responsibility and community involvement. Comparison of the book's contents with contemporary usage shows that though More coined the term utopia, his text no longer anchors its meaning. And, ironically, that is so primarily because of his book's influence. Somewhere amid the publication of the more than fifteen hundred utopian fictions written since More's *Utopia*,[3] the popular usage of the term utopia became detached from More's original message. Additionally, the distance between the popular definition of utopia and More's usage has increased with the formation of the utopian studies discipline,[4] which has blossomed into an impressive body of criticism and journals.[5]

While popular definitions understandably depart from More's landmark text, surprisingly even critical definitions seem dissociated from More's original project. Because utopian studies is by nature multi- and interdisciplinary,[6] each theorist defining the term or genre emphasizes various details relevant to his or her academic discipline, spanning the literary, philosophical, sociological, and political, and, thus, even significant utopian theorists disagree on utopia's key features, complicating even further an untainted impression of More's book.[7] While these critical definitions are

---

laws, customs, and conditions" and 2.b. "An impossibly ideal scheme, esp. for social improvement").

3. Sargent, "Themes."

4. The Society for Utopian Studies was founded in 1975, and their peer-reviewed academic journal, *Utopian Studies*, began printing in 1978.

5. A *JSTOR* search of the term utopia, for example, returns well beyond 56,000 results.

6. On their "About" webpage, the *Utopian Studies* journal website offers the following description of its contributors: "Contributing authors come from a diverse range of fields, including American studies, architecture, the arts, classics, cultural studies, economics, engineering, environmental studies, gender studies, history, languages and literatures, philosophy, political science, psychology, sociology and urban planning."

7. Any worthwhile bibliography of utopian theory and criticism will include the following names: Lyman Tower Sargent—founding editor of the *Utopian Studies* journal, Darko Suvin—early editor of the *Science Fiction Studies* journal, and Krishan Kumar—author of several tomes on utopianism. The definitions of utopia laid out by these critics are as follows: In "Three Faces of Utopianism Revisited," Sargent calls utopia "a non-existent society described in considerable detail and normally located in time and space" (9). Suvin narrows this somewhat general definition by adding the qualification

helpful for fleshing out the limits of the discourse More began, they are less helpful in understanding More's original work. This is so primarily because these definitions, and the shape that the field itself has taken, emphasize the programmatic[8] nature of utopian literature.

Gregory Claeys and Lyman Tower Sargent, for example, encourage readers of their *Utopia Reader* anthology to understand More's text as a developed plan for the best form of a commonwealth.[9] For, though they include a selection from More's text, that selection comes solely from the second book,[10] Raphael Hythloday's in-depth explanation of Utopian social structure, without acknowledgement or explanation of its placement amidst the first book's vexed question of the right response to political and social corruption and maneuvering. And, as firsthand engagement with More's text shows—apart from its position in the utopian fiction and studies that follow it, only a portion of More's book delineates a social program. While utopian fictional offshoots and their integration into popular discourse encourage readers to accept them as prescribed modes of living, the value of More's work lies in its promotion of critical engagement—with the written word and with other people—and its promotion of human dignity and moral development.

MORE'S PROJECT

The original utopia actually opens with a battle of wits and wills between a fictional More and Raphael Hythloday, advocate of the social order described in the second book. None of the popular or critical definitions, though, account for the inclusion of such an introduction. Instead, as Claeys

---

that this non-existent society must be "organized according to a more perfect principle than in the author's community" (49). And Kumar insists that to be counted as utopian this fictional society must be described in "full operation" so as to encourage the reader's imaginative participation in that world (25).

8. By "programmatic," I mean the features of utopian literature that purport to lay out a plan for perfect social order, from family arrangements to economic structure to government details. These features when read without the context of the first book suggest that the literary work advocates implementation of such structures to correct all social ills.

9. Of course, the book's full title when read without irony suggests this is the case: *On the Best State of a Commonwealth and on the New Island of Utopia*.

10. *Utopia* consists of two main sections, a first and second book, and a prefatory letter to Peter Giles. The first book which introduces Thomas More as a fictional character, his friend Peter Giles, and Raphael Hythloday, More's fictional utopian visitor who reports his experiences in the land of Utopia to More and Giles. This report dominates the second book of *Utopia* proper.

and Sargent's anthology exemplifies, they conceive of utopian literary texts solely in terms of the societies they construct, the details involved in those constructions, the protocols, the governance, and the systems imposed. And, as detailed as the description of Utopian society is in More's second book, divorcing that description from its fictional context—the aftermath of More and Hythloday's disagreement over the benefits or downfalls of public service—alters its significance and suggests a wholly different meaning than More intended.

However, fairness to More demands that we reconsider his *Utopia* in its original state. In fact, More's other work suggests that he requires such a reading from us. After More's friend and fellow humanist co-laborer, Desiderius Erasmus, published his *Praise of Folly*, More defended the work against egregious misreadings. One such defense came in the form of a letter to Martin Dorp[11] who believed Erasmus' work corrupted scripture. This letter argues that Dorp's criticisms are unfair because they are built on what More believes is an improper hermeneutic, one that seeks its own elevation at the expense of the author's message, uncharitably twisting the text being read. For More, a proper hermeneutic insists upon context and reads the original text by its own light. And this, too, is the type of reading that More's *Utopia* deserves and that rewards reader's investment.

Primarily More believes that Dorp's criticism of *Praise of Folly* relies on detaching portions of Erasmus' work from the rest of his text. To do so, More argues, is not merely to commit a minor scholastic error; it reaches a level requiring moral censure because these incomplete readings are unethical in their self-serving and self-centered nature. They disrespect the text, and in turn the author and ultimately, and most significantly for More, the truth. In More's words, readers like Dorp

> flatter themselves to the point that whatever they hear being cited, in whatever context, without ever reading the passage or seeing the book it appears in, without knowing what has preceded or what is to follow the words of the quotation, and without even knowing whether or not the text quoted appears in the quoted location, they think they alone can interpret the writings of all men, and even sacred scripture itself, in whatever sense happens to suit them.[12]

---

11. Dorp was Professor of Philosophy at the University of Louvain. More wrote Dorp in 1515, responding to criticism Dorp leveled at Erasmus through a series of letters.

12. More, quoted in Kinney, "Thomas More's Humanistic Defences," 270.

More's letter to Dorp calls for a respect for the text and for the author, a respect predicated on humility, justice, and communal responsibility. The virtue of proper reading lies in its other-centeredness. In true humanist form, More clearly indicates that reading has moral implications, and reading well demonstrates one's moral commitments, commitments that also drive More's project in *Utopia*. For, although *Utopia* has been historically (mis)understood as More's creation and promotion of a model community, the writer's concern is ultimately with his reader's engagement with the text. In *Utopia* More has crafted, not an ideal community, but a transformative agent that, through careful reading, goads readers into self-examination, rooting out self-deception and correcting self-centered impulses.

Reading *Utopia* as More asks Dorp to read Erasmus—with close attention to More's complexity—shows that we should understand it, not as a programmatic guide to creating the perfect society, but as a means for understanding human identity and human obligations to one another. Contrary to the trend of the genre created in the wake of More's book, examination of human frailties and embrace of human value, not promotion of human perfectibility, are at the heart of *Utopia*. These are the book's real lessons, and More teaches them primarily through using Raphael Hythloday as foil to both his fictional characters and the reader. But one can get to these lessons only by jettisoning the texts trailing after it and reading *Utopia* on its own terms.

As noted earlier, *Utopia* is a text in two parts. The first book[13] recounts More's time in Antwerp while serving as envoy for Henry VIII. The second book[14] describes the social structures of the island nation, Utopia. In the first book, More writes of himself in third person, as though he were simply another character in the text; other characters introduced are his friend Peter Giles and Hythloday, a traveler and explorer come back to Europe with extraordinary tales of other worlds and critiques aplenty of European civilization. More's diplomatic task, coupled with his conversations with Hythloday, convince both More and Giles that Hythloday would be well-suited to serve a royal court as advisor, and this belief creates the guiding narrative of *Utopia*'s first book, their attempt to press Hythloday into public service. Yet, despite his many criticisms of European civilization and his self-reported grasp of alternative modes of social existence, Hythloday is inconvincible.

---

13. Entitled "The First Book of the Communication of Raphael Hythloday, Concerning the Best State of a Commonwealth."

14. Entitled "The Second Book of the Communication of Raphael Hythloday, Concerning the Best State of a Commonwealth: containing the description of Utopia with a large declaration of the politic government and of all the good laws and orders of the same island."

Serving a king is bondage, he says; it is also useless, for Hythloday conceives of kings as tyrants, their court as flatterers, and their laws as provincial. Beneficial change can never occur, Hythloday concludes, so he avoids the attempt, all the while feeling free to criticize European society with impunity and pontificating about Utopia with authority. He stands quite indifferently apart from both Europe, the society he criticizes, and Utopia, the society he promotes, making him a less than admirable character and rendering his promotion of Utopian ideals and structure irrelevant.

Primarily because of the striking and comical contrast between Hythloday's public presentation of himself as purveyor of knowledge and his ultimate disdain of More's public service concerns, I follow Robert Elliott's recommendation[15] that *Utopia* is to be read as satire,[16] an approach that insists on careful attention to More's work on its own terms. Additionally I understand satire according to Matthew Hodgart's definition, "literature as propaganda for right action."[17] However, what More promotes as the right action is revealed only by following Elliott's advice to test the voices of *Utopia*'s speakers "against the norms of the work, weighing each shift of tone for possible moral implication. The meaning of the work as a whole is a function of the way those voices work with and against each other: a function of the pattern they form."[18]

It is here, in such a reading, that *Utopia* provides a vision, not of the good life as static existence, but of good living as a process very much like reading, not through structures of utopian life, which honestly seems awfully oppressive, but through active engagement with texts and with others. In reading *Utopia* we can practice this engagement by testing More's voice against Hythloday's and Renaissance England's realities against the fictional

---

15. According to Elliott, the scene at the Archbishop's dinner table in the first book, with the monk and fool, is overtly satirical: "[c]ertain elements in the scene, however—the spiraling invective, the character of contest and performance, of flyting, the threat of a fatal curse—are of the primitive stuff from which formal satire developed" ("Shape," 323). Additionally, in that same conversation, Elliott claims the hyperbolic description of the sheep run amok in satirical form, as a "beast fable compressed into the grotesque metaphor of the voracious sheep; the reality-destroying language which metamorphoses gentlemen and abbots into earthquakes, and a church into a sheep barn; the irony coldly encompassing the passion of the scene" (324).

16. Dustin H. Griffin also categorizes *Utopia* as satire, explaining that in it "ideas of high principle and worldly accommodation, community good and individual good, liberty and equality jostle against each other in an open and free-wheeling contest" (*Satire*, 110).

17. Hodgart, *Satire*, 16. Hodgart himself labels More's *Utopia* as satire early in his treatise on satire (52), but later disavows that label (184). Of course, I think he's right in his first pronouncement.

18. Elliott, "Shape," 321–22.

Utopia, and the discernment encouraged there will serve one—and his or her society—well after the book is set down. While critical and popular discourse has shifted the utopian focus to describing the ideal living space, the following reading of *Utopia* argues that More was primarily concerned with what type of people we should aspire to be.

More's first book is dominated by two main characters: More and Hythloday. The fictional More suggests the two men are friendly with one another, yet they could not have more opposite values. More establishes himself clearly as a public servant, one who does not shy from responsibilities to the state and to his family. Hythloday, on the other hand, sees such duties as burdens to be avoided, leaving his family to travel the world and shunning the call to the king's advisory council. More seems a man of few words; Hythloday is quite loquacious. More offers praise and encouragement to those he encounters; Hythloday primarily criticizes. More asks questions, seeking knowledge; Hythloday answers authoritatively, suggesting self-sufficiency.

By highlighting Hythloday's flaws against the backdrop of the fictional More's virtues, More encourages his readers to value, not resent, their social entanglements and obligations, their civic responsibilities as the place in which they find purpose and fulfillment. Hythloday's dismissal of social concerns,[19] combined with his belief in the possibility of a perfect social order accomplished apart from personal engagement, become the target of More's satire. While Hythloday understands any service to the crown as "bondage unto kings,"[20] not worth his self-sacrifice even for his family's sake, More, in his prefatory letter, has established himself as the consummate family man, one who realizes his duties, both domestic and civic, thinking of himself as participant in a larger community.[21] Of the two characters, More appears more measured, more thoughtful, and more public minded than Hythloday. He also appears to be less self-centered, less boastful, and less self-deluded. Such a contrast speaks to More's readers, encouraging them to render the proper judgment on Hythloday and to follow More's lead

19. Upon Giles's suggestion that Hythloday put his knowledge of other lands to good social use by advising the king, Hythloday responds that he has already done his part for his family, having divvied up his fortune for their inheritance prior to departing for foreign sites (15).

20. More, *Utopia*, 15.

21. As More explains in his opening letter to Giles, "[A] man must so fashion and order his conditions and so appoint and dispose himself that he be merry, jocund, and pleasant among them whom either nature hath provided or chance hath made or he himself hath chosen to be the fellows and companions of his life, so that with too much gentle behaviour and familiarity he do not mar them, and by too much sufferance of his servants make them his masters" (6).

in sacrificing selfish interests for the public good. Hythloday, More reveals, should not be their example because he is contradictory, full of supposed wisdom but satisfied with standing apart from others.

The opening voice of More's *Utopia* also contributes to its satire. In his prefatory letter to Peter Giles, included with *Utopia*'s first publication, More apologizes profusely for a fictitious situation, projecting an utmost seriousness about his failings to transcribe quickly Raphael Hythloday's description of this "perfect" commonwealth. The misdirection of the letter is revealed through More's confession that the publication's delay was entirely his fault: while the writer concedes that he needed only commit to paper what Hythloday communicated to him, the reader of *Utopia* realizes that More himself invented the world about to be described. Contrary to his fictional confession, More's role went well beyond merely "rehears[ing] those things which [Giles and he] together heard Master Raphael tell and declare."[22] Therefore, when this same More indicates that the truth "is the only mark whereunto [he] do[es] and ought to direct all [his] travail and study herein [in the book],"[23] the question of truthfulness is foregrounded. The truth about which More here speaks cannot be the concrete reality of such a world. Again, missing this multilayered misdirection of More's letter as preface to the text proper violates the complexity of *Utopia*. More's self-deprecating style in light of his role in crafting the tale startlingly contrasts Hythloday's self-promotion in light of his merely being the medium through which Utopian society is depicted to us.

After explaining, tongue-in-cheek, why he had little actual work to do in completing the manuscript of Hythloday's perfect commonwealth, More offers his excuses for not finding even the little time required to do so, all of which concern others: his work affairs, his socialization, his household affairs, his domestic duties, all of these leaving only time for food and sleep—from which he stole to write down Hythloday's story.[24] And, significantly, Hythloday's story of Utopia fantastically does away with all of these demands, presenting a society without worry, without tension, without the burdens of others. In Utopia, Hythloday explains, the demands of daily life—food, clothing, governance, education—no longer fall on individuals but on the communal structure, being described by Hythloday with language that obscures the individual's role in that process. As the following representative passage demonstrates, Hythloday's descriptions of Utopian society rely on collective and general nouns, unspecific pronouns, and passive voice:

22. More, *Utopia*, 5.
23. Ibid.
24. Ibid., 5–6.

> Wherefore, seeing they be all exercised in profitable occupations, and that few artificers in the same crafts be sufficient, this is the cause that, plenty of all things being among them, they do sometimes bring forth an innumerable company of people to amend the highways if any be broken. Many times also, when they have no work to be occupied about, an open proclamation is made that they shall bestow fewer hours in work.[25]

Hythloday here describes a structure that seemingly operates on its own. The individuals are subsumed in the general "they," and although some one person must make the decisions concerning working and leisure hours, Hytholoday's passive voice hazes over those details, giving the reader the impression that Utopian society doesn't require the individual responsibility that More exemplifies in his own life and that Hythloday has deemed unworthy of himself.

The prefatory letter, then, sets More up as judicious, self-effacing, temperate—a direct contrast to Hythloday who speaks in proclamations as self-appointed prophet of the new-world order, all the while shirking public duty and self-sacrifice. Although Hythloday dismisses Giles's encouragement to serve in the royal court, he nonetheless presents himself as enlightened, attributing Giles's incredulity about Utopia's wonders to his naiveté: "[I]f you had been with me in Utopia and had presently seen their fashions and laws, as I did which lived there five years and more, and would never have come thence but only to make that new land known here, then doubtless you would grant that you never saw people well ordered but only there."[26] So, while Hythloday purports to know how to shape a commonwealth for optimum social health and wealth, his account of Utopian life serves only to highlight himself and his experiences.

THOMAS MORE'S FICTIONAL PERSONA

More, the author, underscores the tension between Hythloday and the fictional More through humor and exaggeration. One early example of More's satirical technique comes when More and his companion Peter Giles are more anxious to hear about the "wise and well-governed states" Hythloday encountered in his travels than about sea monsters, since the former are more illusory than the latter.[27] Yet Hythloday seems to miss the joke and extolls the virtues of the Utopian community, so sure of himself and his

25. Ibid., 57
26. Ibid., 46.
27. Ibid., 4.

solution to England's ills. The scene at Cardinal Morton's dinner further reveals some elements of the satire's attack: Hythloday seems unaware that this scene actually disproves his earlier assertion that those in power rarely listen to new ideas, as Cardinal Morton readily accepts, and modifies for possible adoption, Hythloday's advice.

Additionally, while Hythloday praises the collective nature of Utopian life, he flaunts his independence from such social constraints, having left his family at a young age to sail with Vespucci and others, joining one expedition after another to discover "towns and cities and weal-publics, full of people, governed by good and wholesome laws."[28] But these discoveries, again, are only self-serving as Hythloday has no intention to submit himself to others' demands, which is required for any advisory role. Instead, he is flamboyant, an upstart, the ultimate individualist, and as such would not fit into the automaton realm of the Utopian society, much as he praises its structure. Thus his praise of them serves merely to self-aggrandize by criticizing the European status quo.[29] In this way, More's book becomes one of character examination, shining the light inward to the reader's own motives and desires. For one curiosity of utopian literature is its disconnect between the thing described (social structures and community), and the audience to whom that is described (the individual). While utopian literature, modeled after *Utopia*, presents fully developed social structures, individuals read the texts in a solitary activity, and More exploits this disparity by relentlessly pointing his reader, the individual, to his or her integration with, his or her responsibilities to, other people. He does so by contrasting his own character—in the prefatory letter and throughout the first book—with that of Hyloday's.

More's prefatory letter also satirically offers two excuses for Hythloday's ineloquent speech under the guise of explaining why he didn't even need to worry about adding eloquence to the writing style of the book, removing another excuse for his not having finished the book quickly. Hythloday's speech was spontaneous—not premeditated—and he is more fluent in Greek than in Latin. This, too, adds some tension to the work: while More describes Hythloday as "a man better seen in the Greek language than in the Latin tongue,"[30] More presents his character's narrative in Latin. True, Latin was the language of the educated in early Modern Europe, but why the misdirection? More, as his creator, could have crafted a fictional traveler fluent

---

28. Ibid., 14.

29. Hythloday criticizes corruption in royal courts, greediness of the nobility, gratuitous use of the death penalty, and the idleness of the landed class, along with other features he also identifies as distinctive to European life.

30. More, *Utopia*, 5.

in the Latin tongue, needing absolutely no translation. But adding this layer to Hythloday's presentation further complicates the character by promoting him through alignment with the classical era of the Greek philosophers[31] and simultaneously undermining that promotion by separating him from the Renaissance elite's chosen language.

MORE'S DEMANDS ON HIS READER

The translation thus provides More a space for encouraging critical engagement from his readers, requiring them to grapple with Hythloday's character—discerning for themselves his trustworthiness and the wisdom of the society he promotes. The translation More invents is, therefore, essential to the work's content. Beyond striking contrasts in these main characters, the text marks itself as satirical through More's pervasive use of translingual puns, which underscore More's demand for reader participation in adjudicating the questions at the heart of his work—what is the individual's role in community, what is the community's responsibility to the individual, by what means can these be balanced? These puns reinforce the tension between More and Hythloday set up in the first book. For example, though the title *Utopia* has been colloquially translated as "ideal," a closer look at More's work challenges this translation. In More's Latinization of the Greek "ou" and "eu" to simply "u," he elides the distinction between the possible interpretations of "no place" and "good place." In general parlance, the "good place" version of utopia has overshadowed the "no place" reading, as the aforestated definitions testify. Yet to appreciate fully More's purpose, the reader must hold those meanings in tension, for each contributes to the questions he is posing to his reader, questions such as the following: Does Utopia exist? Can it exist? Is its existence desirable? What life is desirable? Can a place make life better for its inhabitants? What role does the individual have in creating that place? Just as scrutinizing Hythloday's presentation of Utopian society reveals to us his suppression of individual responsibility in that world and the disparity between that life and his own character, so, too, does reading closely the disparity within the title's pun reveal the interpretive project of the book.

A quick determination of the title's meaning—whether the reader selects the "no place" definition or the "good place" one—works against More's project. There is a tension inherent in the no place/good place pun of *Utopia*'s title, a tension that expands on reflection and even provides space

---

31. Giles directly compares Hythloday to Plato on page 12, and references to the *Republic* occur throughout the text.

for that reflection to occur, a reflection cut short by elevating one over the other. More's book invites readers to dwell within the tension between the no place/good place of the title's pun, to imagine the possibilities of the good place—its features, its qualifications, its lived experience—within the confines of reality, including the knowledge that any such good place, should the reader determine that the good place can actually exist, is not here yet and that much must be overcome to achieve it. The reader who avoids this tension by selecting quickly one understanding of utopia over the other follows Hythloday's lead in eschewing the difficult work involved in striving for the good place while recognizing it has not yet materialized.

Besides this contradictory title, More includes other puns reliant on crossing linguistic boundaries, which undermine a straightforward reading, reinforcing the text's satirical mode and requiring audience participation to sort out. Many names in the book, of Utopian cities and waterways and neighboring peoples, have etymological origins that undermine their general sense in the book.[32] Anyder, Utopia's primary river, literally means "waterless"; one level of Utopian leadership is called the Ademus, meaning "without people"; the capitol city's name, Amaurote, translates to "dim city." While Hythloday explicitly praises Utopia, its names suggest the country may not, in fact, be praiseworthy.

The ubiquity of More's puns suggests a nuanced message, which at once demonstrates both reliability and instability in the world More invites us to explore. And this contradiction is first felt in the storyteller's name: Raphael Hythloday. The etymological origin of the messenger's first name points to its Hebrew source, the archangel, or messenger, of God whose name means God heals.[33] Yet this "messenger of God" carries another message through his family name. Though Hythloday is the expounder of the wonders of utopian life and seemingly quite rational, his surname translated from Greek means "speaker of nonsense." Again, the linguistic riddle raises the question of whether Hythloday can be trusted, which encourages continued vigilance on the reader's part. This vigilance discourages readers from mindlessly skimming through the text and encourages them to remain engaged and alert, recognizing that Hythloday—like all human beings—is both foolish and wise. Dismissing him—and others—too quickly disallows for his individuality and ignores what good he can offer.

---

32. The Oxford World's Classic edition of *Utopia*, included in their *Three Early Modern Utopias* collection, offers detailed notes explaining the range of More's linguistic playfulness.

33. See the Oxford World's Classic translation for a helpful explanatory note on Raphael Hythloday's name.

While one may suspect, for example, that the nonsense Hythloday peddles is Utopia's promotion of euthanasia, divorce, or other practices repugnant to More's Catholic sensibilities, the reader cannot simply reject everything the traveler shares. For Hythloday does promote elements resonant with Christian practice, ones More would certainly embrace and would hope that his readers would also embrace. Rejection of material wealth, a love of learning, cooperation: these, too, are features of Utopia, ones that exist alongside other, more questionable practices. And Hythloday's name, like his behavior, underscores the complicated nature of his message. Untangling this message is what More calls his reader to do through his complex presentation of Hythloday who can be read as humorous, foolish, confused, deceitful, and wise. But, as with the no place/good place pun of the book's title, isolating details that highlight only one characteristic of this character does injustice to him and to the text as a whole. Selecting only singular personality traits flatten out fully formed human beings, reducing them to pawns, much like Hythloday does in his descriptions of the Utopians.

In challenging us to read Hythloday as a full-bodied character and not a one-dimensional caricature, More requires much of his reader, for Hythloday's bombast can be trying. Hythloday evaluates Utopia as "wiselier governed" with his proof resting on its increased wealth and its advanced educational system. And while he often pretends to be merely describing the world he explored and not promoting it, these pretenses come most often when a questionable element of Utopia is raised. For example, when discussing their religion, Hythloday quickly passes over any objections by preempting such questions: "Wherein whether they believe well or no, neither the time doth suffer us to discuss, neither it is now necessary. For we have taken upon us to show and declare their laws and ordinances, and not to defend them."[34] However, he has called the land the best commonwealth he has seen, and he does so in spite of knowing about their mating ritual, which transform human beings to cattle or livestock.

In this literal stripping of potential husbands and wives, the qualities men and women look for in a spouse are reduced to physical concerns, denying any value or consideration of the mate's character. This scene, and Hythloday's unawareness of its conflict with his supposed concern about elevating human beings, like all satiric techniques, "explode[s] [. . .] inflated pretensions."[35] And Hythloday's later defense of other brilliant Utopian practices, such as their communistic aspects and their reevaluation of gold and jewels, without acknowledgement of the more troubling ones well

34. More, *Utopia*, 85.
35. Hodgart, *Satire*, 122.

demonstrate Hodgart's claim that "[s]atire warns us that man is a dangerous animal, with an infinite capacity for folly [. . .]."[36] And, though we see this folly on full display in Hythloday's character, the careful reader will also identify such folly in his or her own response to the imaginary island described in the second book.

In spite of the contradictions of Hythloday's reporting, there's something compelling about Hythloday's imaginary island. Because we recognize as true the struggles he describes in Book I of living in community, of being subject to the frailties of our fellow humans and often having to bear the burden of the consequences of those frailties, we long, perhaps, for the life free of tension described in Book II. England, Hythloday argues and More's character seems to affirm, suffers from the dictates of self-centered rulers—both kings and landholders. The greed of these powerful men has devastated the livelihoods and lives of their subjects. Hythloday offers what seems to be a rational counterbalance to the excesses of these rulers: abolish the object of these greedy rulers' desire and turn over all property to the people. Subject all to the rigid rule of law so that none can manipulate it to exploit others. Prevent personal strivings by collectivizing society. Again, in light of the truth we see about the difficulties of living in community, the reader of Hythloday's account may well identify it as the Promised Land.

However, to encourage us not to fall prey to this temptation, to remind us that we are more like Hythloday than we might want to admit, More provides satirical clues that something is amiss in such a world. He uses quite frequently what Brian Connery and Kirk Combe identify as "[t]he most common rhetorical figures of satire—irony, paradox, and oxymoron."[37] All of these rhetorical devices, Connery and Combe explain, "maximize the imaginative tension of the text and produce in the reader a consequent sense of discomfort."[38] The source of this discomfort is Hythloday's insistence that his first-hand experience of the perfection of Utopia proves its workability. Who are we to argue with Hythloday's experience, we wonder.

But a closer look suggests that More doesn't endorse such conclusions drawn from Hythloday's claim. First, More's simply having created this character renders false all Hythloday's pronouncements to truth and reliability. While Hythloday proclaims that his experiences in Utopia prove its workability, the reader, upon reflection, realizes that Hythloday—a fictional figure—has had no such experiences; thus, Hythloday's apparent thesis—Utopia has realized the best state that a commonwealth can achieve, and

---

36. Ibid., 248.
37. Connery and Combe, *Theorizing Satire*, 6.
38. Ibid.

its achievements are proven by his experiences there—is rendered baseless. Additionally, More crafted Hythloday as a boasting, self-centered, critical, detached figure. These features make comical his calls for the betterment of society. They also invalidate the suggestions he offers for such improvement.

Such contradictions between Hythloday's statements and outcomes undermine his authority as the mouthpiece for More. And these are the contradictions through which More points his readers to his main concerns of encouraging a full-bodied hermeneutic. The norm of this work comes from More's critical frame—the character descriptions of Book I, the personal interactions More describes, and the insight into actual human behavior all provide a foil for the mechanical nature of Book II. There is something eerily inhuman about More's *Utopia*—so ordered, so clinical, so controlled; what human can possibly survive there? Harry Berger calls these Utopians "walking statues confined in a carefully carpentered world of labyrinthine rationalizations and fortified institutions."[39] Berger argues that the rigidity of Utopian society reveals the misanthropy at the heart of its project.

Berger uses the Utopian family structure as his key example, particularly as compared with the family of Thomas More described in his prefatory letter. While on the surface Utopian society seems to value the family, according to Berger, their obliteration of any personal or private space also dissolves family ties. Utopian families are subsumed in the larger social project through communal meals, childrearing, caretaking, and housing. And, paradoxically, the family seems to be praised—overtly by Hythloday—but is simultaneously undermined, a feature of Utopian society Berger identifies as "misanthropic self-deception."[40] Utopia has codified a contingency that obliterates the self, a connection that belies the actual disconnection and dissolution of the individual.

And Hythloday is chief among the self-deceivers. For example, Hythloday denounces owning private property as the besetting human sin and praises its abolishment in Utopia as the panacea for all social ills, yet Hythloday's own account of Utopia reveals that law-breaking still exists—thievery, fornication, deceit. None of these has been eradicated by the imposed program. And, again, Hythloday seems unaware of his contradictions. Such tensions underscore that the greed, pride, and self-concern More attacks in Book I are not the burdens only of the aristocrat, but also of every person, including his reader who, without careful attention, can easily be tempted, along with Hythloday, to misread the Utopian existence as one-dimensional and, thus, wholly perfect.

39. Berger, "Utopian Folly," 279.
40. Ibid., 271.

MORE'S PARTICIPATORY TEXT

In the end, neither Hythloday, the disengaged, self-consumed individualist, nor the utopians, a regimented and mechanical collective, are preferable to More's moderate approach, his navigation of his asserting a determining self in participation with a larger community—navigating one's way through the world, giving and taking, guided by principles rather than preset, rigid rules. Hythloday cannot be more than More's tool; he is not his mouthpiece because he seems unable to acknowledge the disparity between his own actions and the values supported by the rules of the Utopians, yet More is an unflagging seeker of such disparities, constantly probing himself, others, and his surroundings.

A good example of More's unwillingness to accept what he encounters at face value occurs in his prefatory letter when seeks clarification from Giles about Hythloday's description of the bridge over the river Anyder; he recognizes the disparity between Hythloday's description of the bridge and the impossibility of its meeting those qualifications because of the confines of reality. In fact, More's commentary on this reiterates his commitment to truth: "For as I shall take good heed that there be in my book nothing false, so if there be anything in doubt I will rather tell a lie then make a lie, because I had rather be good than wise."[41] More here elevates goodness over wisdom, again underscoring his awareness of his responsibility to others. His call here to correct his memory of Hythloday's description is not self-seeking; he does so to avoid passing on the mistake. His understanding of goodness, then, is intimately connected to his understanding of the individual's role in community. And his elevation here of goodness over wisdom trumps Hythloday's later promotion of wisdom with little regard for goodness. More suggests in this statement—and throughout the book—that wisdom must serve goodness; wisdom without goodness is vain.

Thus, contrary to popular and critical understanding, *Utopia* is not a program for social reform, not in any detailed way, anyway, but rather it is a call for self-examination. More is seeking a correspondence between individual moral requirements and the good of community, a recognition that what is in one's self interest is to live in harmony with one another. The individual has a responsibility to the group in which he finds himself, and the group has a responsibility to the individual. Despite Hythloday's protestations to the contrary, there is no way to programmatize these relationships. One must live, rather, with the messiness of contingencies. For these contingencies are what ground the individual; what Berger calls the

---

41. More, *Utopia*, 7.

"particularistic attachments that guarantee reciprocity and cooperation"[42] are what More insists give meaning to our lives.

BIBLIOGRAPHY

Berger, Harry. "Utopian Folly: Erasmus and More on the Perils of Misanthropy." *English Literary Renaissance* 12/3 (1982) 271–90.
Claeys, Gregory, and Lyman Tower Sargent. *The Utopia Reader*. New York: NYU Press, 1999.
Connery, Brian A., and Kirk Combe. *Theorizing Satire: Essays in Literary Criticism*. New York: St. Martin's, 1995.
Elliott, Robert C. "The Shape of Utopia." *ELH* 30/4 (1963) 317–34.
Griffin, Dustin. *Satire: A Critical Reintroduction*. Lexington: University Press of Kentucky, 1994.
Hodgart, Matthew. *Satire: Origin and Principles*. Piscataway, NJ: Transaction, 2009.
Kinney, James Daniel. "Thomas More's Humanistic Defenses: A New Critical Edition and Translation of Five Letter-Essays." PhD diss., Yale University, 1983.
Kumar, Krishan. *Utopia and Anti-Utopia in Modern Times*. New York: Blackwell, 1987.
More, Thomas. *Utopia*. In *Three Early Modern Utopias*, edited by Susan Bruce. Translated by Ralph Robinson. Oxford: Oxford University Press, 2008.
Plato. *Phaedrus*. Translated by Robin Waterfield. Oxford: Oxford University Press, 2002.
Sargent, Lyman Tower. "Themes in Utopian Fiction in English before Wells." *Science Fiction Studies* 3/3 (1976) 275–85.
———. "Three Faces of Utopianism Revisited." *Utopian Studies* 5 (1994) 1–37.
Suvin, Darko. *Metamorphoses of Science Fiction: On the Poetics and History of a Literary Genre*. New Haven: Yale University Press, 1979.

42. Berger, "Utopian Folly," 282.

4

Desiring Utopian Subjects
Collectivity and Its Discontents

—Holly White

The status of literary utopias at the turn of the third millennium is fraught with productive complexity. Often used colloquially to deride impractical or vaguely hopeful social arrangements, the term "utopia" is still employed to signal a representation of society based on principles that direct human satisfaction. Literary theorist Krishan Kumar reflects that while utopianism is still a lively part of social and cultural life, literary utopia has waned, occluded by its alter identity—dystopian literature.[1] While others contemplate the decline of myth generally or the modern myth of progress specifically, Kumar suggests that utopian fiction may be eclipsed at this moment in history by a diffusion of utopia into culture, writing, "[w]hat seems important today is to understand why it is so difficult for us to contemplate utopia, and the consequences of failing to do so."[2]

This essay tracks, in part, the nature of this difficulty. Utopian literature is frequently mistaken as a blueprint for a better, and thus more desirable, society, one that signals collectivity either through content or form. This representation of collectivity is confusing to contemporary Western readers taught to privilege individualism and assuage desire through possession. I

---

1. Kumar, "Utopia and Anti-Utopia," 264.
2. For an analysis of other reasons for the shift in utopia's reception, see Schaer, "Utopia," 6. See also Kumar, "Utopia and Anti-Utopia," 266.

argue that utopian literature, in representing collectivity to modern readers and then positioning that collectivity as an object of desire, triggers ambivalence towards the genre. Contemplating utopia means considering how utopian literature has come to capture this position of reflecting the desire for collectivity in an age that, first, is suspicious or even dismissive of collective social organization and, second, suspects the sources that fund such a desire.

The first step in contemplating utopia requires seeing utopian literature not as an object to be replicated but as an opening for thinking about the self in relation to others. The second is considering how utopian literature stands within the logic of modern subject-object desire. In this way, the genre opens both the modern ambivalence towards collectivity and the conflicts of desiring what is impossible to possess and unacceptable. This offers a possible route for straddling these disconnects without seeking resolution. Through these points, I argue that contemplating utopia either requires deliberate engagement with the contradictions structuring both desire and utopia or finding other ways to think about desire and collectivity that are not abstract or contradictory but instead are immanent and connected. These two frames of desire and of collectivity give a lattice for contemplating the production of utopian literature, generating ideas for better social arrangements at the level of social totality. This is the task at the center of Kumar's warning. From here, one can see what is at stake in failing to contemplate utopia—the failure to imagine positive collective social arrangements that constitute life lived together in ways that both satisfy human needs and give way to living without fear of one's longings.

UTOPIAN LITERATURE AND MODERN COLLECTIVITIES

Used to denote aesthetic and political forms, "Utopia" as a noun and "utopian" as an adjective convey a better social order and can lie either in spatial or in temporal relation to the present society. Seeing the concept spread across various times and places, utopian scholars such as Lyman Tower Sargent see the universal quality of utopia and analyze its "transformation of generalized hope into a description of a non-existent society."[3] Sargent points to a range of literatures and examples, from the explicitly political works of Plato to the religious images of the New Jerusalem and the golden ages mapped in the religious texts of India, to show how the human imagination throughout history has produced stories and political plans that outline

---

3. Sargent, *Utopianism*, 8.

better, even optimal, societies. But treating utopia as a universal category of human expression evades discussion of the unique conditions that inspired Thomas More's distinctive text known simply now as *Utopia* (1516) and the evocative neologism he coined.[4] The word "utopia" carries with it the meaning of both "good" (eu-) and "no" (u-) place, a play that was crucial to More's satire. Seeing the concept of utopia as an effect of a specific literary genre, originating in what has been periodized as the early modern era, can lend insight to how it retains some of the concerns and contradictions that motivated the inaugural text, why it would proliferate at the dawn of the twentieth century, and why the genre may have receded in popularity in the twenty-first.

A Better Collectivity Somewhere

In presenting an alternative society, the genre of utopian literature derives its energy from proposing a fictional community that is both similar to and different from others, retaining elements that are constitutive of human society generally but also reminiscent of societies contemporary to the fictional work. They may foreground a particular political form or prioritize forms of social relation to emphasize sexual, economic, familial, or occupational organization—Depending on how the authors framed the social problem of their day.[5] The utopian community may not be an ideal or even an aspirational community. Abstracting from the literature, the word "utopia" has expanded across aesthetic, political, and religious works, with both descriptive and prescriptive directions. Distilling the concept of utopia from its proliferated contexts has brought forward features that can give insight into the ambiguous status of utopia and its literary form. What I identify as valuable about the concept of utopia is the contrast it provides for critiquing or motivating change, and its role in presenting society as a total system. In these two respects, utopian literature carries, through narrative, a representation of a better society.

A crucial first step in contemplating utopia and discovering its lost political charge involves considering the comparative qualifier "better." This aligns with the "eu" of utopia, and, as already noted, can be located

---

4. More, *Utopia*.

5. "[S]ocialist, capitalist, monarchical, democratic, anarchist, ecological, feminist, patriarchal, egalitarian, hierarchical, racist, left-wing, right-wing, reformist, free love, nuclear family, extended family, gay, lesbian and many more utopias, and all these types were published between 1516 and the middle of the 20th century, before diversity really took hold" (Sargent, *Utopianism*, 35–36).

in a of variety aesthetic, political, and religious forms, spanning a range of complimentary and even contradictory contents. More than looking to the contents or forms of utopias, social scientist Ruth Levitas privileges the function of utopia as central to its concept: whatever else utopia looks like, utopia alternately functions to critique, compensate for, or supplement present circumstances, or to catalyze action towards alternatives.[6] What is often confused in utopia's representation is the assumption that the society-at-hand—the community being described in the novel or the city or building measured and mapped—is the "better" one. This may be the author's intent, but it may also be that the "better society" is one yet to be realized, may only exist in an imagination, or can only be encountered as an event and not sustained. In the case of utopian literature, the representation of the "better society" may only be evoked in hints, not even appearing in print—a representation "off screen" that is constituted through repetitions of similarity and difference between textual description, reader imagination, and material social relations.

If utopian literature reflects Western society's coming-to-terms with the self as an individual within the nation-state, then it follows that the literature functions to hold space for this work of re-vision. Political philosopher Judith Shklar brings this function to light in her consideration of the utopian form. She notes that, in minimizing the founding event, and by highlighting the details of daily life, utopian writers produce an aesthetic and intellectual tension between what might be and what will be.[7] However, she explains that the energetic fervor of mass movements since the French Revolution, their brutality and their discourses of inevitability, have washed away the more intellectual mood of utopia and replaced it with its modern revolutionary character. The mundane nature of utopia, along with the narrative focus on description over plot, once provided a space for contemplation and inspiration, and was not meant as a blueprint or roadmap.[8] This is now gone, replaced with a call for revolutionary action. From Shklar's perspective, if modern individuals relate ambivalently to utopia, it is in part because they harbor nostalgia for a classical appreciation of thought and ethical formation.

The second step for contemplating utopia is to ask about the constitution of a better *society*, recognizable as a whole or bounded entity,

6. Levitas, *The Concept of Utopia*, 34.
7. Shklar, "The Political Theory of Utopia," 370.
8. This description of classical Utopias that intentionally exploits the gap of the distance between probability and possibility is an aesthetic mode, but, according to Shklar, one that is foreclosed to moderns. Her article, published in 1965, is pre-1968 and thus, can be reconsidered in terms of the reactions to the European social change movements.

functioning to sustain not only human life but human life-in-cooperation. The trope in the genre of the island or of a land in isolation constructs its inhabitants as residents of a common territory, having this resource in common. This distinguishes utopia from nirvana-like states of bliss. While images of pastoral arcadias, along with the mystic's accounts of ecstatic states, employ fantasy and imagination for addressing worldly, existential suffering, fictional utopias recount group effort with their citizens pegging their hopes on shared cooperation with or without divine aid. Whatever their form, utopias anticipate the means by which human life is sustained mutually, by and with others. And this feature of "with others"—as mutual, willing cooperation in a distinct political economy that is coherent to itself and in contrast to its originating society—is what makes utopia a representation of collectivity.

Human relations in utopian societies are solidified not through mere affiliation but through allegiance, grounding economic communalism in shared principles. A survey of the genre demonstrates how the travel-narrative convention highlights this feature and stimulates it to greater effect. As a travel report, the view of the utopian group is filtered through the visitors to the community, the "outsiders" who stumble upon the scene to find a society operating effectively through unfamiliar means. In More's *Utopia*, Hythloday accounts for the Utopians' communitarian ways. A European ship lands on Bensalem in Bacon's *New Atlantis* (1629) and its crew receives a tour of the isolated ideal scientific research community. In Edward Bellamy's *Looking Backward* (1888), Julian West travels not in space but in time to a future Boston, Massachusetts and finds his country transformed into a cooperative socialist paradise where the previously-thought-sour human nature is found to be sweet when nourished. The male survivors of a plane crash debate about the workability of the all-female society they encounter in Charlotte Perkins Gilman's *Herland* (1915), and in Aldus Huxley's *Island* (1963), the journalist notes the rational-yet-gentle cooperation of the women and men, who prioritize their relationships, in contrast to his own selfishness. The subjection of individual will to the collective happens effortlessly for these utopians, and through the eyes of the outsiders, the happy community is brought under suspicion through the outsider's point of view.[9] Thus, collectivity is defined not only by its forms of social relations but also through the form of the novel itself, where the group is contrasted to the travel-narrator's loneliness. Because of the structural dependence on

---

9. Some of the anti-utopian or dystopian novels reverse this convention and have a single person grow up within the confines, eventually departing the enclave, disillusioned. See Johnson, *The History of Rasselas, Prince of Abissinia* (1759) and Huxley, *Brave New World* (1932).

the outsider-perspective of the society, as well as the seeming smoothness of social relations, the utopian community takes on the character of a total, self-sustaining system, constituting its citizens as parts of a whole—a perspective only abstractly available to people within their own social milieu, and always incomplete. Ultimately, how the reader perceives the attractions, weaknesses, and limits of collectivity depends on the reliability of the traveler-narrator and the reader.

These aspects of utopia—its comparative quality and its imaging of society as a whole—lead me to argue that utopian literature has waned because of the narrow reading of representation and the negative perception of collectivity as constructed as an impoverished alternative to Enlightenment individualism promoted through Anglo-American culture and context. Untangling utopian ideals for contemplation begins with considering how utopian literature presents collectivity, not as a conclusion but as a problem, an aspect that is suggested by the non-place of "u-topia." This loosening of collectivity from its imperative connotation recasts collectivity not in opposition to, but as constitutive of, the individual.

Modern Individualism/Modern Collectivity

The role of utopian literature to represent a better social order puts forward the collective qualities of society and underscores how cooperation makes for better living. The most dominant model of utopian collectivity involves shared wealth based on shared principles. Belonging and shared resources were not novel to Thomas More, who saw many examples of collective activity in the monasteries of his time. But instead of leaving the collective behavior to the cloister, More situated it in the broader society, applying the forms of shared resources and activity to the realm of families and secular life. This has led Philip Wegner to argue that More produces a way of relating people to their society that comes to be recognizable as the modern nation-state.[10] In More's Utopia, the former castes and classes are wiped away in favor of a flattened subject in a more regular relation to the social totality, what Wegner recounts as a framework for the emergent European bourgeoisie.[11] The early modern era sees the hold of the church and the feudal lords replaced by monarchies which, in turn, become the republics of Europe. Emerging from More is a foretaste of the modern individual who

---

10. Wegner, *Imaginary Communities*, 55–59.

11. "The spatialized national subject formed in the Utopian narrative thus serves as one of the original forms of the collective subject of class—for it is by way of national identity that the bourgeoisie comes to 'identify' itself" (ibid., 60).

identifies with a political entity and is bound, through practices and loyalty, to principles instead of God or King.

By foregrounding how the individual is cast in relation to society both from within and without, literary utopias reflect the European Enlightenment's proposed and refined characterizations of the self in relation to society. The form complements modern political philosophy and its arguments of how societies serve individuals and yet function as cooperative wholes, following a line of thinking from Aristotle, through Rousseau, Burke, and Hegel, and into more contemporary thinkers such as John Rawls.[12] These arguments were moved into practice through revolutionary declarations and documents such as the *Rights of Man* and the US Constitution. Emerging from these events were the value of liberalism and the formation of the individual's rights in relation to an increasingly neutral state, seen as both protecting and promoting individual engagement. As the Enlightenment movement matured, and colonialism shifted the global landscape, the nation-state emerged over the nineteenth and twentieth centuries as the premier form of social relation. Substituting for God and King, individual citizens worked in cooperation with other citizens and their citizen-representatives. As is all-too-well known, however, the rights of individuals are not secured for every human within the nation-state: many are excluded from the beginning, and the procedures for adding others are slow and politically arduous.

It is important to note that modern collectivity is not contained by nation-state formation: other forms of cooperative activity exist within national borders, such as religious and fraternal affiliations. But the form of the nation-state produced the individual as a unique political entity endowed with "certain unalienable rights" that remapped the potentials of that particular variety of self along social, political, and legal lines. Utopian literature reflects the questions of this self under revision through a particular fictional form and thus offers an alternative perspective for viewing this transition to the political entity now widely regarded as the liberal individual. Some of that literature is not directly fictional but is constructed through sanitizing historical narratives, collapsing the real into an ideal commonwealth through particularly editorial procedures. One such procedure is to ignore, erase, or occlude violent or ugly events that were a part of the nation-state's founding.[13] It is helpful to recall that More's Utopia had

---

12. Avineri and De-Shalit, *Communitarianism and Individualism*, 1–4.

13. Of course, historiographical impulses need always be contextualized, and more often than not, these utopian interventions have occurred within strictly bounded and shared disciplinary frames for writing history, i.e., romantic nationalist, consensus, or progress-driven historical narrative. For a critical account of practices of US

no such bloody beginning, only the peaceful establishment by the brilliant Utopus. Such a convention can be in service of a government's ideology and legitimizing narrative.

Another such procedure is what Wegner labels "operations of neutralization": how collectivity becomes utopian when it reduces or sterilizes the threats from emergent classes, ethnicities, and groups.[14] These operations within utopia are recognizable as the uniformity of taste through clothing or restricted interests or schedules: what once may have been a tempering of vice comes to be regarded in the twentieth century as a potential threat to the unique expressions of the individual human spirit. Utopian literature expanded in style in this century to integrate the stages of nation-state formation, and as states worked to integrate their internal sub-communities, utopian writing proceeded to register different levels of willingness to participate in this process, ordered by different types of state authorities. Dystopian literature expanded on this fear, taking up a concern with coercive collectivity. Science fiction can be said to be a related genre, where the utopian being is often rendered as an alien but situated in relation to counterparts in such a way to resemble human society, often in another stage of social formation.

Contemplating utopia at the beginning of the twenty-first century requires noting the content and form of utopian literature and where it reflects the questions of its political contexts, particularly of the self as a part of the political imaginary of the nation-state. Utopian literature raises the concerns of belonging to and participating within the society as it recasts the self as a particular kind of individual. By analyzing the genre as an archive for this transition, I want to propose that utopia can instruct its readers and researchers in the ways that modern society functions collectively despite its emphasis on individuality, and that the varieties of utopian societies are analogous to the varieties of collectives and their configurations. Utopian literature, in this way, is an inroad to an analysis of the self-in-relation, both to other selves and to the self projected into what it might be, into its potentials, either positive or negative. The ambivalence to individualism that constitutes utopian literature points not only to its ascendency but to its isolation and fissures. Collectivity may be better approached not as an opposition to the individual but as a constitutive of the self. When the individual is seen as a process of individuation, the static nature of the literary utopian community can be seen to be an effort to capture what is actually fluid and less determined.

---

historiography and its relation to utopia, see Mohawk, *Utopian Legacies*.

14. Wegner, *Imaginary Communities*, 61.

Individuation—Self in Process

As already noted, authors use utopian travelers to contrast the individual with the social totality. Also, as mentioned, the founding text and its evolving genre have justified the emergence of the individual in relation to the nation-state. Unlike modern liberal political philosophy, which has focused on the inviolability of the individual, utopian collectivity foregrounds the social and political body over the individual. Alongside utopian literature and the political philosophy of individualism, other theorists have assembled their own accounts of the relation between society and self. Modern philosophers such as Hegel, Marx, and Freud have offered tools for explaining the gaps exposed through the liberal assumptions of autonomy and self-sufficiency. Modernity, with its distinctive political and economic modes, generates contradiction within the self when it reifies individuality. Excluded from such an account are the procedures of individuation and socialization, processes that show how groups, governments, language, and norms—along with bodily necessity and affective connection—contribute to both the formed self and ongoing self-formation. By reviewing how the economic and political forms of the social relations of modernity create dissonance and contradiction for the modern self, I want to propose that individuality is one of many concepts produced from procedures of individuation and socialization. Collectivity, then, need not be opposed to the individual but seen as constitutive of her. The reification of individuality has isolated her from the conditions of her becoming and sustaining. These critiques of self-sufficiency and self-identity permit a wider view of collectivity and further open the way to see utopian fiction as a cipher for collective belonging and its potentials for collective action.

Hegel's theories of history are well-known, and his interpretations of the self in relation to society are fundamental to his persisting influence. The political subject under the conditions of the modern state is not first autonomous and then submissive to the social contract but instead is shaped through contests of power. While there is an interest on the part of the self to see itself as distinct and autonomous, Hegel introduces the important philosophical correction that autonomy depends on being recognized by an other. The psyche forms through a series of encounters with micro operations of projection and doubling of recognition.[15] An important aspect of this procedure for Hegel is the implicit or explicit threat in this formation,

---

15. While the formation of the self is thought to be the action of the self, the self can only be made conscious of itself through a procedure whereby an other comes to the self as seemingly autonomous and independent (Hegel, "Independence and Dependence of Self-Consciousness," 11).

with a self emerging through defense and action: while there may be an individual who is recognized as a person, only through putting her life at stake will the individual come to know herself as a "being for self."[16] Thus, what is seen from the liberal perspective as a self that knows itself as a will with rights given to others like himself is, in Hegel's framework, only ever self-knowing because of external entities. Simply stated, what is thought to be private or internal is made up of outsides, of contests, of relationships.

The liberal individual is, through Hegel, refigured as a subject in formation: the individual is no longer is just an actor in a social world but is seen as shaped by that world in ways that resituate an external reality as constitutive of an internal, or psychic one. Second, Hegel shows how the fascination with the individual is an effect of history: individuals are products of an emerging middle class that must divorce themselves from embeddedness in the social totality in order to preserve agency and autonomy. Hegel writes,

> the individual human being must repeatedly, in order to preserve his own individuality, make himself a means for other people, serve their limited ends, and transform them into means in order to satisfy his own narrow interests. The individual, therefore, as he appears in this world of daily life and of prose, does not draw his principle of activity from himself as a totality, is not comprehensible in himself, but only in relationship to other people. For he finds himself dependent on external influences, laws, political structures, domestic relationships which preceded him and to which he must yield, whether he has been able to interiorize them or not. Furthermore, the individual subject is no totality for other people, but appears from their point of view only in the context of their own immediate and isolated interests in his actions, wishes and opinion.[17]

In sum, what is known as an "individual"—a political and legal concept emerging from the French Revolution and integrated into the episteme of nineteenth-century bourgeois identity—can only be maintained by a series of obfuscations. The result is alienation, an alienation that Marx then saw running through all of life lived in the mode of production of capital.[18]

---

16. This formation of identity through struggle grounds what is familiar of Hegel's contribution to theories of history as a "master-slave" contest (ibid., 13).

17. Hegel, from *Aesthetik I* in Jameson, *Marxism and Form*, 353–54.

18. Marx's revisions of Hegel most notably include the recognition of not just the trials of the bourgeois subject but his construction within capital. "Let us provisionally say just this much in advance: Hegel's standpoint is that of modern political economy. He grasps *labour* as the *essence* of man—as man's essence in the act of proving itself: he

From the perspectives of Hegel and Marx, becoming a self is an arduous and incremental procedure of power always nested within a series of contests of history. The fuel for the modern reader's ambivalence towards collectivity, then, is not merely a fear of deprived liberty: it is an ambivalence produced by distinguishing oneself from others, reproduced by those who benefit from the individual's disavowed connection to the social order and its parts.[19]

Marx and Hegel were not alone in giving an account of the alienation of late modern society. Sigmund Freud's theories of the unconscious have provided popular culture at large with an interpretation of the division of the psyche and its undoing by its libidinal attachments and social development. The fully conscious, stable self, was, through Freud, seen as constantly plagued by its internal "other" that held the memories of its secret wishes. This repressed self would readily disturb the conscious self through neurotic and psychotic behaviors, or, less dysfunctionally, in dreams. What unites all three theorists is a critique of the stable, intending self of liberal humanism. Each provides a substantial case for why the autonomous individual is a fiction that is both laborious and dangerous to sustain. They also explain that debilitating psychic frictions are not isolated personal conflicts but social events being played out through the self. Together with their interpreters, they show that the contradictions of collectivity are not to be repressed but must be acknowledged as an essential operation of self-formation and a process to be engaged with, lived through, endured, and resisted.

The Function of Desire in Utopian Collectivity

Although utopian literature has lessened in popularity, it still provides an occasion to analyze the political, philosophical, aesthetic and cultural forces that, unresolved, have dispersed across Western society and spread along lines of global exchange and nation-state building. Utopia's continued cultural currency for signifying collectivity over individualism provides a

---

sees only the positive, not the negative side of labour. Labour is man's *coming-to-be for himself* within *alienation*, or as *alienated* man. The only labour which Hegel knows and recognizes is abstractly mental labour" (Marx, "Economic and Philosophical Manuscripts of 1844," in Marx and Engels, *The Marx-Engels Reader*, 112).

19. In Hegelian and Marxist analysis of this subject, the alienation felt from the collective is a construction for the purposes of a few—an alienation that will be overcome, according to Georg Lukács, when the minority who benefit from commodity culture come to see how rationalizations that make for economic efficiencies break apart and isolate one from one's own experience. See Lukács, "Reification and the Consciousness of the Proletariat."

means to investigate the longing for non-alienated social life. I turn now to investigate longing itself and how utopian literature represents desire to its readers, exploring how the eclipse of utopian literature signifies difficulties with expressing longings rather than the end of a desire for collectivity.

Utopia has been applied to many aesthetic and political forms, from architecture to political treatises. In many cases, its work compensates for failures in the present society. As mentioned above, sociologist Ruth Levitas identified a central function of utopia as a compensatory one: to fill in what is absent. But not all utopias function in this way: some critique society through their alternative account—holding up a mirror to reflect back the inadequacies without offering solutions. Others add to or supplement the society. Levitas sees the function of utopia as an overlooked aspect of its definition and concludes that what animates the concept broadly is a desire for a better way of living and that these desires are grounded in specific needs that arise from human nature. Levitas does not defend that this is a universal, ahistorical human nature, but instead claims that different societies will circumscribe human need differently through social process.[20] She does, however, mark human need as the basis of utopia, and thus implies that need and desire go together. But a glimpse at human behavior in contemporary developed Western countries discloses that what is needed and what is desired may not be so closely linked. Or, more precisely, that what constitutes desire in this historical moment has the potential to detach from need. Desire is currently funded from a broader set of reference points than biological survival, and Levitas offers no direction for thinking through what may be special about desire for readers of her text.

Freud was not responsible for the creation of desire, but, through him desire became an object for analysis. Desire in Freud has a repressive aspect, depends on transgression, and turns on the building blocks of unconscious wishes and the restrictions of society.[21] Freud offers a world of subjects who desire and objects of that desire, thus recounting the self as a series of utilitarian encounters whereby a maturing self moves in relation to the unconscious. For Freud, desire begins with the libido that is attached to its primal familial objects from its infancy until is it redirected, through sublimations, to the more socially-acceptable habits of its surroundings.[22] Civilization is a good thing overall, but is constantly threatened by instinctual aggressiveness that must be controlled by psychic reactive formations. Desire then, is the circuitous yet productive route of the libido towards objects of at

20. Levitas, *The Concept of Utopia*, 182–83.
21. Jameson, *The Political Unconscious*, 65–68.
22. Freud, *Civilization and Its Discontents*, 29–30.

least some social standing so as to avoid the treacherous routes outside of civilization that are fraught with violence. From this perspective, a utopian community would only be possible through a homogenous group, formed through aim-inhibited love and preserving a channel of aggression to outsiders.[23] As a form of art, utopian literature issues from an artist fashioning his private fantasies for broad consumption. Under this rubric, utopian literature is only a narcissistic wish, a daydream, and while perhaps useful to the artist who finds some relief in the presence afforded by the fantasy of the return of some lost object, it pales compared the explanatory function of psychoanalysis.[24]

Utopian literature, read with Freud, is funded by fantasies that surface from the inaccessible nature of the unconscious and its repository of inexpressible longings. This fits well with the "impossible" quality—the "u"—of "utopia." Utopia fits less well with Freud when an abstract society takes the center stage as the object of desire, when the well-being of others of different families, related to one another through impersonal, rational principles, becomes the longed-for fantasy. Literary theorist Fredric Jameson frequently turns to this question in his analysis of utopian literature. He sees Freud's psychic architecture in many places as related to utopian literature, specifically where gratuitous details of the utopian society signal the individual author's repressed erotic attachments. These may appear in such quirks as More's description of gold chamber pots or B. F. Skinner's loving detail of the trays in the cafeteria in his *Walden Two* (1948).[25]

Seeing the repression on a grander scale, Jameson calls out the utopian literary form itself as a symptom of a repressed longing for collectivity that has been pushed from reach through modern economic and political social formations. He labels this repressed material the "political unconscious" because it reveals what has been repressed due to capitalism's transformations. Jameson cautions that the political unconscious is not a solid or coherent story, not a "master-narrative" but a construct: "it exists nowhere in empirical form, and therefore must be re-constructed on the basis of texts of all sorts, in much the same way that the master-fantasies of the individual unconscious are reconstructed through the fragmentary and symptomatic 'texts of dreams, values, behavior, verbal free association, and the like."[26]

23. Ibid., 65–66.

24. Donald Capps describes this connection between the melancholic and the utopian author in Capps, "Melancholia, Utopia, and the Psychoanalysis of Dreams," 85–104. At the conclusion of this essay, Capps quips that "[Freud's] book, *The Interpretation of Dreams*, was his map of utopia" (102).

25. Jameson, *Archaeologies*, 50, 189.

26. Ibid., 283.

The reconstruction begins with the cultural products of our time, especially fiction, which, with its investments in narrative, is a priviledged site for history-becoming-conscious—historicity itself.[27] What one finds in this unconscious are the remnants of life lived outside of capitalism, memories of belonging to something other than the apparatuses of the state. To summarize: the stories that groups tell themselves, left in the fictions that are written and read, should be analyzed not only for their contents but also for their narrative shape or genre.

The structures belie repressed desire. Historical fiction, memoir, romance, and mystery each reflect something of the struggle of the collective to articulate itself as it undergoes its historical transformation. They each exhibit, through their form, societal-level wishes for alternative social arrangements. And for Jameson, the genres with the most telling fragments of the political unconscious are utopias and their post-industrial counterpart, science fiction. In utopian and science fiction, the forms of social life and economic relation pushed underground by the forces of capital find their way into material culture and uniquely into fiction. Utopian literature read symptomatically gives the modern audience its only access to past and future potential modes of relating to one another and of providing for our survival.

This symptomatic reading of texts is a generative approach for interpretation but leaves intact Freud's work that supposes a chasm dividing consciousness, leaving one to question how reliable dreams or literature are in bridging it. Others have followed who have worked to refine Freud in order to explain the passage between fantasy and reality and to suggest that satisfaction is possible, thus making utopia more about possibilities and less about distortion. Ernst Bloch observes that Freud's petite bourgeois concerns, erupting in the formula of the Oedipal triad, mirror his particular Victorian milieu. Bloch expands his frame away from the personal to consider the ontological: desire is only as relevant to Bloch as it is capable of exposing the more expansive quality of time and its unconditioned future—the not-yet-conscious. Bloch reorients the source of the wish from Freud's buried illicit past to the unknowable-yet-expectant future.[28] Herbert Marcuse reverses Freud's theories of libidinal sublimation to use the libido as the organizing energy of civilization. Concerned with the repressive aspects of advanced industrial society, Marcuse makes room for the erotic in everyday interactions, not through a Freudian sublimation, but by claiming that the repressed memories of primal need satisfaction are accessible when

27. Ibid., 285.
28. Bloch, *The Principle of Hope*, 83–113.

one partakes in playful production.[29] Art, then, instructs the attentive artist into what is truly needful and how to meet that need. A new "rationality of gratification" surfaces from within commodity culture, using the technological advancements of modern life not for exploitation but for coordinating the individual needs of all.[30] In these versions of Freud, desire's urge still indicates a lost object, a repressed fantasy, or a need never met, but, according to Bloch and Marcuse, the self has the potential to be sated. Both theorists carry forward the cooperative goals of psychoanalysis and Marxism's aims of exposing the procedures of psycho-social development and mapping the limits of knowledge, either through the function of time, in the case of Bloch, or through the human body, in the case of Marcuse. These limit-cases of time and body are then the engines of desire, as they both hold the position of the unknowable horizon toward which humans need only be positively oriented.

Utopian literature not only signifies an object of fantasy, but also structurally resembles Freud's account of how humans are beholden to their repressed fantasies, forever working to make them present—re-presenting them—and thus only finding satisfaction through the efforts of aesthetic production. The utopian novel epitomizes the impossibility in longing, if one follows Freud, as Jameson does. While Jameson sees utopian literature as capturing both the structure of Freudian desire and the questions of collectivity set into motion through modernity, his account preserves Freud's pessimism and distrust of the libido. It also fails to address how women are essentialized in Freud and restricted from the subject position of desire, and it preserves the contradiction of desiring what one cannot have—a contradiction that can impede thought and action with relation to topics that utopian literature raises, such as how to live well with others and how to structure social forms to satisfy libidinal needs.[31] Voices like those of Bloch and Marcuse contribute to utopian studies through disclosing the possibility of an "education of desire" as, through their critiques, they map the potential for humans to achieve, as Nietzsche proposed, a transvaluation of values, or as Marcuse describes, a new "rationality of gratification." This re-education of satisfaction leads me to suggest that the contemplation of utopia depends on one's willingness to manage contradiction or to recast desire without the types of oppositions central in Freud.

29. Marcuse, *Eros and Civilization*.

30. Ibid., 205.

31. Luce Irigaray has done much to disrupt the dominance of Freud in the philosophical use of psychoanalysis. For a re-reading of the history of philosophy with her critiques, see Irigaray, *Speculum of the Other Woman*.

DESIRING COLLECTIVITY AND CONTEMPLATING OTHERWISE

Jameson helps to untangle utopia from its ambivalent status by showing that utopian literature is built on contradiction, that it derives its attraction from this contradiction and thus should be read for it. This is an uncustomary approach. As noted above, utopian contents reflect the variety of wishes and needs of the funding communities. While Levitas and Sargent have advanced the fields of utopian studies, the typologies central to their work harmonize and contain the field: Jameson leans into the ambiguity of utopia and draws out the contradictions inherent to the form. Whereas Sargent works at the surface of contents, explaining why some literary utopias emphasize work while others leisure, why some are in cities and others identified with nature, Jameson directs attention to the paradox that the form simultaneously depends on specific historical conditions for its rise and fall in popularity and yet creates a type of ahistorical society.[32] Levitas finds that the function, more than the form or content of utopia, is what unites the concept. Jameson uses function to trace how utopian literature spans desire at multiple levels and, in doing so, excites the genre.

Contemplating utopia, following Jameson, means to work with texts as a study of contradictions and with the antinomies that arise in modern life and to preserve these contradictions instead of resolving them. The ambivalence arising from utopia gives occasion for thinking with the complexity of the self and society in relation, the historical configurations of text and context, and the structures of affect and bodies that surround intellectual, political, and aesthetic productions. The challenge becomes to sustain attention in the midst of the contradiction or at least to manage interpretation that does not seek easy resolution. This is not Shklar's classical pensivity, though it preserves space for thought as a function of utopian literature; thinking the contradictions has the explicit political goal of addressing the sources of contradiction, leveraging interpretation to reduce alienation.

Thinking the contradictions is one way we sustain contemplation when the instrumental pressures of advanced industrial society would prefer that we turn to other tasks. If utopias are "by definition ... never real fulfillments of desire" and thus, are always marked by absence and failure, then utopian

---

32. "It is a paradox that a form so absolutely dependent on historical circumstance (that it flourishes only in specific conditions and on certain rare historical occasions) should give the appearance of being supremely ahistorical; that a form which inevitably arouses political passions should seem to avoid or to abolish the political altogether; and that a text so uniquely dependent on the caprice and opinion of individual social dreams should find itself disarmed in the face of individual agency and inaugural action" (Jameson, *Archaeologies*, 37).

literature is, by definition, a place for investigating the production of fantasy and how to manage its disappointments.[33] The longing for utopian collectivity presents the opportunity for encountering the Reality Principle of politics, wherein global capital creates massive wealth and poverty and nation-states unequally distribute their rights to their citizens. Also, if utopian literature stands at the crux of a modern reader's disavowed desire for collectivity, as Jameson avers, then it can be read for the symptomatic sparks of this repressed desire, and so, can only be known through the subtle forms of interpretation and encounter usually reserved for dreams. The tentative and frustrated paths through utopia are productive because they counter the logics of consumption and speed prevalent in modern society. Building a patience for utopian literature's failures and misfires as it works through its representation of a better social order can provide gratifications that are not about acquiring an object, but that instead invite us into a confrontation with the impossible.[34] While perhaps not hopeful, contemplating contradictions may be productive and, in that way, offer a route to affirmation.

As one contemplates the failure of utopian literature to sustain its audience in the twentieth century, one comes in contact with other failures and possibilities. Dominated by the logic of individualism and the simultaneous objectification of thought and the means to turn it towards capitalist production—to treat reason as an instrument for ends other than itself—contemplation of utopia will be difficult to sustain and will be thought to be a waste of time. Yet, as I have argued here, utopian literature has with it a resistance to easy reception or transparent understanding, and thus sends its readers to other shores for its explication. Philosophical and psychological questions surface when considering the self as a subject who is both constituted by and constitutes others. Historical methods yield an understanding of how the genre emerged as a response to its surroundings, and aesthetic analysis directs one to the formal properties of the genre to show the novel as a distinctive kind of text with a particular role in producing thought. The methodological diversity available to the discipline-crossing concept of

33. Ibid., 83.

34. "We need a nobler word than *frustration* to evoke the dimension of Utopian desire which remains unsatisfied, and which cannot be felt to have been fulfilled without falling into the world and becoming another degraded act of consumption . . . what is wanted is a concept which will not transfer the theory of the split subject to the collectivity; nor will it encourage an apolitical mysticism of the infinite or the unattainable. The desire called Utopia must be concrete and ongoing, without being defeatist or incapacitating; it might therefore be better to follow an aesthetic paradigm and to assert that not only the production of the unresolvable contradiction is the fundamental process, but that we must imagine some form of gratification inherent in this very confrontation with pessimism and the impossible" (ibid., 84).

utopia builds networks and connections that give rise to thinking concepts outside of their disciplinary bounds.

NEW UTOPIAN TERRITORIES

Contemplating utopia, then, can take a path through revisions of the concepts of collectivity and desire. Instead of following an inherited logic of desire as a consciousness-resisting libidinal taboo or as a lack in constant search of its fulfillment, I want to suggest that we might rely on another way of figuring desire—one that places us not as chasing desire but as resting within desire's stream. This view of desire would also constitute us as composed of collectivities and capable of recombining into other collectives or assemblages of desire instead of as beings limited to recalling or hoping for an amorphous and distant collectivity.

I have discussed how the classical Enlightenment formula represents the subject in relation to the collective—as an individual, as a member of a whole. Marxist interpretations ask a different question—how the collective represents the subject to himself and emphasizes the regimes of representations for delivering different subjects. Hegel and Marx both saw the shared language and structures of society as a part of an iterative process of individuation. From this perspective, I want to consider another approach to collectivity—one not of a whole individual living with other individuals but of a dispersed and pulsating self formed as a collective, moving in cooperation with other collectives in whole or in part. These nesting and overlapping selves are not threatened by others but are energized through established and potential relations. In this enriching way, then, needs are satisfied through social relations instead of deferred or as treated as separate from desire.

This view of collectivity would be based in a desire that organizes and connects, continuing life and motivating its destruction equally instead of being based in a desire for objects. As a motivating force of relations through which fragmented objects come to be associated, desire operates prior to some form of subject. This shifts the emphasis from objects to the types of relations between objects or, more precisely, how the libido directs and collects parts for its use and extension.[35] From this refiguring of desire,

35. French philosopher Gilles Deleuze provides a means for considering collectivity as a function of desire itself. Unlike Lacanian desire based on lack and absence, Deleuze calls desire as that which flows and as the motivating force of association. Whereas desire in the psychoanalytic frame produces fantasies, Deleuze sees this as an impoverished account of desire, for while desire can produce fantasies, it produces at the smallest scale the assemblages of that go on to form other units recognizable for their

motion, interaction, and sensation are primary, giving rise to forms. In this framing, the desire for utopia is understood not as a desire for the missing experience of collectivity but as a perspective within a network of desiring collectivities. From here, one may desire collectivity again—and allow that revisioned collectivity to critique or supplement the present society.

Utopian literature, by leading its readers into representations of better societies, has for centuries worked at the limits of representation in constructing a social order both similar to and differing from actual societies. In reserving the right of impossibility, the utopian order in the text resists the status of blueprint but also excites speculation as to what might be. As utopian literature consolidates questions of the modern period of what life might be like lived in cooperation with others different from one's own endogamous family, connected through principles supported through the legal and political structures of the nation-state, it also brings forward philosophical questions about the subject in modern society—its formation, allegiances, cohesion, and fragility. It also centers modern assumptions about desire and how society forms itself around seeking satisfaction of needs. The desiring subject struggles in knowing itself disrupted by its desires, suspicious of its attachments. This situation can lead in several directions. In the case of Kumar's warning about the failure to contemplate utopia, the suspicion of utopia can mean a reluctance or refusal to figure out social improvements for the collective and the welfare of those who are other than a familial or social sub-group. It is an anxiety about the failed idealism of liberal society and the promises of republican revolutions. By extension, the waning of utopian literature signals a suspicion of imagining anything so ambitious as universal claims to human rights or material security for all.

Contemplating utopia means wading again into these impossible spaces of hope and politics, longing and fantasy. It may require an iterative process of working dialectically through the contradictions and mapping the points of connection and dislocation in order to find what is obscured from view through procedures of power. It may include attempts to remap concepts such as desire and collectivity in order to offer ontologies more tuned to immanence and becoming than transcendence and static being. It may also mean involvement in failed political movements of resistance or efforts in novel writing that risk being labeled as narcissistic wish-fulfillment. Contemplating utopia is not a recipe for modern success, but the assurance that alienation is not the only or final mode of the individual. It is also not a hopeless exercise, but an invitation to court disappointment in exchange

---

relations. "Desire and its object are one and the same thing: the machine, as a machine of a machine" (Deleuze and Guattari, *Anti-Oedipus*, 26).

for the promise of other gratifications. Contemplating utopia begins with contemplating utopian literature and the ways that authors have intimated a better society through descriptive language. Whether or not they have outlined a society worth working towards, through their work, they signal that the distance between what is, and what might be a territory worthy of inhabiting.

BIBLIOGRAPHY

Avineri, Shlomo, and Avner De-Shalit. *Communitarianism and Individualism.* New York: Oxford University Press, 1992.

Bacon, Francis. *New Atlantis; and, The Great Instauration.* Arlington Heights, IL: H. Davidson, 1989.

Bellamy, Edward. *Looking Backward, 2000–1887.* New York: Signet, 2000.

Bloch, Ernst. *The Principle of Hope.* Translated by Neville Plaice, Stephen Plaice, and Paul Knight. 1st American ed. 3 vols. Studies in Contemporary German Social Thought. Cambridge, MA: MIT Press, 1986.

Capps, Donald. "Melancholia, Utopia, and the Psychoanalysis of Dreams." In *The Blackwell Companion to Sociology of Religion*, edited by Richard K. Fenn, 85–104. Malden, MA: Blackwell, 2001.

Deleuze, Gilles, and Félix Guattari. *Anti-Oedipus: Capitalism and Schizophrenia.* Translated by Robert Hurley, Mark Seem, and Helen R. Lane. Minneapolis: University of Minnesota Press, 1983.

Freud, Sigmund. *Civilization and Its Discontents.* Translated by James Strachey. New York: W. W. Norton, 1961.

Gilman, Charlotte Perkins. *Herland: A Lost Feminist Utopian Novel.* New York: Pantheon, 1979.

Hegel, G. W. F. "Independence and Dependence of Self-Consciousness." In *Identities: Race, Class, Gender, and Nationality*, edited by Linda Alcoff and Eduardo Mendieta, 11–16. Oxford: Wiley, 2003.

Huxley, Aldus. *Brave New World.* London: Grafton, 1977.

———. *Island.* London: Grafton, 1976.

Irigaray, Luce. *Speculum of the Other Woman.* Translated by Gillian C. Gill. Ithaca, NY: Cornell University Press, 1985.

Jameson, Fredric. *Archaeologies of the Future: The Desire Called Utopia and Other Science Fictions.* New York: Verso, 2005.

———. *Marxism and Form: Twentieth-Century Dialectical Theories of Literature.* Princeton: Princeton University Press, 1972.

———. *The Political Unconscious: Narrative as a Socially Symbolic Act.* Ithaca, NY: Cornell University Press, 1982.

Johnson, Samuel. *The History of Rasselas, Prince of Abissinia.* Edited by Thomas Keymer. Oxford World's Classics. New York: Oxford University Press, 2009.

Kumar, Krishan. "Utopia and Anti-Utopia in the Twentieth Century." In *Utopia: The Search for the Ideal Society in the Western World*, 251–66. New York: Oxford University Press, 2000.

Levitas, Ruth. *The Concept of Utopia.* Syracuse, NY: Syracuse University Press, 1990.

Lukács, Georg. "Reification and the Consciousness of the Proletariat." In *History and Class Consciousness*. Translated by Rodney Livingston. 1967. https://www.marxists.org/archive/lukacs/works/history/index.htm.

Marcuse, Herbert. *Eros and Civilization: A Philosophical Inquiry into Freud*. Humanitas: Beacon Studies in Humanities. Boston: Beacon, 1966.

Marx, Karl, and Friedrich Engels. *The Marx-Engels Reader*. Edited by Robert C. Tucker. 2nd ed. New York: Norton, 1972.

Mohawk, John. *Utopian Legacies: A History of Conquest and Oppression in the Western World*. Sante Fe, NM: Clear Light, 2000.

More, Thomas. *Utopia*. Edited and translated by Robert M. Adams. Norton Critical Edition. New York: Norton, 1975.

Sargent, Lyman Tower. *Utopianism: A Very Short Introduction*. Very Short Introductions. New York: Oxford University Press, 2010.

Schaer, Roland. "Utopia: Space, Time, History." In *Utopia: The Search for the Ideal Society in the Western World*, 3–15. New York: Oxford University Press, 2000.

Skinner, Burrhus F. *Walden Two*. Indianapolis: Hackett, 1974.

Wegner, Phillip E. *Imaginary Communities: Utopia, the Nation, and the Spatial Histories of Modernity*. Berkeley: University of California Press, 2002.

Part 2

Historical and Literary Utopian Visions

5

John Calvin, Geneva, and Godly Patriarchs

Hope and Reality in the Creation of a Christian Utopia

—*Ezra L. Plank*

On 17 January 1544, Pierre Rosset appeared before the ecclesiastical disciplinary tribunal in Geneva—the *consistory*—and was questioned regarding his treatment of his wife, Anthoyne. The previous week, she had testified that he regularly beat her. When confronted, Pierre claimed that, in fact, he did "not want to live except according to God;" the problem was that his wife did "not want to do what he command[ed] her." He further asserted that Anthoyne insulted him, demonstrating that she "want[ed] to be the master." In a strong assertion of patriarchal sovereignty that modern readers find appalling, he insisted that he would "beat her wherever he finds her when he has forbidden her someone's company and she goes there; he will beat her in front of everyone."[1] Similar passion was displayed a decade later when the consistory confronted Claude Galleys for harshly beating his son; Galleys retorted that "there was not one who could keep him from punishing and beating his child, not even the *Messieurs* themselves."[2]

---

1. Lambert et al., *Registres du Consistoire de Genève*, fol. 156v.
2. As cited in Spierling, "Father, Son, and Pious Christian," 110.

These two examples from early modern Geneva are surprising in light of the authority which the church consistory possessed. Clearly these two householders felt so strongly about their right and duty to discipline their families that they directly challenged a body which had the power to excommunicate them and even recommend their expulsion from the city. Rather than considering Rosset and Galleys as cruel fathers and imperfect Christians, I propose that they be viewed as seeking to embody—however erroneously by many standards—a key component in Geneva's utopic vision. These fathers were following the directives of John Calvin (1509–64), the influential reformer of Geneva at the time, whose writings presented an exalted view of fathers and strongly advocated for their divine role as leaders in their families. Although Calvin and the consistory did confront this excessive and brutal discipline, Rosset's and Galleys' determined expressions call for a closer examination of the role of Genevan fathers' regulation of their households in realizing a Genevan utopia. This chapter initiates this effort through consulting theological ideas within Calvin's sermons and commentaries and comparing these with their practical application as evidenced in the early Genevan church discipline records (1542–44).

CALVIN'S UTOPIC VISION FOR HUMANITY

Few manifestations of utopic societies remain as prominent in the historical imagination as sixteenth-century Geneva under the control of John Calvin. Indeed, over forty years ago J. H. Hexter began drawing comparisons between Calvin's work in Geneva and Thomas More's *Utopia*.[3] Calvin took seriously his perceived divine mission and held lofty hopes for the reform of his city. While he did not use the language of "utopia," the latter half of his career was given to creating a New Jerusalem in Geneva. Calvin's understanding of a utopic society was envisioned primarily in religious terms, in which the lives of its citizens would be wholly conformed to the will of God. If this was accomplished, all other political and social considerations would be resolved, because human beings who lived in harmony with the Creator would live in harmony with one another.

David Nicholls' description of French Protestants—that they "were only rarely in a position to try and impose their religion and ways of life upon an uncommitted or hostile population,"[4]—provides a needed contrast and reminder regarding the nature of Geneva. Unlike France where Protestants remained a persecuted religious minority, Geneva was a self-contained

---

3. Hexter, "Utopia and Geneva"; Hexter, *The Vision of Politics*, 107–17.
4. Nicholls, "France," 120.

city-state which lended magisterial support to enacting Protestant ideals. Calvin and the church had power and the support of civic officials to (in Nicholls' language) "impose their religion and ways of life" on the Genevans. Calvin's efforts were enough to impress many. The famous reformer of Scotland, John Knox, applauded Calvin's efforts and boasted in 1556 that Geneva was "the most perfect school of Christ that ever was in the earth since the days of the Apostles," declaring elsewhere it was "the most godly Reformed church and city of the world."[5] John Bale, expelled bishop of Ossory, wrote a similar glowing report not long after, claiming,

> Geneva seemeth to me to be the wonderful miracle of the whole world: so many from all countries come thither, as it were a sanctuary, not to gather riches but to live in poverty.... Is it not wonderful that Spaniards, Italians, Scots, Englishmen, Frenchmen, Germans, disagreeing in manners, speech and apparel, sheep and wolves, bulls and bears, being coupled with the only yoke of Christ, should live so lovingly and friendly, and that monks, laymen and nuns, disagreeing both in life and sect, should dwell together, like a spiritual and Christian congregation.[6]

Evidence for these claims were apparent to those such as Knox and Bale, manifested by the closure of municipal brothels, mandatory catechism for children and the unlearned, and the presence of the consistory to guide the beliefs and behavior of its citizens.

THE FOUNDATION FOR UTOPIA: GENEVAN FATHERS AND TRANSFORMED HOUSEHOLDS

One the most important factors for Calvin in creating a Christian utopia was the condition of society's fundamental units: families. Calvin conceived of ideal, "godly" households, characterized by their hierarchal relations, purity, and educational focus. The central figure in creating these spiritualized households was the father. The Genevan reformer asserted the patriarch was divinely-established as the head of his family, and, as the father embraced a proper leadership role within his home, the Church and all of society would experience a true reformation of piety.

The model, godly father would excel in three principal areas: first, he would bring order to the home. Calvin viewed the world as one ordered by God but pushed toward disruption and chaos by the sinfulness of humanity.

---

5. Knox, *The Works of John Knox*, 4:240; Knox, *History of the Reformation in Scotland*, 1:283.

6. As quoted by McNeill, *History and Character of Calvinism*, 178–79.

Christians needed to reclaim order in all realms of life, and Christian homes played a central role in this effort as they established clear, recognizable lines of authority. In Calvin's understanding of the divine, "inviolable" hierarchy of the household, fathers were to hold a near-absolute rule: he asserted, "For we know there are masters and servants, Magistrates and subjects: in a household there is the good man which is the head, and the good wife which ought to be subject. We know then that this order is inviolable, and our Lord Jesus Christ did not come into the world to make such confusion as to abolish that which was established by God his father."[7] Godly patriarchs would firmly establish this hierarchy by willingly embracing their own role and demanding members of the household submit to their respective authorities.

For Calvin, the evidence of this order was abundant. Both the Hebrew Bible and New Testament contained examples of ideal patriarchs. The Gen. 17 story of Abraham imposing circumcision on all male members of his household demonstrated that his house was well-instructed, obedient, and "under holy discipline."[8] From the New Testament, Calvin applauded fathers such as Nymphas whose home was so well-regulated that it was called a "church" in Paul's letters.[9] Not surprising for Calvin was the fact that the ordered home was so important that it was one of the primary qualifications for the role of elder in the church.[10] Finally, the very title of "father" revealed the divine mandate for patriarchal leadership. In his discussion of the Fifth Commandment ("Honor your father and your mother,"), he moved beyond advocating mere reverence for the father's position. God, he claimed, "shares his name with those to whom he has given pre-eminence." Calvin saw great significance in the relationship between fathers and God based on this shared title, concluding that "in him who is our father we should recognize something divine because he does not bear the divine title without

---

7. Calvin, *Sermons on Galatians*, Gal 3:26–29, 352; Calvin, *Commentary on the Gospel According to John, Volume 1*, John 13:7, 56; Calvin, *Tracts and Treatises, Volume 1*, 242. Regarding the reclamation of order in the world, reference Calvin, "The Form of Prayers and Songs of the Church, 1542," 160. For Calvin's view on fathers' role, reference Calvin, *Sermons on Galatians*, Gal. 3:26–29, 352; Calvin, "On Shunning the Unlawful Rites of the Ungodly," 408; Thompson, *John Calvin and the Daughters of Sarah*, 110.

8. Calvin, *Commentaries on the First Book of Moses Called Genesis*, Gen 17:23, 1:464–5. Also see Calvin's comments on Gen 18 in ibid., Gen 18:6, 1:471.

9. Calvin, *Commentaries on the Epistles of Paul the Apostle to the Philippians, Colossians, and Thessalonians*, Col 4:15, 230. Also reference Calvin, *Commentaries on the Epistles to Timothy, Titus, and Philemon*, Phil 3, 349; Quick, *Synodicon in Gallia Reformata*, 1:79.

10. Calvin, *Commentaries on the Epistles to Timothy, Titus, and Philemon*, 1 Tim 3:4, 82. Also reference ibid., Titus 1:6, 292–93.

cause."[11] Order was fundamental to the nature of God and God's original intention: therefore, if fathers were to create the foundation for utopia, they must bring order to their families.

Second, Calvin's godly home was characterized by a father who worked to ensure its moral purity. Homes of the faithful were extensions of God's sanctuary, and consequently they needed to be kept pure.[12] The challenge for ecclesiastical leadership was the secluded and private nature of homes; they could be the site of domestic violence, games and gambling, dancing, fornicating, ambiguous marriage promises, and a host of other activities deemed immoral. Calvin viewed the tedious laws of the ancient Jewish people which addressed diseases as immediately relevant to the domestic lives of Genevans: as God ordered mass quarantining of the diseased and dead outside of the camp so the people would develop an awareness of and desire for purity, the reformer's contemporaries should develop a sensitivity to spiritual disease in the home.[13]

Calvin directed this responsibility for keeping the home pure directly at fathers. For example, in his sermons on Deuteronomy he argued, "Seeing that G[od] hath given [the father] sovereignty in his own house, it behooves him to deal in such wise as G[od] be honored there, and as no filthiness be mingled with the pure religion, but that all be rid quite and clean away."[14] This charge extended to the purity of belief and practice for all members in his home, including the servants. Calvin's concern for the context (he refers to the area as a "country of Idolaters") clearly was part of his motivation for this instruction; if pollution was allowed to be present in the home, he maintained, it would lead to "havoc." As an essential component of a Christian utopia, moral purity had to reign in each family, and it would be the father who would ensure each family member's compliance.

Finally, the godly father took seriously the spiritual education of his household.[15] Calvin's utopic vision was grounded on the belief that each individual would know and embrace the pure truth of Christianity. While the transmission of this truth to each individual was the church's aim, Calvin placed it at the heart of the Reformed family—parents passing the truth of the Gospel on to their children, and they to their children. There was little

---

11. Calvin, *Institutes of the Christian Religion*, 2.8.35.

12. Calvin also tied the purity of the Church to the Jewish temple in his *Commentary on the Gospel According to John, Volume 1*, John 2:16, 93.

13. Calvin, *Commentaries on the Four Last Books of Moses, Volume 2*, Num 5:2, 12; Lev 14:34, 27; Lev 11:13, 66–7.

14. Calvin, *The Sermons of M. Iohn Calvin upon the Fifth Booke of Moses called Deuternomie*, Deut 12:1–5, 492.

15. Spierling, "Father, Son, and Pious Christian," 96.

doubt that this system of transmission worked—to the church's dismay, the ecclesiastical discipline records are full of testimonies by congregants who said their prayers and the confession like the "papists" (in Latin), just as their parents had taught them.[16] Parents were a powerful, formative force in the lives of their offspring, and the consistory expected fathers to lead in this effort.

While both parents had a duty to provide religious instruction, Calvin viewed the father as primarily responsible, and the instruction of children by fathers is a constant theme of his writings.[17] He asserted that

> fathers were not led to instruct their children in these truths under the mere impulse of their own minds, but by the commandment of God. . . . The decree then is this, That the fathers being instructed in the doctrine of the law themselves, should recount, as it were, from the mouth of God, to their children, that they had been not only once delivered, but also gathered into one body as his Church, that throughout all ages they might yield a holy and pure obedience to him as their deliverer.[18]

For Calvin, the clearest indicator that fathers took the education of their families seriously was that they were able to bring about confessional homogeneity in their households. Abraham again emerged as an exemplar because of his ability to bring his entire household into the covenant.[19] Whereas Calvin commonly argued that the baptism of a child of a faithful parent subsumed the child in the parents' covenant, he interpreted the Abraham story even more liberally: non blood-related members of the household (namely, servants and slaves) were "embrace[d]" and "adopt[ed]" by God.[20] Calvin's argument was further illustrated in discussing New Testament examples such as Cornelius (Acts 10) and the unnamed jailor (Acts 16) who converted their entire households.[21] All Reformed fathers should secure not only the commitment of their children for the Reformed church, but also any others who might be included in the household. In places like Geneva and France, where contact with Catholic relatives, friends, and

---

16. Lambert et al., *Registres du Consistoire de Genève*, fol. 116v, 26 April 1543.

17. For additional reading on the obligations of parents, see Spierling, "Making Use of God's Remedies."

18. Calvin, *Commentary on the Book of Psalms, Volume 2*, Ps 78:5, 230–31. Also reference Watt, "Calvinism, Childhood, and Education," 447–48.

19. Calvin, *Calvin: Commentaries*, Gen 17:23, 404.

20. Calvin, *Commentaries on the First Book of Moses Called Genesis*, Gen 17:12, 455.

21. Calvin, *Commentary upon the Acts of the Apostles, Volume 1*, Acts 10:2, 407; Acts 16:33, 122.

neighbors occurred regularly, producing confessional conformity in the home was difficult—which made it all the more important for Calvin. His pressure on patriarchs to create Reformed households pressed the hope for an ideal society onto the local level of families: fathers became agents of religious conformity, responsible for their family, servants, and any others who might enter their home.

THEOLOGICAL TENSIONS: LIMITED KNOWLEDGE AND THE UNREFORMABLE

Calvin's view of a Christian utopia, however, was never simple or straightforward. At the heart of his *programme* of reform and hope for a Christian utopia lay discordant and contradictory beliefs. One such belief was his doctrine of predestination—a conviction that from the beginning of time God had predested some to eternal salvation and others to eternal damnation.[22] This theological tenet colored all other beliefs because it informed his fundamental understanding of the entire human race. Predestination, he held, was exercised by the divine mind apart from the knowledge of humankind (the identity of the saved and reprobate lay hidden within "the sacred precincts of divine wisdom"[23]), preventing speculation regarding the final election or damnation of individuals.[24] For this reason, Calvin could distinguish between two understandings of the "Church" in his *Institutes*: the group known to God (who were truly the elect/saved) and the group known to humans (the whole undifferentiated mass of people who identified as Christian, composed of both elect/saved and reprobate/damned individuals). He asserted,

> In this [second understanding of the] church are mingled many hypocrites who have nothing of Christ but the name and outward appearance. There are very many ambitious, greedy, envious persons, evil speakers, and some of quite unclean life. Such are tolerated for a time either because they cannot be convicted by a competent tribunal or because a vigorous discipline does not always flourish as it ought. Just as we must believe, therefore, that the former church, invisible to us, is visible to the eyes of God alone, so we are commanded to revere and keep communion with the latter, which is called "church" in respect to men.[25]

22. Calvin, *Institutes of the Christian Religion*, 3.21–24.
23. Ibid., 3.21.1.
24. Ibid., 3.22.1.
25. Ibid., 4.1.7.

Without knowledge of identity of the saved and damned, Calvin considered it imprudent and presumptuous to treat someone as if they were among the damned. As a consequence, all people were to be treated as saved and called to live as such, despite the fact that many were not. The proper response toward the doctrine of predestination was to seek out the highest potential in human beings and hope for the transformation of the world. Thus, in Geneva, *all Reformed Christians* were called to reconcile with their neighbors, learn the Lord's Prayer, Creed, and Ten Commandment, attend sermons, and participate in the Lord's Supper. In particular, Calvin urged Genevan fathers to embrace their Christian vocation and establish homes marked by order, purity, and Christian education. The deep irony remained that as a pastor he was compelled to strive for the reformation of all people, even the unreformable damned.

Furthermore, while Calvin expressed faith in fathers' abilities to bring order, purity, and understanding to the home, his commentaries and sermons contain contradictory undercurrents. For example, Calvin echoes Protestant themes of the powerlessness of humanity and the necessity of the grace of God. When this emphasis emerged in his discussion of the depravity of King David's household, it served to elevate God's role in history and diminished David's culpability for his family's condition by highlighting the impotence of human action. Even though David "took pains to have [his children] instructed and taught the requirements of the Law,"[26] his children were some of the most immoral in the Hebrew Bible. Therefore, Calvin urged parents to pray to God to guide their children because "all their labour, industry, and vigilance will be useless unless it is blessed by his Spirit."[27] Parents should release their children to the sovereignty of God, "recognizing that they will never reach their goal, and their pain can produce no good fruit unless God takes the whole matter in hand and controls it."[28] Such a message implicitly discredited fathers' ability to succeed on their own efforts and contradicted his earlier encouragement for fathers to instruct their households.[29] This tension between God's sovereignty and human effort brought the role of human effort in producing a utopic society into question entirely.

---

26. Calvin, *Sermons on 2 Samuel: chapters 1–13*, 2 Sam 8:9–18, 426.

27. Ibid., 2 Sam 8:9–18, 427.

28. Ibid., 2 Sam 6:20–23, 280.

29. "Farther, although fathers ought diligently to form their children under a system of holy discipline, yet let them remember that they will never succeed in attaining the object aimed at, save by the pure and special grace of God" (Calvin, *Commentary on the Book of Psalms, Volume 3*, Ps 127:5, 112).

A further tension can be witnessed in Calvin's interpretation of Psalm 78, a psalm in which the central theme was praising fathers for their role in transmitting the faith to their children. The author boasts that he told his descendants the great things God had done in the past so they would trust in God. While Calvin here affirmed the need for fathers to follow this example, a conspicuous thread of suspicion wove its way through his comments : "If it was incumbent upon the fathers to recount to their children the things here spoken of, these things ought, of course, to have been familiarly known to all the people, yea, even to those who were most illiterate, and had the weakest capacity."[30] However, the presence of multitudes of religiously ignorant individuals provided concrete evidence that domestic instruction was ineffective: Calvin asserted that some families passed on the Truth while others peddled "forgeries."[31] Fathers often transmitted their own vices, immorality, and unorthodox ideas.[32] The Jewish people demonstrated for Calvin that imitation was dangerous when the models were morally and doctrinally deficient: Jews that claimed that they were like their fathers were right, but not in the way God desired.[33] Ironically, Calvin turned the psalm on its head and used it to provide justification for the role of ministers in catechizing—rather than fathers! He argued that—since "the law was given not for one age only"—ministers were God's instruments of propagating the Gospel. Ministers could ensure "a continual succession of persons to communicate instruction in divine truth."[34] While originally this duty belonged to fathers, Calvin argued, God shifted this responsibility to priests and teachers at the close of the age of the patriarchs (Abraham, Isaac, and Jacob).[35] While this did not relieve fathers of their duty to instruct their families—for Calvin encouraged them to do so![36]—he asserted that fathers could not guarantee the longevity of the knowledge of God in the manner that these ministers could.[37] While fathers were to play a critical role in this

---

30. Calvin, *Commentary on the Book of Psalms*, Volume 2, Psa 78:3, 228.

31. ". . . all fathers are not here spoken of indiscriminately, but only those who were chosen to be God's peculiar people, and to whom the care of divine truth was entrusted," (ibid., Ps 78:3, 229).

32. Calvin, *Commentary on the Book of Psalms*, Volume 3, Ps 95:9, 42.

33. Calvin, *Commentary on the Book of Psalms*, Volume 2, Ps 78:8, 234–35.

34. Ibid., Ps 78:6, 231. Jane E. Strohl identifies a similar shift in the life and work of Martin Luther (Strohl, "The Child in Luther's Theology"). Also reference Pitkin, "The Heritage of the Lord," 169.

35. Calvin, *Commentary on the Book of Psalms*, Volume 2, Ps 78:6, 231–32.

36. Ibid., Ps 78:6–7, 232–33.

37. Ibid., Ps 78:6, 232.

utopic religious society, Calvin viewed them as unreliable in their central task of transmitting the faith.

DYSTOPIC REALITIES

Despite Calvin's aspirations for Reformed fathers to transform their homes and usher in a golden era of religious purity, fathers failed to perform the role he envisioned. The reoccurrence of issues of domestic disorder in discipline records reveals that although the consistory assumed that fathers were responsible for imposing order on household members, it remained a contested subject.[38] Genevan fathers often failed in two ways: they did not embrace their own vocation by fulfilling their basic responsibilities, *viz.*, providing materially for their families. Wives' frequent complaints suggest that husbands wasted household goods and left families destitute.[39] In addition, fathers improperly imposed discipline upon family members: they were either too lax or excessively harsh. Some fathers let their wives skip the sermon service or talk too much to neighbors. The aforementioned cases of Pierre Rosset and Claude Galleys were not unique: one husband threatened his wife with physical harm,[40] another threw his wife out of a window while she was naked,[41] and yet another beat his wife with a broom so badly she "lost an eye and [could] see nothing."[42] Although fathers embraced Calvin's call to establish their patriarchal leadership in their families, their abusive treatment of wives and children revealed they failed to understand his important caveat: this authority was given by God and to be exercised with

---

38. Spierling, "Father, Son, and Pious Christian," 100. Also reference Lambert et al., *Registres du Consistoire de Genève*, fol. 90v, 22 February 1543; vol. 1, fol. 181–181v, 27 March 1544; vol. 1, fol. 22, 20 April 1542; vol. 1, fol. 62v, 5 October 1542; vol. 1, fol. 86v, 1 February 1543; vol. 1, fol. 90v, 22 February 1543; vol. 1, fol. 93, 8 March 1543.

39. Spierling, "Father, Son, and Pious Christian," 96, 99, 108. Reference Lambert et al., *Registres du Consistoire de Genève*, fol. 85–85v, 25 January 1543; vol. 1, fol. 141, 15 November 1543.

40. In this notable case, Pierre Rosset "threatened to cut off [his wife's] head if she returned to this place of the Consistory" (ibid., fol. 181v, 27 March 1544.). Also see ibid. vol. 1, fol. 143v, 6 December 1543.

41. Ibid., fol. 128, 30 August 1543. Jaquemaz Papilliez claimed her husband wanted to throw her out of the window into the Rhone, and that "in the winter he threw her out of his company pregnant. He threw a bucket of water on the fire so she would not get warm and so she might die. And he beats her more often when she is pregnant than other times . . ." (ibid., vol. 1, fol. 197, 15 May 1544.).

42. Ibid., fol. 52, 17 August 1542. Also reference ibid. vol. 1, fol. 105, 29 March 1543; vol. 1, fol. 138v, 8 November 1543; vol. 1, fol. 196v, 8 May 1544. Ibid., 29 March 1543; 8 November 1543, 287; 8 May 1544, 394.

clemency.[43] In actuality, however, fathers were attempting to create order in the domestic kingdom by means similar to those employed by the men who controlled the city-state. Genevan ecclesiastical leaders and civil magistrates resorted to strongly coercive—even violent—methods to bring about a utopic reality; however, fathers were prohibited use of the same methods to transform their families. Without reformed fathers, committed fathers, and fathers who could bring about conformity without violence, ordered homes would never serve as the foundation for a utopia.

Regarding purity in the home, fathers failed to serve as its guardian. The consistory was scandalized that householders opened their doors to guests of questionable character, heretical beliefs, and all types of immoral behavior (games, gambling, bawdy songs, swearing). While consistory cases do little to reveal moral and compliant individuals in Geneva, Calvin expressed an overall displeasure with fathers and their unwillingness to keep their homes pure. In his sermons on 2 Samuel, he discussed the infamous story of the rape of Tamar. After warning his audience to guard their homes carefully (because "it only takes a day, or even a minute, to reverse what they have faithfully carried out [in] one or two, or even ten years,"), Calvin turned on Genevan patriarchs with a scathing reproach:

> Now how many husbands are there—I am not talking about somewhere far off, but in this very city—who would like there to be dances? Now what does such a request mean, if not that they are wanting to open a bawdy house, which are seen around here only too often? That is the real reason that there are husbands who would like their wives and daughters to dance. Why? So they can fornicate, which means that they will go to perdition, and receive perpetual shame. Even though we can see that fornication is forbidden before both God and man, how many people, in fact, are there who go to all lengths for their wives and daughters to be in style? Yet we know that this kind of thing tempts people to fornication. Thus, it is obvious to me that they are ultimately wanting to be pimps for their wives, they must want to be covered with an awful shame that there is nothing that they could ever do to blot it out.[44]

It was one thing for a well-meaning father to be surprised by Satan's attacks on his home. It was quite another—and completely unacceptable—for

---

43. Thompson, *John Calvin and the Daughters of Sarah*, 110. Also reference Calvin, Calvin, *Sermons on the Epistle to the Ephesians*, Eph 5:22–26, 570–71; Spierling, "Father, Son, and Pious Christian," 108, 116; Calvin, *John Calvin's Sermons on the Ten Commandments*, Deut 5:16, 143.

44. Calvin, *Sermons on 2 Samuel: chapters 1–13*, 2 Sam 13:1–14, 625.

fathers to be channels of immorality into their homes. Calvin's goal of reformed homes assumed moral purity, but its moral state was undermined by these lax and immoral fathers.

While Calvin charged fathers with the duty of instruction of their households, his misgivings of father's instructional capabilities were clear. Jeffrey Watt notes that the consistory's demand that Genevan youth attend catechism at the church stems from the fact that "Calvin obviously did not entirely trust the ability of fathers—and still less of mothers—to fulfill their roles in the religious education of the young."[45] Karen Spieling affirms this, adding, "Both Council and Consistory depended on these fathers to help maintain the stability and disciplinary structure of the church and city, but both bodies also at times found themselves disciplining children whose parents had not held their offspring to Reformed standards. . . . [I]n cases where the Consistory was directly disciplining children, they were at the same time *casting doubts on the authority, and perhaps even the family honor, of the parents of those children.*"[46] Just as Calvin casted doubt on the father's role in transmitting the faith (by transferring it to ministers), it was here again compromised by the consistory executing parental discipline. Rather than solving the problem of religiously-uneducated families, Genevan fathers themselves represented a hindrance to realizing a New Jerusalem.

A final obstacle to fathers creating homes which would transform Geneva was their personal capacity for learning the faith: householders repeatedly admitted to the consistory that they could not understand or remember sermons, others confessed that they could not recite the confession, and some that they did not know the prayers.[47] Even while pressing fathers to teach their households, the consistory recognized their ignorant state and assigned ministers and schoolmasters to domestically tutor congregants who failed to grasp doctrinal rudiments.[48] This concession can be interpreted as both an acknowledgement of fathers' inadequacy to carry out their pedagogical responsibilities—and possibly even the ineffectiveness of catechism (or churches' inability to coerce children to attend catechism!). Actions such as this passively acknowledged that the high hopes for fathers which rang from pulpits were half-hearted and would likely never be enough.

45. Watt, "Calvinism, Childhood, and Education," 454.

46. Spierling, *Infant Baptism in Reformation Geneva*, 212 (emphasis mine). Also reference ibid., chapter 6, especially 194, 205–209; Pitkin, "The Heritage of the Lord," 178.

47. For example, see Lambert et al., *Registres du Consistoire de Genève*, fol. 50–50v, 17 August 1543; vol. 1, fol. 68, 26 October 1542; vol. 1, fol. 105, 29 March 1543.

48. For example, see ibid. vol. 1, fol. 11, 30 March 1542; vol. 1, fol. 100v–101, 22 March 1543; vol. 1, fol. 148v, 20 December 1543.

PRESERVING THE TENSION

Ultimately, Calvin's hopes for Genevan father were illusory, but unsurprisingly so. This example exposes a deeper tension in a dualism at the heart of the Christian faith. In Christianity, heaven exists in distinction from—and opposition to—earth and vice-versa. Even without platonic and neo-platonic notions of the inherent evil nature of matter, heaven exists as a utopic, perfected vision of earth—essentially, a non-earth. In Reformed (Calvinist) theology as well as other traditions, all of humanity is fallen and deformed by Original Sin.[49] This even includes individuals who have been predestined by God to be saved. Calvin certainly held no lofty illusions regarding human nature. He argued that even the elect were not chosen based on their merit; while their election would lead to their eventual holiness, they remained sinful, imperfect individuals.[50] Thus, even fathers who were counted among the elect would not perfectly live out their vocation as the head of the household. The temporarily-imperfect nature of the elect and essentially fallen nature of the reprobate would therefore create a reality in Geneva where many fathers appeared to lack discipline and a drive toward sanctification. This clearly preserved the heaven/earth (holy/unholy) distinction.

However, this separation of the holy and profane was not absolute. The doctrine of the Incarnation was "exhibit A" in this regard, asserting that God in the form of Jesus came to live on earth. Indeed, the core of the Christian message is that the Kingdom of God has come to earth. Furthermore, there is an expectation that Christians are supposed to become more like God, even in this life (e.g., "Be perfect, therefore, as your heavenly Father is perfect," Matt 5:48, NIV). The idea of perfection—striving for a utopia where "all things are made new" (2 Cor 5:17; Rev 21:5)—is central to the biblical text: resignation is never presented as the solution to this tension of earth/heaven, imperfect/perfect, and darkness/light. Calvin embodies hope and the expectation for a utopia despite this dualism. It is hardly surprising, then, that he challenged these imperfect fathers to embrace their callings to remake their homes into "Little Churches."[51]

Even while acknowledging this pull toward heaven-on-earth, the idea of a Christian utopia is problematic. Perfection of human nature on earth would blur this fundamental dualism, thereby compromising the divine/human distinction and the impetus for the Christian message. This message demands human failure; to exist as Good News (gospel), it demands a

---

49. Calvin, *Institutes of the Christian Religion*, 1.15.4; 2.3.5.
50. Ibid., 3.22.2–3.
51. Quick, *Synodicon in Gallia Reformata*, 1:79.

dystopic reality on earth. Calvin and Geneva provide a marvelous example of this tension: even while Calvin chastised fathers for their corruption, he did not abandon his elevated view of patriarchal potential. With such a tension at the heart of his theological ontology, it is not surprising that Calvin could simultaneously hold a view of fathers that was both utopic (where fathers could act as divine agents in reforming their families) and thoroughly disillusioned (where the fallen, corrupt nature of fathers made them desire to be "pimps for their wives").

BIBLIOGRAPHY

Calvin, John. *Calvin: Commentaries*. Translated by Joseph Haroutunian and Louise Pettibone Smith. Philadelphia: Westminster, 1958.

———. *Calvin: Institutes of the Christian Religion*. Edited by John T. McNeill. Translated by Ford Lewis Battles. Philadelphia: Westminster, 1960.

———. *Commentary on the Book of Psalms, Volume 2*. Translated by James Anderson. Calvin's Commentaries 5. Grand Rapids: Baker, 1996.

———. *Commentary on the Book of Psalms, Volume 3*. Translated by James Anderson. Calvin's Commentaries 6. Grand Rapids: Baker, 1996.

———. *Commentaries on the Epistles of Paul the Apostle to the Philippians, Colossians, and Thessalonians*. Translated by John Pringle. Calvin's Commentaries 21. Grand Rapids: Baker, 1996.

———. *Commentaries on the Epistles to Timothy, Titus, and Philemon*. Translated by William Pringle. Calvin's Commentaries 21. Grand Rapids: Baker, 1993.

———. *Commentaries on the First Book of Moses Called Genesis*. Translated by John King. 2 vols. Calvin's Commentaries 1. Grand Rapids: Baker, 1996.

———. *Commentaries on the Four Last Books of Moses Arranged in the Form of a Harmony, Volume 2*. Translated by Charles William Bingham. Calvin's Commentaries 2. Grand Rapids: Baker, 1996.

———. *Commentary on the Gospel According to John, Volume 1*. Translated by William Pringle. Calvin's Commentaries 17. Grand Rapids: Baker, 1996.

———. *Commentary upon the Acts of the Apostles, Volume 1*. Edited by Henry Beveridge. Translated by Christopher Fetherstone. 2 vols. Calvin's Commentaries 18. Grand Rapids: Baker, 1996.

———. "The Form of Prayers and Songs of the Church, 1542: Letter to the Reader." Translated by Ford Lewis Battles. *Calvin Theological Journal* 15/2 (1980) 160–65.

———. *John Calvin's Sermons on the Ten Commandments*. Translated by Benjamin W. Farley. Grand Rapids: Baker, 1980.

———. "On Shunning the Unlawful Rites of the Ungodly and Preserving the Purity of the Christian Religion." In *Tracts and Treatises in Defense of the Reformed Faith, Volume 3*, edited by Thomas F. Torrance, 359–411. Translated by Henry Beveridge, Grand Rapids: Eerdmans, 1958.

———. *The Sermons of M. Iohn Calvin upon the Fifth Booke of Moses called Deuteronomie: faithfully gathered word for word as he preached them in open Pulpet: Together with a preface of the Ministers of the Church of Geneva, and an admonishment made by the Deacons there. Also there are annexed two profitable Tables, the one containing*

the chiefe matters; the other the places of Scripture herein alledged. Translated by Arthur Golding. London: Printed by Henry Middleton for Iohn Harison, 1583.
———. *Sermons on the Epistle to the Ephesians.* London: Banner of Truth Trust, 1973.
———. *Sermons on Galatians.* Translated by Kathy Childress. Edinburgh: Banner of Truth Trust, 1997.
———. *Sermons on 2 Samuel: chapters 1–13.* Translated by Douglas Kelly. Carlisle, PA: Banner of Truth Trust, 1992.
———. *Tracts and Treatises on the Reformation of the Church, Volume 1.* Edited by Thomas F. Torrance. Translated by Henry Beveridge. Grand Rapids: Eerdmans, 1958.
Hexter, J. H. "Utopia and Geneva." In *Action and Conviction in Early Modern Europe: Essays in Memory of E. H. Harbison,* edited by Theodore K. Rabb and Jerrold E. Seigel, 77–89. Princeton: Princeton University Press, 1969.
———. *The Vision of Politics on the Eve of the Reformation: More, Machiavelli, and Seyssel.* New York: Basic, 1973.
Knox, John. *History of the Reformation in Scotland.* Edited by W. C. Dickinson. New York: Philosophical Library, 1950.
———. *The Works of John Knox.* Edited by David Laing. Edinburgh: Johnston and Hunter, 1855.
Lambert, Thomas A., Isabella M. Watt, Robert M. Kingdon, and Jeffrey R. Watt, eds. *Registres du Consistoire de Genève au temps de Calvin (1542–1544).* Geneva: Librairie Droz, 1996.
McNeill, John T. *The History and Character of Calvinism.* New York: Oxford University Press, 1954.
Nicholls, David. "France." In *The Early Reformation in Europe,* edited by Andrew Pettegree, 120–41. Cambridge: Cambridge University Press, 1992.
Pitkin, Barbara. "'The Heritage of the Lord': Children in the Theology of John Calvin." In *The Child in Christian Thought,* edited by Marcia J. Bunge, 160–93. Grand Rapids: Eerdmans, 2001.
Quick, John. *Synodicon in Gallia Reformata: Or, The Acts, Decisions, Decrees, and Canons of Those Famous National Councils of the Reformed Churches in France.* 2 vols. London: T. Parkhurst and J. Robinson, 1692.
Spierling, Karen E. "Father, Son, and Pious Christian: Concepts of Masculinity in Reformation Geneva." In *Masculinity in the Reformation Era,* edited by Scott H. Hendrix and Susan C. Karant-Nunn, 95–119. Kirksville, MO: Truman State University Press, 2008.
———. *Infant Baptism in Reformation Geneva: The Shaping of a Community, 1536–1564.* Burlington, VT: Ashgate, 2005.
———. "Making Use of God's Remedies: Negotiating the Material Care of Children in Reformation Geneva." *The Sixteenth Century Journal* 36/3 (2005) 785–807.
Strohl, Jane E. "The Child in Luther's Theology: 'For What Purpose Do We Older Folks Exist, Other Than to Care For . . . the Young?'" In *The Child in Christian Thought,* edited by Marcia J. Bunge, 134–59. Grand Rapids: Eerdmans, 2001.
Thompson, John Lee. *John Calvin and the Daughters of Sarah: Women in Regular and Exceptional Roles in the Exegesis of Calvin, His Predecessors, and His Contemporaries.* Geneva: Librairie Droz, 1992.
Watt, Jeffrey R. "Calvinism, Childhood, and Education: The Evidence from the Genevan Consistory." *The Sixteenth Century Journal* 33/2 (Summer 2002) 439–56.

6

Fruit, Fossils, Footprints
Cathecting Utopia in the Work of Miyazawa Kenji

—Melissa Anne-Marie Curley

Essays on the Japanese writer Miyazawa Kenji (1896–1933) often begin with an inventory of his interests and accomplishments. The list is irresistible: he was a poet and author, particularly remembered now for his children's stories, but also a soil scientist, a high school teacher, and a sometime fertilizer salesman. He was the head of an agricultural cooperative founded on the basis of his own theory of peasant aesthetics. He was an amateur geologist, a student of Esperanto, and a cellist. He was an avid hiker and cataloguer of things observed while hiking. He was a devout Buddhist and an inspired reader of the Lotus Sutra, one of the keystone texts in Japanese Buddhist thought. And like others of his generation, he was a thoroughgoing utopian.

One thing sometimes omitted from lists of this sort is the fact of Kenji's membership in the National Pillar Society (Kokuchūkai), a Lotus-derived new Buddhist movement founded by lay evangelist Tanaka Chigaku. Such omissions reflect Tanaka's bad reputation: George Tanabe, Jr. characterizes Tanaka's ideology as "Lotus nationalism"[1]; Eishirō Itō goes further, calling it "Lotus fascism."[2] To be associated with Tanaka is to be associated with wartime ultranationalism. Some scholars interested in the Buddhist sources from which Tanaka drew his inspiration have taken pains to point out that

---

1. Tanabe, "Tanaka Chigaku," 192.
2. Itō, "Nationalism in Ulysses," 51.

he departs from these sources in significant ways, pressing the point that it is Tanaka who is the problem, not the Lotus Sutra or its earlier Japanese interpreters. Similarly, some scholars interested in Kenji have taken pains to distance him from Tanaka and thus resolve what Hiroaki Satō refers to as the "nagging question" of "guilt by association."[3] They are helped along in this by the particulars of Kenji's life: he spent less than a year in Tokyo around Kokuchūkai headquarters before permanently returning to his hometown in rural Iwate prefecture far from Tanaka's ambit, and he died in 1933 before the state's mobilization of its citizens and subjects for total war was fully underway, giving him "practically no chance to get involved in any such activity."[4] Jacqueline Stone suggests that Kenji in fact broke with Tanaka ideologically later in life[5]; Roger Pulvers suggests that he was too naive to engage ideology effectively in the first place.[6] The impulse here seems the same in either case: the further away we can place Kenji from Tanaka—whether geographically, philosophically, or temperamentally—the better.

The question I take up in this chapter moves out on a slightly different trajectory. What is at once troubling and compelling about Tanaka is that there is nothing exceptional about the movement of his intellectual life: he started out a utopian and ended up a totalitarian. We see utopianism curdle into totalitarianism in other modern Japanese thinkers inspired by the Lotus Sutra, and in modern Japanese thinkers inspired by other religious texts and traditions. We see it in modern Japanese thinkers inspired by sources other than religion. And of course we see it outside of Japan too, in the grim aftermath of other revolutionary utopian projects undertaken across Asia and Europe.

Anti-utopian critics reflecting on this pattern take it as evidence that there is a totalitarian drive inherent in all utopias, waiting to ripen. Karl Popper argues that the will to overturn the existing order and enact utopia requires the utopian to "purify, purge, expel, banish, and kill"[7]; Frédéric Rouvillois characterizes utopias as "harbingers of totalitarianism" and totalitarianism as "the tragic execution of the utopian dream"[8]; Leszek Kolakowski warns us that "the victory of utopian dreams would lead us to a totalitarian nightmare and the utter downfall of civilization."[9] In the anti-utopian view,

3. Satō, "Miyazawa Kenji," para. 12.
4. Ibid.
5. Stone, "Japanese *Lotus* Millennialism," 265–66.
6. Pulvers, *Strong in the Rain*, 17.
7. Popper, *The Open Society*, 156.
8. Rouvillois, "Utopia and Totalitarianism," 316.
9. Kolakowski, *Modernity on Endless Trial*, 145.

whenever we encounter a utopian imagination, we are encountering a totalitarian imagination—if we apply this to the case at hand, the problem is not with Tanaka as a personality but with utopianism itself. This leaves Kenji vulnerable to critique regardless of his association with the Kokuchūkai.

On the other hand, utopia still has its defenders. In a letter written not long after the events of 9/11, Ruth Levitas briskly summarizes her opposition to the anti-utopian position:

> All political movements have utopian elements, insofar as they encompass views of what a good society might be like. Some of these political movements are dangerous and genocidal. *But it is not 'utopianism' that makes them so. The problem about totalitarianism is not its utopianism, but its totalitarianism.*[10]

Elsewhere, Levitas lays out a different way of imagining utopia. It is both possible and desirable, she says, to understand utopia as "a method rather than a goal, and accompanied by the recognition of provisionality, responsibility, and necessary failure."[11] In understanding utopia as a method, Levitas aligns herself with theorists Raymond Williams, Tom Moylan, and Fredric Jameson, for whom "what is most important about utopia is less what is imagined than the act of imagination itself, a process which disrupts the closure of the present."[12] At the same time, Levitas emphasizes something that in her view they do not—she wants a utopia with pluralism, but not what she calls "a kind of pathological pluralism" that "undermines the capacity to occupy, even critically and provisionally, a ground of one's own, so that commitment is impossible."[13] So, on the one hand, provisionality, and on the other hand, responsibility (or, on the one hand, rupture, and on the other hand, ground): "The effective synthesis of provisionality and responsibility may be the condition of keeping utopia open as a space in which to reach out to the real possibility of a transformed future."[14] This combination resonates with what Darren Webb refers to as "reterritorialising hope," or a mode of hoping that both opens the present to ongoing critique and "emphasises the necessity of transforming society in light of the liberating utopia."[15]

---

10. Levitas and Sargisson, "Utopia in Dark Times," 26.
11. Levitas, "Looking for the Blue," 290.
12. Levitas, "For Utopia," 39.
13. Ibid., 40.
14. Ibid.
15. Webb, "Modes of Hoping," 38.

In the pages that follow, I will try to show at some length how Kenji's utopia speaks to the first requirement and, briefly, how it speaks to the second. Like his utopian contemporaries, Kenji has an image of an ideal world different from the real one and a powerful wish to mobilize a collective in order to realize this ideal; unlike them, however, he does not imagine utopia permanently overwriting the real, foreclosing on the possibility of future transformation. I will argue that this is because he is attuned to an element of the traditional Buddhist spatial imaginary that his contemporaries—Tanaka among them—are not. For this reason, he imagines utopia differently.

LOCATING UTOPIA IN THE LOTUS SUTRA

Both Tanaka and Kenji are inspired by the Lotus Sutra's image of the *jōjakkōdo*, the radiant land of eternal tranquility that is the true home of the historical Buddha and the best of all the buddha lands. The buddha lands described in the Lotus share certain generic features: the ground is made of lapis or crystal; they are perfectly level, without mountains or valleys; they are free from all manner of filth, including the stench of latrines; all beings who dwell within them flourish and all beings who look upon them are filled with joy; and roads criss-cross them in eight directions, marked by golden ropes—this last detail is important because it means that above the road is an eight-spoked wheel, symbol of the Buddhist law, signifying the way in which these lands are ordered by that law, radiating from the enlightened body that has established itself at the center. Our world—the *saha* world, or world of enduring suffering—has none of these features: it is "uneven, high in places, low in others, and full of dirt, stones, mountains, foulness, and impurity";[16] like a rotting house, it is piled with garbage and stinks of excrement.[17] This is not a place for buddhas—in the eleventh chapter of the Lotus, the historical Buddha prepares for a visiting host of buddhas from other lands by swapping out the bad place for the good place. It takes him only a moment:

> The *saha* world thereupon immediately changed into a place of cleanness and purity. The ground was made of lapis lazuli, jeweled trees adorned it, and ropes of gold marked off the eight highways. There were no villages, towns or cities, great seas or rivers, mountains, streams or forests. . . . the members of this

16. Watson, *Lotus Sutra*, 291.
17. Ibid., 62–63.

assembly alone were gathered there, all other heavenly and human beings having been moved to another region.[18]

When he finds he does not have enough room, he just expands the borders of his empire—"in order to provide seats for all the Buddhas that were arriving, [he] once more transformed two hundred ten thousand million *nayutas* of lands in each of the eight directions, making them all clean and pure."[19] Here the good place and the bad place are set in opposition to one another; it is a mark of the compassion of the historical Buddha that he consents to be in this bad place with us.

In the sixteenth chapter, however, the Buddha declares that in reality the suffering of the *saha* world is an illusion and he is always in a pure land: when for us the world is consumed in flames at the end of time, "My pure land is not destroyed"—indeed it is not even disturbed.[20] So where the eleventh chapter suggests that this world can be displaced by a pure land, here the implication is that this world, perceived correctly, is itself pure. Medieval Japanese interpreters of the Lotus take the position that the sixteenth chapter supersedes the eleventh, and therefore hold that the Lotus ultimately affirms the identity of this world and the pure land—for those who have eyes to see, this bad place is always already a perfectly good place. The correct attitude is thus not one of despising this world but of realizing its perfect goodness.

For later Buddhist modernizers, this option proves attractive. It is difficult to reconcile the other-worldly pure lands of the premodern spatial imaginary with Copernican cosmology; trading that spatial imaginary in for something more readily understood as a metaphor for a particular way of ordering this world is appealing for this reason. More than this though, the idea of a transcendent pure land is seen as bound up with a tradition of world renunciation that has had the ill effect of inculcating an attitude of passive hope rather than the active engagement in the public sphere modernity demands of good citizens. Borrowing from Max Weber, we might say that the Buddhist modernizer needs to recast Buddhism as oriented not around "contemplative 'flight from the world'" but rather "active ascetic 'work in this world.'"[21] Toward this end, the identity of this world and the pure land is read by modernizers like Ikeda Daisaku as affirming such active work as the proper duty of the Buddha and his disciples: "'Pure land,' in other words, means 'purify the land.' It indicates taking action to improve

18. Ibid., 173.
19. Ibid., 174.
20. Watson, *Lotus Sutra*, 231.
21. Weber, *Sociology of Religion*, 290.

the environment and construct a better society. . . . The true heritage of Buddhism is found in the spirit to transform the actual land in which we live for the better."²² But the Lotus Sutra offers more than one way of imagining this immanent utopia.

When Tanaka imagines an immanent utopia, he imagines it taking hold everywhere through the transformation of the realm itself into a buddha (*kokudo jōbutsu*)²³ or a "this-worldly land of tranquility" (*sekai no jakkōdo*).²⁴ Such a transformation will not be "like heaven or the [transcendent] Pure Land, which are never actually expected to appear before our eyes. We predict, envision, and aim for it as a reality that we will definitely witness."²⁵ This transformation is to be effected through the harmonizing of imperial law and Buddhist law in Japan (the center of the world), the construction of a seat of authority from which the law will be disseminated at the base of Mount Fuji (the center of Japan), and the subsequent spread of the Buddhist law from this epicenter to the eight corners of the earth: "the light of our country will fill the universe and instruct the people of all nations. This will accomplish the spiritual unification of the world, without need of a single soldier or sword."²⁶ So the utopian reordering of the world starts at the center and radiates outward; peace is established through the leveling of all difference as every nation accepts the law delivered by the Lotus Sutra, which Tanaka understands as identical to the Japanese body politic (*kokutai*).²⁷ Tanaka's spatial imagination is concerned most acutely with maintaining a stable center; establishing Japan everywhere is for him a way of preserving the core of Japanese identity. This is a totalitarian vision, obviously, but it's also a Buddhist vision: it is the image of the wheel of law that organizes the pure land. Japan is here charged with assuming the role of the enlightened body at the center of the world, immanentizing utopia through the expansion of its borders.

Kenji, on the other hand, is writing from the middle of nowhere. Iwate is a rural place, far removed from metropolitan Tokyo; it was (and remains) economically and politically marginalized, and is culturally identified with the hardscrabble north rather than the refinement of the capital. It makes sense then that Kenji's spatial imagination does not much resemble Tanaka's—where Tanaka seeks a stable center, Kenji tends to decenter. He

22. Ikeda, "The 'Saha' World," para. 32, 36.
23. Stone, "By Imperial Edict," 200.
24. Iguchi, "Nichirenism as Modernism," 156.
25. Stone, "By Imperial Edict," 200.
26. Ibid., 201.
27. Tanabe, "Tanaka Chigaku," 203.

imagines an immanent utopia concealed within the real that might appear fully developed anywhere and at any time. In developing this vision, he seizes upon a different spatial image from the Lotus: an image of eruption.

The Lotus presents two such images. The transformation of the realm described in the eleventh chapter comes on the heels of one eruption, describing a vast reliquary "that rose up out of the earth and stood suspended in the air;"[28] the reliquary contains the full-body relic of a buddha called Many Treasures who, in an earlier life, had vowed that even after he passed into nirvana, his reliquary would appear wherever the Lotus Sutra was preached, so that he could praise its efficacy. A second eruption takes place in the fifteenth chapter, which describes a host of enlightened beings emerging from the earth: "the earth of the thousand millionfold countries of the *saha* world all trembled and split open, and out of it emerged at the same instant immeasurable thousands, ten thousands, millions of bodhisattvas and mahasattvas. The bodies of these bodhisattvas were all golden in hue, with the thirty-two features and an immeasurable brightness."[29] The historical Buddha tells the human audience witnessing this event that these bodhisattvas have been concealing themselves beneath the earth for countless eons, "dwelling in the world of empty space underneath the *saha* world."[30]

In both cases, the basic event is the same: enlightened bodies, singly or as a mass, suddenly erupt into the *saha* world from below, illuminating this world with their radiance. This works to literalize the notion that the Buddha's pure land lies immanent within and concealed beneath this world of suffering;[31] this at any rate is how the image of the bodhisattvas emerging from the earth is read by interpreters who take "the empty space in its lower part" as referring to the *jōjakkōdo*.[32] And it works to suggest that a pure land might disturb the order of the *saha* world, not sweeping it away but rather taking place within it—this is about a world of rupture, as Gerald Iguchi puts it,[33] rather than a world of unity. Both concealment and revealment are important aspects of this image; it makes poetic sense that the figure of the full-body relic is deployed in the other version of this image, because the relic too points to absence and presence simultaneously.

28. Watson, *Lotus Sutra*, 170.
29. Ibid., 213.
30. Ibid., 219.
31. See Leighton, *Visions of Awakening Space and Time*, vii.
32. See Kanno, "Bodhisattvas of the Earth," 116.
33. Iguchi, "Nichirenism as Modernism," 154.

Gayatri Spivak refers to this dynamic of concealment and revealment as invagination—"the supernatural in the pocket of the natural."[34] Invagination describes neither a strictly transcendent divine, nor a strictly immanent divine; instead, she proposes, it represents the way in which an "active polytheist imagination negotiates with the unanticipatable yet perennial possibility of the metamorphosis of the transcendental as supernatural in the natural."[35] In the working of such an imagination, everything is open to "cathexis by the ulterior,"[36] and anything can be "contaminated by the supernatural, by alterity."[37] So the real has no claim to stability. But neither does the divine—"rather unlike any sustained notion of incarnation," Spivak says, the moment of cathexis is not meant to be "sustained into stabilized worship."[38]

Where Spivak talks about beings, we can talk about spaces. The image of eruption suggests that the utopian space of the pure land is neither strictly separate from this world of suffering nor strictly identical with it; rather, it is folded into this world in such a way as to produce a chiasm: the supernatural site where the transcendent opens up within the natural. This chiasm can be coaxed into revealing itself when the right words are spoken (obviously the message of the Lotus Sutra is that those words are the words of the sutra itself). Then the human audience should find itself in two places at once: both in the world of suffering *and* in the Buddha's pure land. Here the bad place is not abjected by the good place but momentarily cathected by it; the human being tasked with coaxing this moment of opening up into existence participates in the ongoing process of realizing utopia through disrupting the closure of the present.

For medieval Japanese Buddhists, who have active polytheist imaginations, this cathexis seems easy to produce. They understand both the transcendent buddhas and their transcendent pure lands as "perhaps already descended in what surrounds us,"[39] or *both* "up-there" and "come-down."[40] Unsurprisingly, they also operate in a world in which relics are abundant.

For most modern Japanese Buddhists though, cathexis is difficult and the supernatural itself becomes a source of embarrassment.[41] Kenji is un-

---

34. Spivak, "Moving Devi," 124.
35. Ibid., 123.
36. Ibid.
37. Ibid., 124.
38. Ibid., 123.
39. Ibid., 124.
40. Ibid., 123.
41. See Figal, *Civilization and Monsters*.

usual in part because he is enchanted with modernity—his work is rich with images drawn from chemistry, astronomy, archaeology, geology—but still very good at imagining utopia as enfolded within the real, welling up from below. His name for the site of this invagination is Īhatōvu.

THE DREAMLAND ĪHATŌVU

Kenji imagines Īhatōvu as hidden underneath the real, represented for him by Iwate. Īhatōvu is the site—and, as he presents it, the source—of his children's stories. What is it like in Īhatōvu? This is how he describes it in an advertisement for the story collection *Restaurant of Many Orders*:

> There, everything is possible. A person can in an instant leap above the ice and clouds, travelling north on the great atmospheric current, or talk with the ants underneath the red bowls of the flowers. There, even sin and sadness shine in a way that is sacred and lovely. Deep forests of beech, wind and shadows, evening primrose, wondrous cities, rows of lightpoles stretching to Bering-shi: a truly mysterious and blissful realm.[42]

This account invokes a number of the standard features of a pure land. One such feature is translocation—the residents of buddha lands are able to travel effortlessly across vast distances, and in Īhatōvu, we can leap through the air across the sky. Another is translocution—in buddha lands, the plants and trees and animals all constantly preach the Buddhist dharma in a language every resident understands, and in Īhatōvu, we can talk with the ants; in the foreword to *Restaurant*, Kenji will explain that all of his stories about Īhatōvu have been transmitted to him by non-human narrators: "These stories of mine all came from the rainbows and moonlight, in the woods and fields and along the railroad tracks."[43] And a third is radiance—buddha lands shine with the illuminating power of the buddha bodies out of which they are manifested, and Īhatōvu too is suffused with radiant light.

But Īhatōvu is not a transcendent pure land. It overlaps with the real Iwate technologically: the radiant light that limns it comes from electric lights, not a miraculous body, and the circulating current on which we travel is an atmospheric tide, not a river of *qi*; elsewhere, Kenji will play with the image of an intergalactic railway as a substitute for the rainbow-colored clouds that facilitate the passage from the world of the living to the world of the dead in the traditional imaginary. It overlaps with the real

---

42. Miyazawa, "Kōkokubun," para. 4–6.
43. Miyazawa, *MKZ*, 8:219.

Iwate geographically too: features of Iwate's landscape, both natural and human-made, frequently appear in Kenji's Īhatōvu stories, and he suggests that anyone looking for Īhatōvu should plot a course northeast of Tagore's fairy tale desert of Tepantar and east of Tolstoy's fairy tale kingdom ruled by Ivan the Fool,[44] thus fixing his dreamland Īhatōvu northeast of a dreamland India and east of a dreamland Russia. And it overlaps with the real Iwate existentially—there are sins and sorrows there. The image of those sins and sorrows made to shine with radiant light is a way of talking about the intertwining of the good place and the bad place.

This intertwining is important to Kenji. In the advertisement for *Restaurant*, he describes his intention as a writer in explicitly utopian terms, with an important proviso: "These stories have been presented," he says, as "materials for forming a new, better world"; the world he has in mind, however, is "not an ashen-colored utopia kneaded together in a deformed manner, but a miraculous development of the world itself . . ."[45] The organic quality of this image makes sense here, given Kenji's framing of the stories themselves as products of the landscape—"These are the fresh produce of the countryside. From out of the wind and light of the countryside, along with the gleaming fruits and green vegetables, we offer these mental sketches to the world," for they contain "the seeds of truth and its beautiful sprouts."[46] The new, better world Kenji has in mind is the dehiscence of an ancient utopia concealed beneath contemporary Iwate. His work is marked by repeated efforts to imagine this dehiscence through three related figures—fruit, fossil, and footprint—each of which he reads in relation to the Lotus's images of eruption.

Fruit

Kenji's description of his stories as, like fruit, made from wind and light is connected to other images he deploys of consuming wind and light. In the foreword to *Restaurant*, he writes "Even if we don't have as much rock candy as we want, we can eat the pure, transparent wind and drink the lovely peach-colored morning sunlight. . . . I like that kind of pure food,"[47] and in his novel *Night of the Milky Way Railroad*,[48] he imagines luminous herons "flickering like fireflies" that are captured and hung "in the water-light of the

44. Miyazawa, "Kōkokubun," para. 1.
45. Ibid., para. 9.
46. Ibid., para. 11, 8.
47. Miyazawa, *MKZ*, 8:219.
48. Ibid., 10:229–300; trans. Strong, *Milky Way Railroad*.

Milky Way's silver river,"[49] transforming them into a candy that tastes "even better than chocolate."[50] Sarah Strong offers a compelling interpretation of this image as connected to Kenji's Buddhist dream of a truly non-violent diet—because the herons are just motes of light, "the cheerful bird catcher is no more guilty of taking life than is a child scooping sand at the seashore."[51] But the image of food as a concentrated form of light is also appealing to Kenji as a way of thinking about the radiance of the buddha's enlightened body being absorbed by and refracted through ordinary things.

He makes this point more explicitly in a story about fruit, "The Porcelain Berries and the Rainbow."[52] In the ruins of an ancient castle, a cluster of porcelain berries grows on a square heap of earth. After a brief summer rain, a rainbow appears in the sky "like a dream-colored bridge"[53] stretching from the castle to the mountains in the distance. The berries, overawed by the beauty of the rainbow, work up their nerve and ask if it won't accept their veneration, but the rainbow says in fact the berries are much finer than it is—its colors will shortly fade away, but the berries will surely last. The berries cry that this is not the case; they will be scattered by the autumn wind, buried by the snow, and lost underneath the cut grasses in spring. The rainbow smiles and allows that this is true enough—nothing is permanent, and yet, it says, endless life (*kagirinai inochi*) consists of nothing but such fleeting moments. As the rainbow starts to fade, the berries beg to come along, but the rainbow insists that even as it disappears, it isn't really leaving: "I'm not going anywhere. . . . People who live with each other in the light of truth are always together."[54]

The Buddhist symbolism here is clear. The distant mountains represent nirvana, the true abode of the buddhas (as mountains do in the traditional Japanese Buddhist imaginary), and the rainbow represents the clear light of nirvana manifesting for a moment in the *saha* world, in the form of the historical Buddha—in fact, the rainbow's speech to the berries is a spin on one the Buddha gives his disciples in the Lotus, in which he reveals that although he appears to vanish into nirvana, in truth he is always here. The berries—fragile and impermanent and not even good to eat—represent suffering beings. But the reader is supposed to realize that the berries are also the cathected body of the buddha. The rainbow tells the berries so: when

---

49. Strong, *Milky Way Railroad*, 45.
50. Ibid., 44.
51. Ibid., 101.
52. Miyazawa, *MKZ*, 7:37–41.
53. Ibid., 7:38.
54. Ibid., 7:40.

they say that the grasses and flowers and birds all sing the praises of the rainbow, it replies "Those songs are also for you—whatever makes me shine makes you sparkle too."[55] And Kenji tells us so, pointing out that the color of the ripening berries is "like a rainbow," and planting them on that square heap of earth (*shikkakuyama*)—literally a four-cornered mountain.[56] This refers to the old name for a real place in Iwate but also suggests the image of the square mountain that sits at the center of the universe in traditional Buddhist cosmology, and the square base of the traditional Buddhist reliquary. So the berries here function precisely as relics do: they are a site in which a divine radiance is concentrated.

In the premodern Japanese imaginary, relics conceal within themselves the radiant power of an enlightened body that is otherwise gone; when the relics are activated—unearthed or opened up—that radiant power spills out, transforming the degenerate order of the present. In Kenji's imaginary, fruit conceals within itself the sunlight of a growing season that is otherwise finished; when the fruit is activated—picked and eaten—that sunlight spills out and so too do the seeds that will eventually produce new fruit; the gloomy present order is thus disrupted by the presencing of the bright past and bright future. Where fruit literally refers to fruit grown in Iwate, it contains all the wholesomeness of the soil (which figures the past) and nourishes the bodies of children (which figure the future); the chiasm opens up in the act of eating. Kenji's stories are like fruit in that they record the utopian pattern of life he fancies as having obtained in an ancient Iwate, and contain the blueprint for rebuilding that utopia in a future Iwate; the chiasm opens up in the act of reading.

Fossils

Kenji imagines fossils as another *sanbutsu* yielded up by the ground of Iwate—here the chiasm opens up in the act of digging. He spent two summers doing archaeological digs in the Kitakami river bed with his students, at a site he christened the English Coast.[57] In a poem remembering those summers, he writes of "Looking for long pointy fossils of walnut shell" and

> ... Digging the footprints of ancient beasts
> Out of thinly clouded grumbling water[58]

---

55. Ibid., 7:40.
56. Ibid., 7:37.
57. Strong, *Milky Way Railroad*, 100.
58. Pulvers, *Strong in the Rain*, 65.

He returns to this image in *Milky Way Railroad*. Here the setting has moved to the "Pliocene Coast" and the Milky Way or, in Japanese, the Amanogawa—literally the River of Heaven. Our two young heroes, Giovanni and Campanella, discover a cache of fossilized walnuts embedded in the river bank. Treasures in hand, they meet an archaeologist supervising a dig:

> The boys looked and saw an enormous pale-colored animal bone that seemed to have fallen over on its side and broken. It was more than half dug out from the soft white rock around it. Then they noticed that some of the stone that bore the footprints of cloven-hoofed animals had been neatly cut out into ten square pieces with a number attached to each piece.
>
> The professorial gentleman turned toward the boys, his glasses flashing. "You've come to observe, I take it," he said. "I expect you saw lots of walnuts. Those are roughly one million two hundred thousand years old. Very recent as these things go."[59]

Kenji uses the same image once more in *Spring and Asura*. Again, there is a cosmically-scaled archaeological dig taking place:

> ... Perhaps, two thousand years from now,
> an appropriately different geology may win the time ...[60]

But now the footprints belong to us:

> ... fresh bachelors of arts may excavate
> wonderful fossils from the top stratum of the atmosphere ...
> or discover the enormous footprints of an invisible mankind
> among the Cretaceous sandstone strata.[61]

Like fruit, the fossil too concentrates a span of time—here geological time rather than agricultural time. (Although notice that Kenji imagines geological time as cyclical, like agricultural time: if now we are the archaeologists digging up fossils, eventually time will bury us, making way for new archaeologists.) In *Milky Way Railroad*, the boys ask if the professor wants the animal bone as a specimen (*hyōhon*); he says no, he wants it for proof (*shōmei*). Mita Munesuke reads this as pointing to a distinction between the thing in itself and the thing as part of a larger order of things—the bone specimen proves the existence of the animal that is now gone; the animal specimen proves the existence of a world of animals that is now gone; the

---

59. Strong, *Milky Way Railroad*, 37.
60. Satō, *Spring and Asura*, 7.
61. Ibid.

human footprint will eventually prove the existence of a humankind that will eventually be gone. "'Specimens' and related items such as 'fossils,' 'footprints,' and 'transparent beings,'" Mita writes, "are first and foremost *proof of the existence of non-existent things*."[62] We could also say they re-present unpresent things, at once confirming and disturbing the temporal order—the fossil is the presence of the past.

In exploring the river bed, Kenji plays one spatial metaphor for time against another. The conventional Japanese Buddhist metaphor for time comes from Kamo no Chōmei's *Hōjōki* and its famous image of the flowing river: "The flow of the river is ceaseless and its water is never the same. The bubbles that float in the pools, now vanishing, now forming, are not of long duration: so in the world are man and his dwellings."[63] What gets emphasized here is one aspect of impermanence—despite our grasping for a fixed order, everything we try to hold onto will be swept away in time; the present is at every moment giving way to the future. In Chōmei's river, nothing persists.

In Kenji's dry riverbed, however, everything persists. Against the image of time flowing, he gives us an image of time piling up in layers, so that the past is concealed without wholly disappearing. The temporal order of the past is retrievable through the fossil. This is impermanence seen from another angle—the order of the present might at any moment be disrupted by the past. And because Kenji imagines the past that lies concealed below the ground of Iwate as a utopia, the possibility that the past might disrupt the present is also a source of hope for the future; thus the fossil is, for him, oriented toward the future as well as the past.

Fossils are, of course, connected to relics in an obvious way—they are both the material remains of once-living things. But they are also connected to Buddhist relics in a particular way for Kenji. My contention here hinges on the link between fossils and footprints.

Footprints

You will have noticed already that when Kenji talks about fossils, he talks about footprints. This is surely in part because when he was digging at Kitakami, he really was finding shale footprints. But footprints are also constellated within a network of Buddhist images. The footprint is read variously as an aniconic image of the historical Buddha and thus a relic of

---

62. Strong, *Milky Way Railroad*, 89.
63. Keene, "An Account of My Hut," 197.

commemoration, as a relic of use, and as a relic of embodiment.[64] Coming into contact with a footprint relic is understood to have the same salutary effects as coming into contact with the Buddha—one of the inscriptions on a set of carved Buddha footprints held by Yakushiji, for example, tells us that "Whoever shall come to gaze on these most sacred footprints, for him shall the sins of a thousand ages be wiped out . . ."[65]

Kenji makes the connection between the fossilized footprint and the holy footprint clear in a poem about Koiwainōjō, a farm at the base of Mount Iwate that Hoyt Long notes served as "a critical entry point for Western methods of crop production, dairy farming, and livestock operations."[66] Kenji identifies Koiwai as having a holy place within it—

> somehow
> I want to call it
> *der heilige Punkt*[67]

At Koiwai, he senses the presence of two celestial beings, whose feet "shine a pure white . . . like shells"[68]:

> . . . how long it has been since I last saw
> your huge, pure white unshod feet
> How I searched for your archaic footprints
> in ancient beaches of Cretaceous shale . . .[69]

And he makes the connection between these shining white footprints and the feet of the buddha clear in the story "The Shining Feet," the work in which, as Sarah Strong has pointed out, he most explicitly draws on the Lotus Sutra.[70]

"Shining Feet"[71] tells the story of two young brothers, Ichirō and Narao, who go out to gather firewood on the mountain and lose their way in a mountain pass at twilight; blinded by the falling snow, they find themselves trapped in a hell realm for lost children—here Kenji borrows from an existing Japanese Buddhist image of a purgatory for dead children in a dry

64. See Kinnard, "The Polyvalent Pādas," 38–42.
65. Mills, "The Buddha's Footprint Stone Poems," 240.
66. Long, *On Uneven Ground*, 246 n. 60.
67. Strong, "Miyazawa Kenji and the Lost Gandharan Painting," 177.
68. Ibid., 177.
69. Ibid., 197.
70. As noted in her paper for the Spring 2012 Lotus Sutra Seminar, hosted by Rikkyō University. This seminar paper in particular, and Strong's rich body of work on Kenji generally, has deeply informed my reading here.
71. Miyazawa, *MKZ*, 9:228–258.

riverbed in the netherworld. In Kenji's version, the children are whipped by demons and forced to march back and forth across sharp stones; Ichirō tries to shield his younger brother from the descending whips, and as he does so, he senses something in the air that reminds him of a phrase—in the story, he is not aware of its meaning, but in fact the phrase is "chapter on the lifespan of the Tathāgata" the title of the sixteenth chapter of the Lotus; as we noted above, this is the chapter in which it is revealed that the Buddha is always present in this world. On impulse, Ichirō repeats this phrase once and everything stops; he repeats it once more and over the horizon appears a very tall, very splendid-looking person: "The person's feet seemed to shine white. He came walking quickly, straight toward them. Those pure white feet shining. . . . He had huge bare feet that shone white like shell. His heels glittered and pressed into the earth. He had huge pure white bare feet."[72]

Throughout the story, Kenji emphasizes images of feet in contact with the ground. When the boys are lost in the mountain pass, icy thorns cut at their feet like knives; as the mountain pass resolves into the hell realm, the ground transforms into a blanket of jagged stones and fire; when the figure with shining feet comes to the children, "those soft feet stepped across the sharp shards of agate and the burning red fire and were not cut or burned at all"[73]; and when he reaches the children and gently brushes their heads, all of their wounds are healed. "The ground is made of swords here," the figure says, "and so it tears at your feet and your bodies. That's what you're thinking. But this ground is completely flat—come, take a look."[74] The figure then transforms the land: the ground becomes a lake, green as malachite, perfectly still and level, with splendid trees and buildings floating suspended on top of it, flags flying from them like rainbows, shining bridges connecting them, and celestial maidens hovering in the air above them dropping blue and gold flower petals down to the ground. This is the Buddha's pure land. (It also, very charmingly, has certain qualities that would most appeal to children: a museum that has specimens of everything in existence, a library, and a playground; when a really small boy says that what he'd like most is some chocolate, one of the celestial maidens descends bearing a bowl full of candy.)

The story suggests that the mechanism for summoning the figure with shining white feet is Ichirō's repetition of the phrase from the Lotus Sutra, in keeping with the Lotus's own suggestion that preaching the sutra will trigger the manifestation of a buddha. The mechanism for transforming the

72. Ibid., 9:251.
73. Ibid., 9:251.
74. Ibid., 9:252–53.

ground, however, is not just the presence of an enlightened body but the contact between his feet and the ground—where for Ichirō and Narao the ground is hard and unyielding, for the Buddha, it is soft: he is able to imprint it with his qualities, which has the effect of reordering space. As we read the story, we move through four different spaces: the family's house, the snowy mountain pass, the dry riverbed, and the Buddha's pure land. Kenji signals each shift with a subheading: (1) The Little Mountain Hut, (2) The Mountain Pass, (3) The Twilight Country, (4) The Shining Feet, and (5) The Mountain Pass. This too is a signal, I think, that we should be imagining the good place as constituted in relation to those feet: wherever those feet make contact with the ground, the good place is established.

At the end of section 4, the Buddha tells Ichirō that it is time for him to go home: "Your feet, which have been torn once, can go barefoot once more over the hateful thicket of blades. . . . Many people have gone to your country from here. Search well and find the true path."[75] Then a fog rolls in, obscuring the landscape, and as section 5 opens, we are back in the mountain pass with Ichirō waking up under a blue sky; Narao, lying beside him, has frozen to death overnight. The implication here is that the boys have not moved over the course of the night, and yet it would be a mistake, I think, to suppose that Kenji intends us to understand that within the frame of the story, the mountain pass was real and the hell realm and pure land just imaginary. Rather, the shift from one spatial regime to the next is accomplished in each case through a reorganization of the environment surrounding the boys: icy thorns resolve into sharp stones; the buddha appears at the horizon and walks toward the boys; and fog covers the landscape, lifting to reveal the mountain pass. The story thus suggests not that the boys are in transit across three contiguous realms, but instead that the three realms are overlaid on top of each other, so that as the boys remain in place, the hell realm opens up within the mountain pass, and the pure land opens up within the hell realm. When the pure land gives way to the mountain pass, it is concealed without wholly disappearing. The spatial order of the pure land is retrievable through the path that Ichirō is charged with discovering—that is to say, it is retrievable as an accumulation of footprints.

So in the same way that fruit concentrates the verdant landscape of Iwate, the footprint concentrates space—it is literally produced through the compression of the ground, and for Kenji it figures the site in which the fact of the good place concealed within the bad place makes itself known. And

---

75. Ibid., 9:256.

in the same way that we activate the fossil by excavating it[76], we activate the footprint by discovering the path.

Fruit, fossils, and footprints are all *sanbutsu*; they are all yielded up by the earth. And like the enlightened body or relic welling up from the ground, they all figure the sudden eruption of an invaginated utopian counter-order within the real. This way of imagining utopia has a number of effects. Where his contemporaries tend to imagine a stable utopia, Kenji imagines a utopia that is only temporarily and even elusively established. Where his contemporaries imagine a centralized utopia that radiates outward displacing the real, Kenji imagines utopia and the real as interfolding such that utopia might open up anywhere. And where his contemporaries imagine utopia in terms of homogeneity and totality, Kenji imagines it in terms of heterogeneity and at least sometimes in terms of multiplicity. Thus I would contend that—appropriately for a dreamland—Īhatōvu stands for provisionality against fixity. Although we cannot know whether or not Kenji would ultimately have followed his contemporaries into totalitarianism, we can say that his image of the invaginated utopia mitigates against a totalizing vision of utopia in this respect.

THE RESPONSIBILITY OF RETURN

Levitas tells us that provisionality is not enough on its own; her utopian method also requires commitment to transformation of material and social structures. I'd like to close this chapter by addressing one way in which Kenji attaches a call for commitment to his image of the dreamland, once again drawing on the Buddhist imaginary.

"Shining Feet" ends with elder brother Ichirō waking up alive in this world and younger brother Narao remaining in the buddha's pure land. *Milky Way Railroad* has a similar ending: after traveling across the milky way to the fields of heaven, Giovanni wakes up on a hill high above town and learns that while he was sleeping, Campanella has drowned in the act of saving a classmate who had fallen in the river. The motif of one child dying and remaining in a heavenly realm while the other returns to this world reflects Kenji's own grief at the death of his younger sister. But in developing this motif (and perhaps in making sense of his own experience), he weaves in a suggestion that the child who returns is tasked with a particular responsibility to help those still living in the *saha* world.

---

76. For another treatment of Kenji's use of excavation as figure for disrupting the present order of space and time, see World of Kenji Miyazawa, "Archetypal Beings Who Appear in Visions," para. 24ff.

Ichirō has already experienced pain in trying to protect Narao. But rather than rewarding him by allowing him to stay in the pure land as we might expect, the Buddha tells him he must go through pain once more, and find the true path that connects the pure land and Ichirō's own country. In *Milky Way Railroad*, the purpose of this return to the world is spelled out in more detail. While Giovanni and Campanella are on the train together, Giovanni swears "I really am going to go and search for the true happiness of everyone. Let's go on together, on and on and on forever."[77] Campanella makes the same promise but becomes distracted at the sight of "the real heaven."[78] Half-waking from his dream and realizing that Campanella is gone, a tearful Giovanni encounters a strange professor who tells him he must not give up: "It is wisest . . . to do as you thought earlier and seek the best happiness of all people. . . . Only in that way is it really possible for you to go on forever with Campanella."[79] Giovanni fiercely affirms that he will, and the professor gives him a final piece of encouragement: "Soon you will no longer be on this dream railway but must walk boldly with straight, unswerving strides through the fire and violent waves of the real world."[80]

The figure Kenji is invoking here is the figure of the bodhisattva. If the Tathāgata belongs in his pure buddha land, and the ordinary person properly in the ordinary world, the bodhisattva belongs in the chiasm between the two. Introductory textbooks on Buddhism often describe the bodhisattva as a figure who vows to put off crossing into the enlightened realm of the buddhas in order to save ordinary beings, but in the Japanese imagination at least, the bodhisattva is better understood as a figure who elects to return to this world from that enlightened realm (as in the example of the bodhisattvas emerging from beneath the earth). The bodhisattva thus opens the path between the buddha land and the *saha* world so that everyone can follow it. When the Buddha tells Ichirō that there are "lots of people" who have made this trip, Kenji is pointing to the figure of the bodhisattva returning to the world, and when Giovanni swears that he will go on and on forever in order to find the true happiness of everyone, Kenji is pointing to the bodhisattva's commitment to save all beings.

If this somewhat abstract religious commitment reminiscent of the Buddhist commitment to save all sentient beings was all Kenji had in mind, it would be grand but not very concrete. It seems to me, however, that Kenji is concerned with connecting the utopian bodhisattva ideal to material,

77. Strong, *Milky Way Railroad*, 75–76.
78. Ibid., 76.
79. Ibid., 150.
80. Ibid., 152.

bodily reality. This concern comes through in the tasks he has his bodhisattva figures undertake. Giovanni's model for bodhisattva activity in *Milky Way Railroad* is a scorpion who regrets not sacrificing its own body to a hungry weasel and so at the time of his death prays that in the next life he will "not throw my life away in vain like this, but, rather, use my body for the true happiness of everyone";[81] he is reborn as a burning signal fire. In another story, "The Life of Gusuko Budori,"[82] Kenji models his protagonist on the figure of the Bodhisattva Never Disparaging, who is described in the twentieth chapter of the Lotus as making a practice of bowing to everyone he met despite the constant mockery and abuse he received at their hands as a result. Kenji's endlessly good-natured Gusuko is orphaned, robbed of his land, forced into hard labor, and beaten up; the story ends with him discovering a way to force a volcanic eruption in order to prevent a cold summer from destroying the harvest, saving everyone's life but his own—here the bodhisattva is effectively recast as a self-sacrificing agricultural scientist. Giovanni's first act upon returning to the world as a bodhisattva is spurred by his realization that he had set out that evening on an errand to pick up milk for his mother: "With a rush of feeling he had remembered his mother waiting at home, still waiting to eat her supper . . ."[83] He runs to the dairy farm, finds the milk man, and heads back home, "wrapping his hands around the still-warm bottle of milk."[84] The common motif that emerges here is that the bodhisattva works to feed other beings: his hero, in each case, is motivated by a consciousness of someone else's hunger.

This has a deep connection to Kenji's own conception of how arts and agriculture should relate to each other, and what a farm should be—the same injunction to seek the true happiness of everyone that comes in the final chapter of *Milky Way Railroad* appears in the first section of his manifesto on art for farmers: "Until the whole of the world finds happiness, there can be no individual happiness. . . . Let us search for the true happiness of the world."[85] Other commenters have interpreted Giovanni's milk delivery in terms of cosmology, taking the bottle of milk as representing a microcosmic version of the Milky Way, and in terms of cosmopolitanism, taking the bottle of milk (where a Japanese reader might expect instead a thermos of tea) as one of a number of gestures through which Kenji indicates that Īhatōvu floats somewhere between the east and the west. I would argue that

81. Ibid., 69.
82. Miyazawa, *MKZ*, 10:185–228.
83. Strong, *Milky Way Railroad*, 76.
84. Ibid., 77.
85. Miyazawa, *MKZ*, 11:10.

it is meant to point us back to the real dairy farm, Koiwai, which for Kenji is both a place of imagination and a place of real agricultural production. On the one hand, as a writer Kenji is interested in imagining or envisioning dazzling buddha lands welling up from beneath the earth—this is rupture. On the other hand, as an activist he is interested in mobilizing new technologies in order to farm more efficiently, more cooperatively, and more humanely—this is ground. As a writer, he generates a hopeful vision of utopia out of the landscape that surrounds him, and as an activist, he attempts to (literally) reterritorialize that vision.

CONCLUSION

There are reasons to be cautious about how Kenji's utopian vision is deployed outside of the context in which it develops. It is one thing to urge self-sacrifice when addressing the self, and something else to urge self-sacrifice when addressing others. Kenji's sensitivity to this distinction is apparent in his attitudes around eating—he valorizes offering the body to be eaten but is deeply unhappy about having a body that itself needs to eat. But when he is presented now as a saintly figure from the rural north, it is sometimes to the effect of valorizing self-sacrifice in order to avoid questions about the structures within which such sacrifices take place. We have seen some of this recently, for example, in the way that Kenji's work was invoked in the rhetoric of noble endurance surrounding the March 11 disaster in Tohoku, as exemplified by the narratives that sprang up around the nuclear plant workers who volunteered to remain in Fukushima despite the danger to themselves; in a statement sharply critical of these narratives, the Freeter General Union characterized this as "the ugliness of praising the workers as if they were Gusuko Budori": "We must move away from a coldheartedness so disgusting as to demand that the nuclear plant workers, 'in order to save thousands of lives,' do a job we would never do ourselves. We should instead support the *refusal* of work that compels the death of the worker."[86]

In the context of its historical moment, however, Kenji's utopianism represents the transformation of an old impulse toward the supernatural into something new and surprising. Using his gift for thinking chiasm, he finds ways to figure utopia that don't end with a collapsing of utopia and the real in which utopia is firmly established everywhere with no room for difference. Instead, he is able maintain a generative tension between utopia

---

86. Furītā zenpan rōdōkumiai, "Seimei: Daremo korosuna," para. 5. Freeter is a Japanese term referring to members of the precariat.

and the real which supports a sustainable process of seeking utopia that can go on and on and on forever.

BIBLIOGRAPHY

Figal, Gerald A. *Civilization and Monsters: Spirits of Modernity in Meiji Japan*. Durham, NC: Duke University Press, 1999.
Furītā zenpan rōdōkumiai. "Seimei: Daremo korosuna." No pages. Online: http://d.hatena.ne.jp/spiders_nest/20110317/1300289557.
Iguchi, Gerald. "Nichirenism as Modernism: Imperialism, Fascism, and Buddhism in Modern Japan." PhD diss., UC San Diego, 2006.
Ikeda Daisaku. "The 'Saha' World Is Itself the Land of Eternally Tranquil Light." No pages. Online: http://nichiren.info/buddhism/library/SokaGakkai/Study/LectLS/Lectur22.htm.
Itō Eishirō. "Nationalism in *Ulysses* and Kenji Miyazawa's Works." *Gengo to bunka* 7 (2005) 43–55.
Kanno Hiroshi. "The Bodhisattvas of the Earth in the *Lotus Sūtra*: Involvement in Human Society." *Journal of Oriental Studies* 20 (2010) 108–28.
Keene, Donald, trans. "An Account of My Hut." In *Anthology of Japanese Literature: From the Earliest Era to the Mid-Nineteenth Century*, edited by Donald Keene, 197–212. New York: Grove, 1955.
Kinnard, Jacob N. "The Polyvalent Pādas of Viṣṇu and the Buddha." *History of Religions* 40 (2000) 32–57.
Kolakowski, Leszek. *Modernity on Endless Trial*. Chicago: University of Chicago Press, 1990.
Leighton, Taigen Daniel. *Visions of Awakening Space and Time: Dōgen and the Lotus Sutra*. Oxford: Oxford University Press, 2007.
Levitas, Ruth. "For Utopia: The (Limits of the) Utopian Function in Late Capitalist Society." *Critical Review of International Social and Political Philosophy* 3 (2000) 25–43.
———. "Looking for the Blue: The Necessity of Utopia." *Journal of Political Ideologies* 12 (2007) 289–306.
Levitas, Ruth, and Lucy Sargisson. "Utopia in Dark Times: Optimism/Pessimism and Utopia/Dystopia." In *Dark Horizons: Science Fiction and the Utopian Imagination*, edited by Tom Moylan and Raffaella Baccolini, 13–28. New York: Routledge, 2003.
Long, Hoyt J. *On Uneven Ground: Miyazawa Kenji and the Making of Place in Modern Japan*. Stanford: Stanford University Press, 2012.
Miyazawa Kenji. "Chūmon no ooi ryōriten kōkokubun." No pages. Online: http://www.aozora.gr.jp/cards/000081/files/43733_17907.html.
———. *Miyazawa Kenji zenshū* [*MKZ*]. 11 vols. Tokyo: Chikuma Shobo, 1956–1957.
Mills, Douglas E. "The Buddha's Footprint Stone Poems." *Journal of the American Oriental Society* 80 (1960) 229–42.
Popper, Karl. *The Open Society and Its Enemies*. Abingdon, UK: Routledge, 2011.
Pulvers, Roger. *Strong in the Rain: Selected Poems*. Tarset, UK: Bloodaxe, 2007.
Rouvillois, Frédéric. "Utopia and Totalitarianism." In *Utopia: The Search for the Ideal Society in the Western World*, edited by Roland Schaer, Gregory Claeys, and Lyman

Tower Sargent, 316–32. Translated by Nadia Benabid. Oxford: Oxford University Press, 2000.

Satō Hiroaki. "Miyazawa Kenji: The Poet as Asura?" *Asia-Pacific Journal: Japan Focus* (2007) No pages. Online: http://japanfocus.org/-hiroaki-sato/2526.

———, trans. *Spring and Asura: Poems of Miyazawa Kenji*. Chicago: Chicago Review, 1973.

Spivak, Gayatri Chakravorty. "Moving Devi." *Cultural Critique* 47 (2001) 120–63.

Stone, Jacqueline. "'By Imperial Edict and Shogunal Decree': Politics and the Issue of the Ordination Platform in Modern Lay Nichiren Buddhism." In *Buddhism in the Modern World: Adaptations of an Ancient Tradition*, edited by Steven Heine and Charles S. Prebish, 193–220. New York: Oxford University Press, 2003.

———. "Japanese *Lotus* Millennialism: From Militant Nationalism to Contemporary Peace Movements." In *Millennialism, Persecution, and Violence: Historical Cases*, edited by Catherine Wessinger, 261–80. Syracuse: Syracuse University Press, 2000.

Strong, Sarah. "Miyazawa Kenji and the Lost Gandharan Painting." *Monumenta Nipponica* 41 (1986) 175–97.

———, trans. *Night of the Milky Way Railroad*. Armonk, NY: M. E. Sharpe, 1991.

Tanabe, George J., Jr. "Tanaka Chigaku: the Lotus Sutra and the Body Politic." In *The Lotus Sutra in Japanese Culture*, edited by George J. Tanabe Jr. and Willa Jane Tanabe, 191–208. Honolulu: University of Hawaii Press, 1989.

Watson, Burton, trans. *The Lotus Sutra*. New York: Columbia University Press, 1993.

Weber, Max. *The Sociology of Religion*. Translated by Ephraim Fischoff. Boston: Beacon, 1963.

World of Kenji Miyazawa. "Archetypal Beings Who Appear in Visions." No pages. Online: http://www.kenji-world.net/english/works/texts/jikuu15.html.

7

Walter Kerr's Utopia of Re-Creation

—Benjamin K. Hunnicutt

Walter Kerr (1913–96) began his career teaching speech and drama at The Catholic University of America, moving on to write about the theatre for *Commonweal* in the early 1950s. Afterwards, he was theatre critic for the *New York Herald Tribune* and then for *The New York Times* until his retirement. He was also a playwright, lyricist, and director of a number of Broadway plays and musicals, the most successful of which was "Goldilocks" (1958), which he wrote with his wife Jean Kerr and which won two Tony Awards. In midcareer, as one of the most influential theatre critics in the United States, Kerr wrote *The Decline of Pleasure* (1962).[1] Throughout his life he had been enthusiastic about the future of the American theatre. But when he wrote *The Decline of Pleasure* he had lost much of his youthful optimism. Something had gone wrong—a reassessment was needed.

    Earlier in the century, leaders of the American theatre such as Percy MacKaye, Robert Edward Gard, Paul Green, and E. C. Mabie had based their hopes on the nation's economic successes. It was clear then that as the nation's wealth grew, more people would have more free time to attend and participate in the theatre. MacKaye was sure that ordinary people, better able to satisfy their material needs, would naturally join together in communities across the nation to create new venues for democratic expression, sharing their lives freely with their words and their stories on local stages.

---

    1. Kerr, *The Decline of Pleasure*. Subsequently, references to this book will appear as page numbers in parenthesis in the chapter above.

The function of professionals and gifted individuals would be, more and more, to instruct, support, and inspire these community theatres of discourse rather than simply showcase their individual talents.[2]

But whereas MacKaye and his contemporaries had seen prosperity, by the 1960s Kerr was witnessing affluence: "By the standards of another generation, and by the standards of the present generation in an alien three quarters of the globe, we might be forgiven for thinking ourselves rich." (4) The "great" American dream was well within practical reach: "One of the great adult dreams of the twentieth century was the dream of leisure." (16–17) The foundation of the nation's renowned work ethic, the "very purpose of work" throughout most of the nation's history, had been "to create occasions for ease." During his lifetime, the "dream stirred." The moment seemed to have come to seize the day: "the world was well mechanized, the money could be made during a five day week . . . [and] given . . . just a few more years . . . [humans might be] free forever" (17).

Kerr recalled watching utopian films during his teenage years when he was an aspiring movie critic—films about the near future, filled with free, "exuberant souls . . . fishing on a riverbank . . . singing the livelong day." By 1960s, "everyone knows how far we have pushed the promise." The forty-hour workweek was years out-of-date. People who should know, such as Boris Pregel, president of the New York Academy of Sciences, were confident "that it will soon be reduced to twenty . . . " Housework was being mechanized so that both the "homebound husband and the chore-free wife" were guaranteed plentiful "liberty" to pursue "pleasure" (18).

With affluence and new technologies came new opportunities: libraries, cheap books, well stocked record cabinets, museums, adult educational possibilities, dance studios, as well as theatres—the list grew daily. Kerr concluded: "The twentieth century has not only realized . . . its dream of leisure time but has also supplied the riches with which to fill it" (20).

Yet he detected something of a national "malaise." In the midst of affluence and expanding leisure "we are vaguely wretched . . . [and] restless" (3). His fellow citizens seemed woefully unprepared for the realization of their American dream. Plentiful leisure had become a "problem."[3] A day off work had become, for far too many, an "empty day," a "menace" from which to escape back to "intensified labor" or into various forms of vapid amusements.[4]

2. See for example, MacKaye, *The Civic Theatre*, passim. See also Benjamin Hunnicutt, *Free Time*, chapter 5.

3. For a more complete account of the 60s and 70s' "leisure problem," see Hunnicutt, *Free Time*, chapter 9.

4. Kerr often wrote of his own struggle to "let go," and enjoy his leisure, free from the guilt of not working. See for example his letter to Miss Gail Gordon, 20 May 1965,

The utopian dream of leisure was being overtaken by its contradiction: a nightmare of total work and total utility in which "pleasure" declined and leisure was regarded as something trivial—a great silliness.[5] The nation had become, as Pregel put it, "leisure smitten."[6]

All the talk in the media about the new leisure and the reduction of work to "its lowest terms" disguised a new reality: "the conviction that only labor is meaningful." Moreover, "although we assume ourselves to be a people possessed of unusual opportunities for leisure, we are actually occupied in more and more work." The "problem of leisure" revealed a paradox, a "situation . . . strange and, in some ways, frightening" in which a people, having realized their dream of leisure, had changed their minds, coming to value work instead (31). Kerr's contemporary, Hannah Arendt, describing the modern "glorification of labor," agreed: "What we are confronted with is the prospect of a society of laborers without labor, that is without the only activity left to them. Surely nothing could be worse."[7]

The most popular explanation for what journalists across the nation were calling the "leisure problem" was the lingering influence of the Puritans. The Protestant work ethic seemed to have retained so strong a hold on American culture that when the long awaited leisure arrived it did not seem quite right. Kerr noticed that he and his friends often felt guilty when they had a day off. Perhaps this guilt was the sign of a Puritan conscience.

But he remained unconvinced: "An ancient Puritanism returned to haunt us? Hardly . . . All the old restraints on freedom including Puritanism and Epicureanism have been 'released.'" Along with corsets, Americans had shed the *Protestant* work ethic years ago when they had come to believe that "very purpose of work" was "to create occasions for ease" (38).

So where did the guilt come from? Why were Americans fleeing the "pleasure" they once longed and worked for, and rushing back to work?[8]

---

box 41, folder 1, Kerr papers.

5. Kerr also often remarked on the modern trivializing of leisure. See for example *The Decline of Pleasure*, 137–38, 301. See also Cousin, "Dimension of a Woman's World."

6. Typescript, Vol. 28, page 353. Kerr papers. Kerr used Boris Pregel's term, "leisure stricken," several times in the draft manuscripts of *The Decline of Pleasure*, but removed them before the final published version.

7. Arendt, *The Human Condition*, 5. Published four years before Kerr's book, *The Human Condition* may have influenced Kerr in his writing of *The Decline of Pleasure*. Even though Kerr never acknowledged her book, he used several of her major themes, as in the quotation above, and toward the end of his book, in his descriptions of what Arendt called the *Vita Contemplativa* and *Vita Activa*.

8. In the first draft of *The Decline of Pleasure*, Kerr wrote: "It is an irony almost too great to be borne that our affluence should have made our pleasure unattainable . . . " box 41, folder 2, Kerr papers.

Why was it that "the twentieth century had been engaged in a long struggle to produce a new kind of man—a man whose sole concern should be his useful work—and, in our children, had successfully accomplished the mutilation" (33).

Kerr concluded that it was true that "pangs of guilt imply patterns of belief . . . " But not traditional religious beliefs. Somewhere along the way, a new secular morality had arisen. The "law of the twentieth century" had become: "Only useful activity is valuable, meaningful, moral. Activity that is not clearly, concretely useful to oneself or to others is worthless, meaningless, immoral" (33). This law, or "article of faith," was a recent revelation. It was not a product of a superannuated Puritan conscience, or even Capitalist greed. It "is something new, and it is something universal," and it was responsible for "the leisure problem" (39).

How then had "so Spartan a notion managed to fasten itself so fiercely upon an age that really hoped to make machines do all the useful work while man enjoyed his freedom? Where did the surprising, contrary, rigid notion come from?" (40). Several of Kerr's contemporaries, noting the international turn from free time back to work at the time, struggled with Kerr's questions, notably Hannah Arendt (the modern "glorification of labor"), Joseph Pieper ("the rise of total work"), Jacques Ellul (the emergence of the "false religion," "*Travail-Bien*"), and Karl Barth (the idolatrous worship of work), each offering answers.[9] But for Kerr, it all started with "a philosophy and its aftermath."

Kerr argued that the source of the new worldview (what he termed, variously, a new "morality," "law," "article of faith," "mutation," and "mutilation") was "utilitarianism": a nineteenth century philosophy that had "won the twentieth century without seeming to have fired a single shot" (43). Jeremy Bentham and other utilitarians based their science on the *a priori* assumption that, as with all other creatures, the selfish seeking of pleasure and avoidance of pain were the basis of human motivation, determining "all we do . . . all we say . . . all we think." Intending to establish his theories on a scientific foundation, Bentham then looked for a reliable, concrete, and objective definition of pleasure—something better than murky subjectivity, something that he could measure. He settled on the *utility* of a product: its "usefulness" that was determined by the objective value the marketplace assigned to it. Kerr concluded that for the utilitarians:

---

9. For a more complete account of the many explanations for what Pieper called "rise of the world of total work" see Hunnicutt, *Free Time*, introduction, chapter 9, and passim.

> Pleasure and profit came to mean the same thing. This identification of happiness with utility, of pleasure with profit [became] absolute. (44)

Obviously such a technical definition of pleasure left out most of what ordinary, unscientific people thought was pleasurable. The utilitarians realized the novelty of their conclusions, and that theirs was a new understanding of human experience. William Stanley Jevons wrote: "Repeated reflection and inquiry have led me to the somewhat novel opinion that value depends upon utility" (40). A broad category of pleasurable, subjective, and non-useful activities was thought to be indispensable during the nineteenth century—autotelic activities such as expressions of conviviality ("disinterested friendship") that were valuable in themselves, requiring no further payoffs. But according to Bentham, "moral systems" that recognized such activities and that gave second place to *utility* as defined by the marketplace, "deal in sounds instead of sense, in caprice instead of reason, in darkness rather than light" (44). It was work that produced utility and value. Value produced worth and wealth. Wealth, in turn, produced more work.

Value could never be an intrinsic part of any particular product, state of being, or activity. Intrinsic pleasures were, by definition, subjective and pointless: silly wastes of time except when they prepared people for productive effort. Rejecting disinterested motives such as friendship and benevolence, the utilitarians formulated "a new maxim for the new age: 'few acquaintances, fewer friends, no familiarities.'" Utilitarianism had "succeeded in excommunicating [intrinsic and subjective] pleasures," ruling that "only useful activity is valuable, meaningful, moral. Activity that is not clearly, concretely useful to oneself or to others is worthless, meaningless, immoral" (48).

Such a "Spartan morality" was initially hard to take—even for its original prophets. John Stuart Mill chafed under the "moral imperative" that only the useful was valuable. Focused entirely on his studies and endless preparations for the future, Mill found that he had lost direction at the age of twenty-one—that he no longer knew what he was working so hard and preparing so diligently for: "The whole foundation on which my life was constructed fell down . . . I seemed to have nothing left to live for." Suffering a "nervous breakdown," Mill then spent several years incapacitated by depression.[10]

Kerr described Mill's "collapse" as "prophetic," a harbinger of a universal moral crisis soon to come, in which the whole point of economic growth for the sake of more economic growth, and of work for the creation

---

10. J. S. Mill, quoted by Kerr, *Decline of Pleasure*, 46

of more work, were called into question. Mill, in what Kerr thought was exemplary fashion, tried to find his way out of the utilitarian iron cage by admitting intrinsic pleasures as meaningful, valuable, and worthy of serious attention, and concluding that "a great many acts [may] be regarded as good in themselves" (45–46, 51). Mill then criticized his utilitarian colleagues for confining the value of activities and things to their "exchange value": to their "circumstantial [extrinsic] advantages rather than in their intrinsic nature." Instead, he insisted that pleasure could be both "taken out of a thing" and "taken in it."

In his autobiography Mill explained how he was able to rid himself of his depression:

> I, for the first time, gave proper place, *among the prime necessities of human well-being*, to the internal culture of the individual. I ceased to attach almost exclusive importance to the ordering of outward circumstances, and the training of the human being for speculation and for action . . . In [Wordsworth's poems] I seem to draw from a source of inward joy, of sympathetic and imaginative pleasure, which could be shared in by all human beings.[11]

Thus Mill insisted that reason and science required economists to take into account normative and subjective issues: the larger context and extraeconomic purposes of the economy. Economic science pointed beyond what it could measure with its calculations and contain by its theories to a realm of free activities, beyond the marketplace, pleasurable in and for themselves. Indeed, the free market, rightly understood as a means to an end, might become the portal to the intrinsic realm of human freedom. If individuals acted rationally they would recognize when they had enough wealth, and freely choose to work less and less, in effect buying their freedom (by forgoing income that might have been used to buy other goods in the market) in order to pursue intrinsic pleasure and subjective happiness, thus imputing a market value to intrinsic activities and states of being.[12]

---

11. Ibid.

12. Mill's utopian vision was founded on the steady increase of leisure: "It is scarcely necessary to remark that a stationary condition of capital and population implies no stationary state of human improvement. There would be as much scope as ever for all kinds of mental culture, and moral and social progress; as much room for improving the Art of Living, and much more likelihood of its being improved, when minds cease to be engrossed with the art of getting on. Even the industrial arts might be as earnestly and successfully cultivated, with this sole difference, that instead of serving no purpose but the increase of wealth, industrial improvements would produce their legitimate effect, that of *abridging labor*" (Mill, *Principles of Political Economy*, 751). Even though Mill hinted that "*abridging labor*" may be understood as having a "shadow price," it was not until Gary Becker developed his "Theory of the Allocation of Time," 483–517, that

Unfortunately, economists had managed to shut firmly "'the escape hatch' that Mill had been working so valiantly to construct..." (51). Jevons countered Mill: "A student of Economy... has no hope of ever being clear and correct in his ideas of the science if he thinks of value as... anything which lies in a thing or object... Persons are thus [mis]led to speak of such a nonentity as intrinsic value." The same applied to acts that were not in the service of individual self-interest. They were pointless in terms of the market and hence meaningless and valueless. The only correct view is that "all value is extrinsic, outside things... Value depends entirely upon utility" and utility is that "abstract quality whereby an object serves our purposes ..." (Jevons as quoted by Kerr, 52 and 55).

By the twentieth century "the utilitarian theory of value, in its strict and most uncompromising sense, had won" (55). Nineteenth century discussions about selfless benevolence and intrinsically rewarding pleasures had been ruled out of bounds by the philosophers. According to Kerr, the "aftermath" of utilitarianism was its gradual "adoption" by the industrial nations, America in particular. Economists such as Bentham and Jevons articulated the tenets of belief that had formed the foundations upon which the capitalist world was built: the primary value attaching to the extrinsic usefulness of a good, service, or experience; the worthlessness of intrinsic enjoyment (pleasure); and the fundamental virtue of pursuing self-interest and personal advantage in a free marketplace (producing the greatest good for the greatest number)—these had become so ingrained in American culture that by the time Kerr wrote his book, they were nearly invisible:

> It is not surprising that a predominately industrial age should have accepted . . . the sobering announcement that the goods of this world constituted the good of this world and that felicity lay in the multiplication of commodities . . . The identification of the worth-while with the practically profitable . . . [became] a matter of conscience" (56).

Unlike Max Weber, Kerr saw a new worldview, a new "Spirit of Capitalism," arising in the *nineteenth* century with utilitarianism rather than in the seventeenth century with the Puritans. This was a new, *secular* work ethic, distinguishable from the *Protestant* work ethic, free from old fashioned God-talk. It was a new morality that valued work and utility as meaningful in themselves, independent of any larger, inclusive context or *telos*. Both work and utility had been uncoupled from their original reasons for being: from subsistence; from Puritan vocation; and then from the nineteenth and

---

this understanding was widely accepted.

twentieth century "dream of leisure." Both work and wealth were now, literally and figuratively, without end.

Thus the twentieth century had "arrived at a contradiction"— the "problem of leisure" that Kerr had identified at the start of his book. The nation was on the verge of mass leisure having had its "conscience" formed "in a manner calculated to make leisure meaningless . . ." (56). Still worse, most people had forgotten the possibility of pleasure in their single-minded devotion to work and had, like a cat chasing its tail, embarked on an eternal and ever elusive pursuit of more work and more wealth—the human chase was perhaps even more absurd than the cat's because it was after a transcendent abstraction, utility:

> The habits of delightful recreation . . . and "unprofitable' pleasure" . . . had been lost. It is terribly difficult to give one's attention to an experience that is supposed to provide pleasure if . . . the pleasure can be neither remembered nor quite imagined. Progressive self-denial does more than damage the appetite; it alters the living tissue . . . The superior joy we are half imaging might indeed refresh; but, given our creed, we must logically and stoically conclude that the refreshment itself would be valueless . . . unimportant, unworthy of man. The word recreation remains in our vocabulary, but we do not think highly of the activity it defines (56).

Moderns were paying a price. Dizzied by their chase after utility, confused by the need to create new needs, numbed by "progressive self-denial" in their obsession with work, bored to death by TV and insipid amusements, *alienated* by the loss of their being that once delighted, guilt free, in intrinsic pleasures, men and women were in peril, running the risk of a "breakdown"—a crisis of faith such as John Stuart Mill had suffered. Increased satisfaction had not followed proportionately upon increased economic well-being. Instead of the contentment of leisure, economic progress perpetually generated new needs, increasing dissatisfactions, multiplying scarcity and insecurity, as well as work. Moderns were menaced "by a near universal ennui" — by a weariness produced by both boredom and "progressive disillusion[ment]." (84)

Like Mill, Americans were beginning to doubt the worth and meaning of economic growth for the sake of more economic growth: of trying to satisfy needs that kept multiplying; of work for the sake of more work; and of wealth for more wealth with no end in sight. The new work-based faith was failing: "It is the power of belief that is grinding to a halt." (139) Yet, at the same time, most people found it impossible to imagine an alternative, having discarded, and then forgotten the traditional solution, and dream of free time for the expansion of "pleasure."

KENNETH KENISTON AND THE DECLINE OF UTOPIAS

Kerr had taken his cue from Kenneth Keniston, then lecturer at Harvard in psychology and social relations. As he was writing *The Decline of Pleasure*, Kerr frequently consulted Keniston's article that had appeared in 1960 in *The American Scholar*, "Alienation and Decline of Utopias," in which Keniston had anticipated many of Kerr's major points and to which Kerr turned for the title of his book.[13]

Keniston maintained that the psychological and historical role of utopia had been to provide a common orientation toward the future: a meaningful order and shared goals to work toward. Community was discovered along the way in the joint, imaginative project:

> Of co-operation based on the acceptance of some common vision of the desired future.... There was a time when "utopian" was, for at least some ... a term of praise, and when utopias were defined as tangible and desired possibilities that men might ... actually set out to realize.[14]

Such visions were essential for "cultural vitality." But the trajectory toward "positive, eductive" values, involving "the joint pursuit of meaning," was being abandoned in the United States. Utopias were being replaced by dystopias of cynicism, leaving men and women "unable to visualize a better future":

> It is precisely the absence of any such positive vision ... that most explains our contemporary alienation.[15]

Keniston noticed a new kind of alienation emerging, expressed most visibly by the youth counterculture of the early 1960s. This was not the simple alienation from work and its products Karl Marx described, but the more profound alienation produced by the separation of people from each

---

13. Keniston, "Alienation and the Decline of Utopia," 161–200. All Keniston quotes that follow are from this article. In the early drafts of *The Decline of Pleasure*, Kerr quoted Keniston extensively. In some of the typescript materials Kerr used as reference for his book, large portions of Keniston's articles had been transcribed. See typescript, vol. 28, Kerr papers,

14. Ibid.

15. Ibid.

other, from history, the future, nature, and the Divine.[16] Bereft of the joint, imaginative search for meaning and for direction that had historically been the glue that bonded people together, citizens of the modern world, led by their children, were experiencing a "growing distance" from all connections. King Solomon had understood long ago: "Where there is no vision, the people perish."

"Above all" for Keniston, alienation is "apparent in the relationship between fantasy and work . . . [in the] *dissociation of fantasy* [from modern jobs]."[17] Transfixed by the technological bluff, Moderns had forgotten what they were working for:

> "Substantive" reason, which can judge the validly of ends and goals, [was being replaced] by "instrumental" reason, which can judge only the efficacy of techniques in attaining pre-ordained ends . . . "know-how" supplants wisdom: "Whither?" has become archaic, but "How?" is on every [person's] lips.[18]

Kerr concurred: "belief is grinding to a halt," cynicism had replaced hope. His and the current generation believed in, and hoped for, nothing. They were rebels without a cause, nihilists, because they could no longer conceive of alternatives to perpetual work, selfishness, or to capitalism's greed. The age seemed impotent against the cancerous spread of the market that was beginning to overgrow authentic human life, and as Kerr feared, choke out "pleasure."

Keniston concluded that in order to heal the human community and the individual soul, work and the economy needed to be reconnected with fantasy, and the utopian vision recovered:

> Concrete reforms, however desirable, will remain extemporizations in the absence of an explicit positive myth, ideology, faith or utopia. Indeed, no lasting or potent reform is ever possible except as men can be roused from their disaffection and indifference by the prospect of a world more inviting than that in which they now apathetically reside.[19]

---

16. Keniston and Kerr both recognized that the selfishness at the heart of utilitarianism and modern economies was bound to set humans one against the other, creating a future of progressive discord rather than conviviality.

17. Italics in the original.

18. Ibid.

19. Ibid.

KERR'S UTOPIA OF RE-CREATION

Kerr agreed. A new vision, a recoupling of work and the economy to fantasy and to utopia and pleasure, was essential. In "the autumn of our discontent," Kerr concluded that the first step to take was to reject abstractions—the arid, paralyzing worlds of the nihilists and the utilitarians—and find a way back to authenticity.[20] What was needed was a practical roadmap to return to the tangible, pleasurable half of human existence that was being neglected. Kerr identified two barriers:

> There are two present causes for our inability to act . . . One of them is a failure of imagination . . . We cannot conceive what specifically intellectual refreshment might be . . . or how to make it work for us. The other is a failure to keep up with our history (140).

Kerr began his utopian reconstruction project by briefly looking to the past. Trying to "keep up with our history," and re-present the traditional, millennia-old utopian vision, he reviewed the wisdom of some historical authorities: Aristotle's, "recreation is more admirable than work;" St. Thomas Aquinas's, "No man can exist without pleasure;" St. Teresa of Avila's, "life would not be tolerable without poetry;" St. Augustine's, whenever the choice was between "the enjoyable and the useful, the useful had to give way as being . . . inferior." He concluded:

> Many of the sober thinkers of the past . . . did not scruple to elevate what they called recreation to a dizzying position in the hierarchy of the worthwhile . . . No man could exist, life would not be tolerable, without such patently superior [leisure] experiences (137).

But Kerr stopped his historical investigation short, confessing that he was confused by such advice:

> The experiences we, in the twentieth century, tend to lump together as recreational forms . . . do not honestly seem to merit the enthusiasm some minds have bestowed upon the act of play (137).

The twentieth century had so thoroughly trivialized leisure/recreation/play/pleasure that "we are confused . . . [and] perplexed, not enlightened"

---

20. Kerr agreed with Keniston's analysis of alienation. However, he grouped the various forms of alienation Keniston described under one general heading, "abstraction." Kerr understood "abstraction" in essentialist terms, as separation of humans from the unchanging needs for community, nature, history, and the "Other."

by "the . . . claims some thinkers . . . have made . . . We are prisoners of our convictions." (136) But instead of listening more carefully to the voices of the past, and consulting *American* "authorities," Kerr struck out on his own trying to overcome the "failure of imagination" that had landed the nations with the "problem of leisure."[21]

Caught between the great silliness that leisure had become and the failing faith in work and utility, bereft of "pleasure," with counsels of despair filling the plays he reviewed, Kerr cried out:

> Surely somewhere in this tantalizing universe an experience awaits us that is richer than canasta or George Harmon Coxe.[22] Would men keep promising themselves some ultimate "pleasure" when all the work is done, would anyone have bothered to equate the pursuit of happiness with such important treasures as life and liberty, if "pleasure" began and ended with barely tolerable aridities with which we occupy our free evenings? An instinct tells us that we were born to something better . . . [I]f we were to envision pleasure proper, pleasure in all the fullness of its eternally beckoning promise, we should ask that it achieve something more for us than an interesting pastime: we should expect it in some way to make us over (134).

Kerr continued his project of rebuilding utopia by examining his own experience and employing his imagination. Following his "instinct," Kerr became increasingly hopeful. Struggling, as had Jonathan Edwards and Walt Whitman and so many others before him, with leisure's autotelic challenge, he continued the long search for the original American dream—for free activities worthwhile in and for themselves that would give purpose and meaning to work's culmination in the arrival of an age of leisure. He tried to envision new ways to think about the freedom of leisure, and imagine new, up-to-date, free activities, hoping to resurrect the perennial utopian vision that would offer a reasonable alternative to an age of cynics.

He first consulted his dictionary. "Recreation" was of little help, reflecting current usage that expected little or nothing from leisure. The definition of the verb "recreate," however, was revealing, preserving some of the word's rich history: "to restore, refresh, create anew; to put fresh life into." In "recreate" was a hint that the leisure most people dismissed as silly offered

---

21. In *Free Time*, I have attempted to advance Kerr's project to "keep up with our past," beginning to re-present the vision of humane and moral progress, cataloging the many voices in the dialogue such as the Lowell, MA mill "girls" of the 1840s and the Kellogg women who held onto "their" six hour day into the 1980s, and recounting what they were doing in and expected from their new leisure.

22. Coxe wrote inexpensive murder-mystery novels.

the opportunity to renew an "instinctive strain in the human personality." "Recreate" might be:

> An echo of an ancient, and now mislaid hope. If there were actually in the universe a regenerative power that could fill us with fresh life, that could add to our very being still more being, shouldn't we be willing to prize it more highly than the labors that seem to drain our being away (138)?

Whereas many people assumed with the utilitarians that humans are, by nature, selfish, competitive and acquisitive, Kerr believed that most people were looking for meaning and purpose in their lives.[23] The "instinctive strain in the human personality" expressed itself as the innate desire to find some meaning, some order in existence. Thus true re-creation, and the most satisfying of pleasures, resulted from the discovery, or creation of meaning/order. Re-creation might be found by allowing "the mind to follow its own bias which is always toward order . . . toward the knowledge of order" (171).

Here was the secret of the theatre. The theatre's appeal was its "special, eternally hospitable . . . world that has been made in man's image," where audiences could briefly experience an extraordinary harmony, and thus beauty, and participate in that more perfect order. Such was the appeal of all of the fine arts. Such was the vital importance of fantasy and Utopia. Kerr quoted T. S. Eliot: "It is ultimately the function of art, in imposing a credible order upon ordinary reality, and thereby eliciting some perception of an order in reality, to bring us to a condition of serenity, stillness, and reconciliation" (155).

Kerr had "believed for a long time in the directly recreative power of the arts" because they offered just such an experience of order, and in artistic "genius" as the ability to rearrange the world in new, satisfying ways. This was the "work" of the playwright—creating, discovering, and communicating order. But the world created by the fine arts could not be experienced simply as utility—as something that artists manufactured and that audiences consumed. The pleasure of the theatre was not a pleasure "taken out of a thing." The theatre could not be "consumed" in the same way as a person "consumed" a pound of hamburger. The pleasure of the fine arts required that "patrons" put something of themselves into the experience, entering the subjective world brought to life by the playwright and actors. Instead of being passively consumed, art re-created individuals by engaging them in its reordered reality, inviting their free participation and creative input, and thus forming a broader, intersubjective order jointly constructed by artists,

---

23. Others writers, such as Paul Tillich, have made similar essentialist points. See also for example, Geertz, "Religion as a Cultural System," 13–14.

audiences, and critics. The discovery of order needed to be a shared experience, thus expressing the "instinctive strain in the human personality." Humans are not only meaning seeking and creating, they are also essentially free, social beings.[24]

Such pleasures were necessarily intrinsic and autotelic. Such pleasures "have to be free," approached "in a spirit of reserved, gentle, and generous disinterest." (172) Casting about for helpful analogies, Kerr settled on play:[25] "In short we are looking for an act that is thoroughly playful." (172) Like play, the creative act of artists and the experience of their audiences required:

> A simple, submissive, eye-to-eye contemplation of the object to be known . . . such knowledge . . . cannot be proved out . . . it cannot be used in our work. Intuitive knowledge is knowledge without a future; it has only a present. The object known is not known for the sake of some other gain; it is known in itself, as itself, for itself alone. The act of knowing is not in this case grasping; it is gratuitous. Its end is not profit; it is love (207).

Kerr cautioned his readers that he was not recommending the contemplative life to the exclusion of hard work, diligent rehearsal, and creative efforts. Satisfying the "dual powers of the mind" required the ability to "move freely and frequently" between work and leisure—between the productive and the gratuitous, reason and intuition, the *vita activa* and *vita contemplativa*, the extrinsic and intrinsic.[26] However there was little danger that the modern theatre-goer or playwright would linger too long among the lotus-eaters. The real, present danger was too much control, too much work.

---

24. Kerr agreed with Aristotle about human essence as the potential to be free, social, and intelligent beings. See Vol. 28, page iv, Kerr papers.

25. Keniston had included a long discussion of the utopian possibilities offered by play in his article. He wrote: "we now have too much time and too little idea of how to play in a way that invigorates and refreshes. We have hardly begun to imagine the possibilities that may exist for a more enhancing interaction between our love, our work and our play."

26. Compare with Hannah Arendt's discussion of *Vita Contemplativa* vs. *Vita Activa* in Arendt, *Human Condition*, passim. The connections between Kerr and Arendt were numerous. Both regularly contributed to *Commonweal* through the 1950s. Sharing many of Kerr's ideas, Arendt wrote: "[Modern man is in] rebellion against human existence as it has been given, a free gift from nowhere (secularly speaking), which he wishes to exchange, as it were, for something he has himself made . . . [Marxists and capitalists share beliefs] which play such a great role in twentieth century thought . . . [they] pretend that man is his own producer and maker . . . even though it is clear that nobody has 'made' himself or 'produced' his existence; this, I think, is the last of the metaphysical fallacies, corresponding to the modern age's emphasis on willing as a substitute for thinking . . ." (Arendt, *Life of the Mind*, 215).

The modern tendency was to go it alone. Having decided that "all value was extrinsic, and that no value was intrinsic"— that play and leisure were silly and productive work was the only thing to be taken seriously— men and women had shouldered a "private responsibility that might well be called intolerable." (306) Moderns had imagined themselves to be in the same position as Atlas, bearing the weight of the world, believing that it was up to them and to their constant efforts to produce "all that was real, all that was worth-while, all that was valuable." They also believed that:

> The moment we stopped supplying [the universe] with fresh charges [of meaning] in the shape of formulas, it would drop. Each of us . . . had perforce to accept the responsibility not simply of knowing but of creating [meaning] . . . and of perpetually maintaining it in the sustained tensions of . . . thought . . . Without being the least egocentric, we had got ourselves in the position of the man who does not trust airplanes and who therefore does one wholly unnecessary thing: he gets a grip under the armrests attached to his seat and helps hold the plane up (307).

Such responsibility, taken seriously, was intolerable. Such a project resulted in mania, born of desperation, followed by the despair and profound depression that followed upon the inevitable collapse of all such attempts to play God. Kerr decided that it was past time to "declare ourselves a bonus":

> We have achieved a high degree of skill in one kind of groping, the hard kind, the theoretical kind. Our futures now depend upon a most attractive activity: upon our developing a matching skill in the easy kind, the loving kind, the arm-in-arm kind . . . our freedom to grow in stature rests unconditionally upon our ability to play . . . [and] produce pleasure (305–6).

For Kerr, genuine pleasure began with the realization that humans are responsible neither for the existence of the universe nor for its meaning, worth, or order—with the realization that there was a fundamental givenness about the world and the human condition. History and the natural world, human nature and human needs, body, birth and death, and God— the ground of existence and the mystery at the heart of all being—were all given, there for us from birth to be enjoyed rather than constantly fretted over, controlled and refashioned to suit our "needs"—needs for which we had, tragically, begun to assume responsibility.

The fountainhead of all pleasure was the recognition, celebration, and representation of found order. Pleasure is:

> An interior experience of the rectitude of things, a seen certainty of the consonance of things. When I become aware that I am in harmony with my own being, I am pleased. When I become aware that I am in harmony with all other, or any other, being, I am pleased. (288–89)

The true artist elicited "some perception of an order in reality" beyond the stage: of an order that flowed "back and forth, in an effortless embrace" between the stage and the world. Authentic art encouraged us to:

> Acknowledge the presence, the independence, the energy, and in some way the reality of The Other [and to] . . . begin to put down the burden that makes us most lonely, most isolated, most exhausted . . . to begin to take pleasure in the comfort, the mutual support, the 'oh, there you are!' of friends. The Other is the warmth in a field that would make the ground thaw and the wheat grow if I never happened by . . . (307).

Instead of utilitarianism's "greatest good for the greatest number," human community depended on the pleasurable, shared recognition of that "submerged oneness"—a recognition that enabled "me to know another form of being nearly as intuitively as I know my own being" (211). Pleasure in such intersubjectivity, not the marketplace or professions, was the glue that would hold people together in community.

Kerr's keen aesthetic sense, perfected during his many years as a theatre critic, had given him a special insight as a critic of American culture, which he panned. American culture was increasingly "artificial" because so many people had come to believe with Jevons and the utilitarians that only the man-made could be true or of any value. People in such a culture faced a nearly insurmountable barrier blocking them from community and authentic living: "a profound requirement of our natures is fixed in our minds as superficial." (301) Our nurture contradicted our nature. Being nurtured to believe that all "pleasure," all intrinsic enjoyment, was idle and never to be taken seriously, moderns plunged ever deeper into the artificiality of manufactured needs, hyper-seriousness, isolation, and depression—into the black hole of self-seeking.

Therefore, the future "depended" on the recovery of pleasure. Such a recovery required giving up the intolerable burdens that moderns had placed, unnecessarily, on their work and themselves. Such a recovery required recreation—the release into a realm of freedom where the intrinsic enjoyment of the world, others, and The Other was possible. Kerr ended his book with a personal testimony, recounting his own understanding and experience of pleasure: "I am pleased in that instant that I discover that I am not alone. My joy, like the discovery, is profound."

CONCLUSION

Kerr is one of the last of a long line of Americans who recognized that free time was as much a normal product of technological progress as increased wealth and consumerism. He would have agreed with the Henry Ford: "Free time will come, the only choice is unemployment or leisure."[27] With so many before him, with Jonathan Edwards, William Ellery Channing, Walt Whitman, Fannia Cohn, Robert Hutchins, Frank Lloyd Wright, and Aldo Leopold, Kerr was moved by a "utopian" vision of what might be accomplished in the opening "realm of freedom." Grounding their vision in the very real economic process of shorter work hours and sharing the assumptions that work was a means to better purposes and a fuller human existence, such men and women predicted the coming of a wide variety of recreations, states of being, and intrinsic activities as diverse as they were numerous.[28]

Kerr, together with many others, also recognized that a new work-based faith and *counter-utopian* vision had recently arisen, and that this faith's derivative, a new politics of "full time, full employment," had emerged out of Franklin Delano Roosevelt's New Deal. This faith and the coming of "JOBS, JOBS, JOBS" as one of the most important political issues, were rapidly eclipsing the traditional American dream of freed time and "pleasure." Whereas Kerr tried to explain the eclipse in terms of utilitarianism's ideological victory, others such as Robert Hutchins, Frank Lloyd Wright, Norman O. Brown, and Herbert Marcuse had alternative explanations. They agreed, however, that the new work-based, hyper-serious utopian vision was a dead end, unsustainable in terms of both natural and human resources, and profoundly alienating.[29]

Thus Kerr, with many others, warned against a future in which "pleasure is lost"—where the worth of intrinsic enjoyment was forgotten and where, as Joseph Pieper feared, people refused "to have anything as a gift."[30]

27. Ford and Crowther, "Unemployment or Leisure," 19–21.

28. See Hunnicutt, *Free Time*, passim, for a more complete account of the "forgotten American dream," its origins and the various voices supporting shorter working hours and preparing for progress into the "realm of freedom."

29. See Hunnicutt, *Free Time*, passim, for a more complete account of rise of the new work-based utopia, the origins of the politics of "full-time, full employment," and for the eclipse of the forgotten American dream.

30. Pieper, *Leisure the Basis of Culture*, 36.

A spiritual famine and a crisis of civility loomed. Eternal economic growth, everlasting job creation, and perpetual "full-time, full employment"—these were the quintessential unrealistic and unsustainable, *dystopian* projects.[31]

BIBLIOGRAPHY

Arendt, Hannah. *The Human Condition*. Chicago: University of Chicago Press, 1958.

———. *Life of the Mind*. New York: Harcourt, 1978.

Becker, Gary. "Theory of the Allocation of Time." *The Economic Journal* 75 (September 1965) 483–517.

Cousin, Michelle. "Dimension of a Woman's World." Transcript of the CBS Radio program, hosted by Betty Furness, box 42, folder 3, Kerr papers. May 30, no year.

Ford, Henry, and Samuel Crowther. "Unemployment or Leisure." *Saturday Evening Post* 203 (August 1930) 19–21.

Geertz, Clifford. "Religion as a Cultural System." In *Anthropological Approaches to the Study of Religion*, edited by Miacheal Banton, 1–46. ASA Monographs 3. London: Tavistock, 1968.

Hunnicutt, Benjamin Kline. *Free Time: The Forgotten American Dream*. Philadelphia: Temple, 2013.

Keniston, Kenneth. "Alienation and the Decline of Utopia." *American Scholar* 29 (Spring 1960) 161–200.

Kerr, Walter. *The Decline of Pleasure*. New York: Time, 1962.

Kerr, Walter, and Jean Kerr. Kerr papers and archives. Wisconsin Historical Society Library Archives, Madison, Wisconsin.

MacKaye, Percy. *The Civic Theatre in Relation to the Redemption of Leisure*. New York: Mitchell, Kennerley, 1912.

Mill, J. S. *Principles of Political Economy*. London: Longmans, 1923.

Pieper, Josef. *Leisure the Basis of Culture*. New York: Random House, 1963.

---

31. See Hunnicutt, *Free Time*, passim, for a more complete account of critiques, such as Kerr's, of the new work-based utopia and political project of "jobs, jobs, jobs."

8

Reframed Hope
Transcendent Technology and Spiraling Subjectivity in Dystopian Cinema

—*Everett Hamner*

In *True Religion*, Graham Ward argues that "the end [of religion] does not signal the falling into disuse or the oblivion of the religious. Rather, it signals exactly the opposite: the extension and hype of the religious as the ultimate vision of the excessive and the transgressive."[1] As he observed over a decade ago, early twenty-first-century society is less the product of religion's disappearance than its immersion in spectacle. Foreshadowing much contemporary scholarship, Ward found religion not just in traditional institutional settings, but "in commercial business, gothic and sci-fi fantasy, in health clubs, themed bars and architectural design, among happy-hour drinkers, tattooists, ecologists and cyberpunks." This led him to conclude that "religion has become a special effect, inseparably bound to an entertainment value,"[2] and that on some occasions, this "liquidation of religion turns itself into enjoying the absence of God."[3]

Ward's claims are difficult to contest. U.S. society has shown a particular willingness to amuse itself to death, to echo Neil Postman; we're even willing to celebrate our nihilism. However, there is a misleading possibility

---

1. Ward, *True Religion*, 34.
2. Ibid., 132–33.
3. Ibid., 151.

in Ward's argument that this chapter would counteract: a potential implication that these settings of the spectacular are *necessarily* host to a vapid, relentlessly-forced euphoria, when sometimes their mixtures of style and substance are much more complex. Here I focus on one of the categories Ward mentions, the "sci-fi fantasy," and specifically dystopian cinema. It may seem obvious to connect the dots between religious idealism and modern utopia, but this chapter considers a subtler tie between the apocalyptic cautions of dystopian film and the transcendent aspirations of contemporary technology. Juxtaposing two films from the heyday of Cold War America, John Frankenheimer's *Seconds* (1966) and George Lucas's *THX-1138* (1971), against two turn-of-the-millennium pieces, Terry Gilliam's *Twelve Monkeys* (1995) and Omar Naim's *The Final Cut* (2004), we will see how all of these works deploy a subdued Christ figure to critique excessive techno-utopian dreams and realign viewers' hopes for the future. At the same time, they also display a remarkable shift: while hyper-technological recreations of human bodies and landscapes prove stultifying in both timeframes, the more recent narratives by which these cautions emerge have become significantly more self-reflexive. By self-consciously revealing their own production and postproduction processes and by recognizing the often arbitrary logic by which we separate the religious from the secular, contemporary dystopian films are interrogating the nearly transcendent hopes we place in emerging technologies.

SECONDS, *THX-1138*, AND THE EXCESSES OF TECHNOLOGICAL UTOPIA

"Is it easier to go forward when you know you can't go back?" asks the kindly old businessman in *Seconds*, who first appears in deep focus over the shoulder of our protagonist, Arthur Hamilton. A loan officer approaching his senior years, this antihero has been lured into the secretive offices of a company dedicated to providing fresh starts in life. Thanks to a cleverly staged and recorded seduction by a female employee, he can no longer return to his stale marriage and unfulfilling career. His future now depends on the company owner, a Colonel Sanders lookalike who makes "reborns" of his half-willing clients via faked deaths, aggressive cosmetic surgery, and rigorous physical conditioning. Through this painful process, Hamilton morphs into Tony Wilson, a painter who appears two decades younger and lives in a Malibu beach home. Unfortunately, the falsehoods of Wilson's utopian existence become impossible for Hamilton to maintain; after starting to adapt to the bacchanalian romps of his new mistress and her set, he drops the ruse and asks for another chance. This is not how the company runs, however, so as the film reaches its climax and he is wheeled toward the operating room a second time, it slowly dawns on Hamilton/Wilson that he will supply the corpse used to simulate another client's death. As the elderly company owner assures him, "we gotta keep plugging away at the dream. The mistakes teach us how, it wasn't wasted, remember that."

While rightly decrying the exploitative methods of various modern religious movements, this dark conclusion also illustrates mid-twentieth-century Hollywood's vulnerability to simplistic treatments of religious hope. The two potential futures in *Seconds*'s superficially utopian America may seem opposites, but they are really just two sides of the same coin: on one face, the New Age chaos of Hamilton/Wilson's girlfriend and other West Coast hippies, and on the other, the empty civil religion performed by the middle-class suburbanites who become the secretive company's clients. In the first case, we watch as Nora Marcus (a name tellingly mimicking a major brand of twentieth-century corporatism) worships the ocean and baptizes her eventual boyfriend with Dionysian wine. The "religious climate out here" which she celebrates is little more than a modernized fertility cult, with the cute additional proviso that its adherents "change sects" every month. When its excesses prove unsustainable for our soon-drunken protagonist and he begins lamenting the incompleteness of his new reality, Nora and other company operatives pin him in a crucifix posture and turn scapegoaters of the first order. They rely on each other to maintain a collective fiction, and Hamilton/Wilson's rebellion threatens the highly artificial but temporarily effective "battle against human misery" their company wages.

The film's second, more traditional religious option is no alternative at all, though. Once the main character's death is assured, the company's elderly owner confesses that he has been discouraged by "a high percentage of failures among his clients," so much so that he "wanted to chuck the whole thing" and shut down the business. In a barb clearly aimed at Christian institutions, he laments that the organization had become too big by the time so many of the "reborns" started returning; indeed his profit-sharing obligations and financial responsibility made the venture too large to fail, even if he could no longer hope to see the New Jerusalem himself. The only option was to maintain his stock of potential cadavers and hope some future customer would be more fully resurrected. In the meantime, the disappointments must be written off with the efficient blessings of a clergyman ordained simultaneously as Protestant, Catholic, and Jewish. The film's conclusion thus finds the minister-for-hire reading the doomed Hamilton/Wilson a series of now all-too-relevant passages from the Gospels: "I am the resurrection and the life. He that believeth in me, though he were dead, yet shall he live"; "He that loveth life shall lose it, and he that hateth his life in this world shall keep it unto life eternal"; "Fear not thou them which kill the body." Hamilton should not seek to escape death, the company avers, because it is the necessary sacrifice enabling another man's artificial, equally impermanent rebirth.

Lucas's first film, *THX-1138*, attacks traditional Christian eschatology even more bluntly than *Seconds*. Rather than aligning religion with liberation, this cross between Fritz Lang's *Metropolis* (1927) and George Orwell's *1984* (1948) is dominated by an extended chase sequence in which an unfeeling, hyper-efficient future underworld attempts to capture a rogue engineer who has gone off his tranquilizers and sought escape. There are subplots involving his female roommate (who refuses the daily sedative, then surreptitiously adjusts her Adam's chemical diet and introduces him to sex), a male and possibly gay superior who forces himself on the eponymous main character, and an African-American hologram who plays a semi-comical Vergil. But the core of the film is the struggle of one man to escape a dystopian hell in which pious robots raise humanity's children to enjoy all the agency of robots. It is a culture of obsessive surveillance in which every hint of spontaneity is disciplined by a maddeningly calm, automatized hierarchy. By the time his robotic pursuer abandons the chase (not due to exhaustion, but because the apprehension effort is more than five percent over budget) and THX emerges into the light of a setting sun (with Bach's St. Matthew Passion playing the ironic soundtrack), the film has starkly distinguished its hero's humanity from the iron hand of religiously rationalized capitalism.

This opposition comes through most powerfully in a series of encounters between THX and a colorless version of Hans Memling's 1478 painting, "Christ Giving His Blessing." This icon appears on the confession booth screens used routinely by off-duty humans, and we listen twice as THX seeks consolation. Indeed we are the only true audience for his mea culpa; the virtual confessor responds only with an unvarying tape of pseudo-empathetic acknowledgments. These soulless interruptions make the illusion far from complete, even risking absurdity. When THX worries that he's dying, the mechanical deity asks, "Could you be more . . . specific?" The supplicant vomits, prompting an automatized benediction: "You are a full believer. Blessings of the state, blessings of the masses; thou art a subject of the divine, created in the image of man, by the masses, for the masses. Let us be thankful we have commerce. Buy more, buy more now, buy . . . and be happy." The scene's bald contention—that Christianity provides the hollow rationale for an unchecked American capitalism—is then amplified by a sequence in which THX's former superior, SEN 5241, finds the soundstage on which OMM's pronouncements are filmed. Renouncing his attempted escape before the larger version of Memling's portrait, SEN is interrupted by an annoyed monk, who ironically objects, "this is no place for prayer." When the would-be penitent knocks the priest unconscious, the camera rests for an extra beat on the unseeing eyes of OMM. In *Seconds* and *THX-1138* alike, religion is technology's puppet, a true opium of the people. Whether represented by an elderly businessman or an indifferent portrait, its priests and deities know only how to enforce others' sacrifices.

Other twentieth-century Hollywood dystopias offer similar critiques of illusory saviors and theocracies, so we might follow this thread much further, from *Soylent Green* and *Logan's Run* through *The Handmaid's Tale* and *Terminator 2: Judgment Day*. The closer we come to the 2000s, though, the more a gradual shift becomes apparent. Dystopian cinema continues to denounce practices of religious coercion, but it also begins questioning the hopes for the future offered by religious and nonreligious sources alike. It does so not just thematically but formally, so that nontraditional narrative structures and cinematic perspectives become interwoven with unconventional theological attitudes. Put another way, films like *Twelve Monkeys* and *The Final Cut* expose how religious and nonreligious hope alike can be manipulated by stagecraft and postproduction effects. In the process, as Michael Kaufmann puts it, these works "take the dynamic and recursive relationship between the secular and the religious as an *object* of inquiry rather than the stable *grounds* upon which that inquiry is based."[4] In their structural self-reflexivity, early twenty-first-century dystopias are becoming postsecular, showing how rigid divisions between the religious and the secular are as contrived as assumptions that new technologies are inherently positive or negative.

SPIRAL TEMPORALITY AND THE UNCERTAIN HOPE OF *TWELVE MONKEYS*

The premise of *Twelve Monkeys* is that in 1996 (the year after the film's release), the vast majority of humanity dies from a virus unleashed by a globetrotting bioterrorist. Following a brief dream-like sequence in which a boy watches a man be shot in an airport, the story begins in a dystopian Philadelphia, decades after the epidemic's onslaught. The remaining inhabitants of this near future live below ground, ruled by a commission of scientists whose devotion to stringent sanitation has preserved what life remains. Members of the underclass like James Cole are forced to ascend

---

4. Kaufmann, "The Religious, the Secular, and Literary Studies," 615 (emphasis original).

to the surface in sealed bodysuits to take samples for experimentation, but Cole's prowess earns him a unique opportunity to serve as guinea pig for the scientists' newly developed time machine. Expecting to travel back to the year 1996, Cole is instructed to determine the source of the outbreak and to procure a biological sample with which the future scientists might produce an antidote.

When Cole instead arrives in 1990, his ravings about the coming apocalypse land him in an insane asylum, perhaps delaying audiences' realizations that Gilliam has a Christ figure up his sleeve, one who is more multidimensional than those employed by Frankenheimer and Lucas. References to second comings are commonplace enough in psychiatric wards that we may nod along when Dr. Kathryn Railly diagnoses Cole with a messiah complex: "you're not going to save the world. You're delusional." Our attention to Gilliam's theological allegory may be further restrained by the fact that an asylum remains one of the few spaces in which the image of a man strapped down in a cruciform posture does not immediately connote Golgotha. Eventually, however, the manic humor of Jeffrey Goines's repeated associations of religion and capitalism breaks through. Without requiring a hired minister or a confession booth, Gilliam allows Brad Pitt's acting to convey the religious dimensions of capitalist excesses in 1990s America: one is to "look! listen! kneel! pray!" in front of the television advertising the Florida Keys, where "you can go to paradise!" The film's allegory is further confirmed by James Coles's initials and by brief glimpses of the letters "CHRIS . . ." on his T-shirt. By the film's conclusion, when we recognize the unblemished department store angel that appears in the much dustier future of the film's opening, *Twelve Monkeys*'s concern with religious commodification and spectacle is inescapable.

Yet the film's spiral narrative structure pushes it beyond more straightforward critiques of religiously rationalized technologies and consumerism. This formal innovation is clearest in the repeated scene in which Cole's childhood self uncomprehendingly witnesses his death as an adult. Inspired by the 1962 Chris Marker film *La jeteé*, this plot element becomes a poignant retelling of Jesus' discovery of his messianic identity and ultimate fate, interpreting him as only partially resigned to his scapegoat role. Its apparent circularity is dizzying enough that some critics see the repeated images as enacting an excessive degree of closure. For example, Elena Del Rio argues that "[*Twelve Monkeys*'s] drive towards realism manifests itself in the persistence with which the film sets up fixed, identifiable boundaries between reality and fantasy."[5] Her widely shared assumption is that the film's climax,

---

5. Del Rio, "The Remaking of *La Jetée*'s Time-Travel Narrative," 386.

in which we most fully witness the airport shooting glimpsed several times earlier in the film, simply brings us full circle. Like Cole, we are caught in a closed temporal loop, or as Gilliam himself summarized this interpretation, "the kid is always going to see himself die. Then he's going to grow up and the world is going to be decimated, he's going to break the law and end up in prison, and it's going to go on and on and on. Just this wheel turning and turning."[6] From this perspective, like a Jesus who never prays in Gethsemane that the cup be taken away, Cole knows that he is predestined to die, has no choice in the matter, and never stops dying, being reborn, and watching himself die.

However, this uptake assumes that Hollywood utopias and dystopias continue to offer fairly direct critiques of religious domination like those found in *Seconds* and *THX-1138*. What it overlooks is the distinction between a circle and a spiral, a shape combining circular and linear elements. When we refer to coming "full circle," in fact, we are really observing the spiral of time: we do not mean that two experiences are the same, but that there is repetition *with difference*. Accordingly, at the airport shooting, Cole's consciousness does not leap the gap between his dying adult self and his observing boyhood self. He experiences the moment only twice, not in an eternal loop. The two experiences are parallel but distinct; it is the audience that is tempted to confuse them, looking up with Kathryn from the dying adult Cole to search the crowd for the child version that must be present. Understanding the film's structure as spiral rather than circular thus negates Del Rio's concern that the story is "ontotheological," overly dependent on an "organizing structure/master narrative, the belief in ultimate truth, and the possibility and power of absolute knowledge."[7] On the contrary, *Twelve Monkeys* rejects mere spectacle by repeatedly gesturing to its constructedness, emphasizing that its messiah possesses not a certain knowledge of the future, but a hopefulness that embraces the unknown. These are among the gifts of a postsecular approach: relief from the assumption that every character wearing the word "Christ" on his shirt is automatically trustworthy or untrustworthy, and opportunity to recognize the immense differences between what constitutes the religious and the secular in various cultures and time periods.

This reassessment of narrative shape delivers still higher fruit: moving from a circular to a spiral structure implies a new relationship between determinism and free will. At first, *Twelve Monkeys* sets us up to accept a fated future. The poem being read upon Kathryn's first appearance, for example,

6. McCabe, *Dark Knights and Holy Fools*, 170.
7. Del Rio, "The Remaking of *La Jetée*'s Time-Travel Narrative," 395f.

is an excerpt from Edward Fitzgerald's translation of "The Rubaiyat of Omar Khayyam," and it creates an immediate sense of predestined, inescapable momentum:

> The Moving Finger writes; and, having writ,
> Moves on: nor all your Piety nor Wit
> Shall lure it back to cancel half a Line,
> Nor all your Tears wash out a Word of it.
> Yesterday This Day's Madness did prepare;
> Tomorrow's Silence, Triumph or Despair:
> Drink! for you know not whence you came, nor why:
> Drink! for you know not why you go, nor where.

Likewise, in Kathryn's theory of the "Cassandra Complex," the prophets of a "Moving Finger" God experience only "the agony of foreknowledge combined with the impotence to do anything about it." And Jeffrey Goines amusingly speculates that his psychiatrists have developed a computer model in which "they generated every thought I could possibly have in the next, say ten years, which they then filtered through a probability matrix to determine everything I was going to do in that period." Even the film's credits feature monkeys revolving in an unbroken circle, and Gilliam felt so strongly about an early scene's nearly imperceptible foreground image of a hamster running on a wheel that he drew out the shot over a dozen takes until the animal could be induced into a properly frenetic pace. Yet all this endless circularity constitutes only a façade: any spiral examined with insufficient depth of field may appear to be a circle.

The film's superficial fatalism is actually questioned from the moment James kidnaps Kathryn in 1996, when they listen to an Ivory Joe Hunter song on her Jeep's radio: "since I met you, baby, my whole life has changed." Like her former patient, Railly *does* change—spontaneously and unpredictably, but of her own accord—which is why she does not abandon Cole when he leaps from the vehicle to point out the Army of the Twelve Monkeys graffiti in Philadelphia. The woman who once diagnosed Cole with a messiah complex ends up insisting to a police detective that "he saved me!" and to James himself, "listen to me: things have changed!" Rather than evidencing Stockholm syndrome, this realization is part of her growing awareness that a laudable dedication to scientific methodology can morph into scient*ism*, a metaphysic that insists upon an absolutist ideology of objective knowledge. Thus when a male colleague condescendingly rebukes Kathryn, "you're a rational person, you're a trained psychiatrist. You know the difference between what's real and what's not," she snaps back, "And what we say is the truth is what everybody accepts, right, Owen? I mean, psychiatry, it's the latest religion, we decide what's right and wrong, we decide who's crazy or not. I'm in trouble here. I'm losing my faith." More precisely, she is abandoning the blinders that had allowed her to separate knowledge and hope from their foundations in uncertainty and intuition, and had made her see time as a closed circle rather than an open-ended spiral.

Twelve Monkeys's unsettling of a determinist temporality becomes most poignant at the film's conclusion. Although easy to miss, we witness here a transformation of the "past" that the future scientists had insisted was impossible—and indeed would be if the film ascribed to a circular, fatalistic universe. The scientists had convinced their enslaved time-traveler that the virus's dissemination could not actually be stopped: as James himself once insisted, "I can't save you. I'm simply trying to get some information for people in the present." However, at the airport, when Cole leaves a final message to the scientists indicating his plan to stay in 1996, José and other toughs from the future appear on the scene immediately. This is crucial: if the scientists can surround Cole with their ambassadors and force their gun on him, there is no reason why they might not also transport forces sufficient to secure a sample of the virus and then return from the future with an antidote, or for that matter, eliminate the virus before it is ever released. In other words, there is nothing that makes the airport scene as we witness it *a final, unalterable present*. Rather, the film lets slip the scientists' own absolutist terrorism and hyper-messianic delusions: they are quite willing to let the virus spread, wanting the power derived from halting it rather than a history in which the epidemic never occurs. As David Lashmet recognizes, "the horde of time travelers in the airport have obviously conspired to slay James Cole, not to stop Dr. Peters [the distributor of the virus]," and "the medical overlords are allowing the death of billions in order to assure their later ascendancy."[8] The scientists' claims that the virus cannot be stopped, that the past cannot be changed because time is an unbreakable circuit, and that their knowledge is absolute, are ultimately power plays. Their dependence on the rhetoric of predestination reveals the very real dangers of a reductive determinism backed by the rhetoric of scientific authority.

This raises perhaps the most crucial strategy by which *Twelve Monkeys* uses its structure to encourage a more nuanced sort of hope. Gilliam's film not only invests heavily in "comic irony,"[9] as Carrol Fry and J. Robert Craig rightly observe, but repeatedly acknowledges the subjectivity of its own editing process. In fact, without understanding Gilliam's investment in questioning the technology of the scientists' future oligarchy, it is very dif-

---

8. Lashmet, "'The Future Is History,'" 62.
9. Fry and Craig, "A Carnival of Apes," 4.

ficult to make sense of several moments of dissonance when the reliability of the camera's testimony comes into question. Like the use of déjà vu in the *Matrix* trilogy, these clues alert us that something is not quite right, that the reality we are witnessing is somehow askew. First, after *Twelve Monkeys*'s opening sequence, the diegetic sound of the airport's public address system in 1996 segues seamlessly into the same voice impossibly broadcast over the loudspeakers of the future prison: "Flight 784 for San Francisco is now ready for boarding . . . at inmate number 87645, Cole, James." If we listen carefully, the two timeframes become equally subjective realities, with the film refusing to make one foundational for the other. Similarly, during Cole's initial escape attempt at the 1990 asylum, we see a security guard sitting near the elevator. After a point-of-view shot showing the young guard reading a tabloid, we look back with Cole to see a much older man—one of the future scientists' henchmen, Scarface—dressed exactly like the young one, sitting in the same position, reading the same magazine. A glance later, the young guard has returned. There are also the moments when Cole converses with a raspy-voiced character who is sometimes incarnate, sometimes ephemeral: one day he seems another agent from the future, telling James how to remove tracking-device teeth and testifying that "science ain't an exact science with these clowns," but another day he is merely a confused, overweight businessman stumbling from a bathroom stall. Finally, Kathryn claims near the film's end not only to have recognized Cole upon their apparent first meeting (which might be explained by his image in a World War I photo), but also to remember him "like this" (as she disguises him), an impossibility even in this film's wild timescape, since she has not yet herself experienced the day of the airport shooting.

The film's most extreme questioning of its own representation of events arrives with the airport scene in which the virus's carrier, Dr. Peters, speaks to the juvenile Cole while escaping the adult version's bullet. In the scene's earliest, most rapid rendition, the speaker is actually *not* Dr. Peters, but Jeffrey Goines dressed as Dr. Peters—or more exactly, Brad Pitt temporarily shifted to the role of Peters. (In fact, because of the disguise, we can only recognize Peters as Jeffrey if we first recognize him as Pitt.) Far from being piously "ontotheological" or shutting down interpretive debate, this scene suggests how heavily Gilliam is relying on his audience's ability to look past the narrative's superficial circularity and recognize the open ends which make it spiral. Goines's message to the boyhood Cole is just as much Gilliam's message to us: "waaaatch iiiit." Beyond a warning about the boy's future, it is an injunction to trade passive consumption of entertainment for the posture of an active, never certain interpreter. It is exactly what the film's grudging messiah models as Kathryn does his makeup in the darkness of a theater screening Hitchcock's *Vertigo*: "I have seen it, but I don't remember this part. Funny, it's like what's happening to us, like the past. The movie never changes—it can't change—but every time you see it, it seems to be different because you're different—you notice different things." The same is true of Gilliam's film: until one grasps how thoroughly *Twelve Monkeys* unseats our expectations of the camera's narrative reliability, it is difficult to appreciate how fully it rejects the spectacle of utopia, whether it claims the authority of religion, technology, or both.

MEMORY, SUBJECTIVITY, AND THE METACINEMA OF *THE FINAL CUT*

More than *Twelve Monkeys*, Omar Naïm's *The Final Cut* immediately advertises its critique of the utopian hopes spawned by new technologies. While Gilliam's dystopian future is consistently rough around the edges, Naïm's debut film offers an initially cleaner vision enabled by the EYE Tech Corporation's wondrous new Zoe implant. As the fictional advertisement in the DVD pre-menu footage suggests, personal transcendence is now available to any who can afford it: once purchased for a fetus, this technology will eternally preserve their entire visual and auditory life. The happy parents receive a congratulatory video beginning, "Welcome to the EYE Tech family. What does that mean? Immortality." By having this "entirely organic, virtually undetectable" chip installed in their child's skull, the couple is assured that nothing of that precious life will ever be lost. When the eventual adult dies, a "cutter" will edit the extracted footage into a feature-length film. Death will have no sting, not because of Donne's hope of resurrection, but because a digital audio and video testimony of the individual's experiences will now be permanently accessible.

Thus summarized, the transcendence ascribed to this innovation may seem naïve, even absurd. However, *The Final Cut* operates not with Gilliam's affinity for farce, but with a more consistently tragic tone. The EYE Tech Corporation's device is treated throughout as a serious possibility, one that instigates an entire subculture of anti-implant fundamentalists who help make the film as strong a critique of religious as secular extremism. Consider the climactic conversation between the appropriately-named videographer Alan Hakman and Fletcher, a former friend and cutter who has turned against EYE Tech's implants. Fletcher now rejects the technology because individuals' memories are being edited by people who never knew them personally, because the fact that anyone could be "recording" at any time is expanding rather than constraining voyeurism, and most importantly because the Zoe chip and the editing process are available only to the rich, who demand cutters portray their family members' lives in the most attractive light possible. Responding to Fletcher's accusation that he "take[s] murderers and make[s] them saints," Hakman extends the theological allegory by explaining that he regards himself as a "sin-eater." A "social outcast" and a "marginal," this messiah finds his greatest satisfaction in "forgiv[ing] people long after they can be punished for their sins." Thus he joins Hamilton/Wilson, THX, and Cole in playing the role of Hollywood Christ, a scapegoated savior whose story testifies to the risks of blurring religious and technological sources of hope.

According to the film's opening sequence, Hakman's primary reason for accepting a self-sacrificial role is his own unaddressed guilt. Much like the repeated airport shooting in *Twelve Monkeys*, the introductory sequence of *The Final Cut*—Hakman's memory of a tragic one-day friendship with a boy he met while traveling with his parents—functions as the specter haunting the narrative. Wandering into a large, abandoned storehouse, twelve-year-old Alan and his new friend had attempted to traverse a plank suspended across a four-story drop, and although our protagonist made it across safely, Louis did not. In Hakman's memory, he taunted Louis into following him, then failed to help when the other boy lost his balance, grasped for safety, and slipped to his death. A crane shot emphasizes the moment's theological allegory: the plank is bisected by a row of support beams, so that viewed from above, the bridge-crossing is figured as a precarious attempt to traverse a cross. As the film then continuously reminds us, Louis's failure to make this passage torments Hakman throughout his life, even motivating his choice of a vocation whereby he can "forgive" others, even if he can never forgive himself.

Indeed *The Final Cut* also reminds us regularly of the relationship between Hakman's technological expertise and the religious associations of his role. That occupation might seem to afford as many blessings as curses, but like other films of the period, including *Pleasantville* and *The Truman Show*, *The Final Cut* warns that utopia for some is usually dependent on dystopia for others. There is a brief anecdote, for instance, about a rebellious young woman who learns on her twenty-first birthday that she has a Zoe implant and eventually her life will be visible to everyone. At first the "complete one-eighty" by which she reforms her behavior suggests that she has been "born again," as the film puts it, but then she leaps off a building, destroying the implant upon impact and saving her privacy at the cost of her future. Even if inactive until after death, we surmise, the observer changes the observed; when that onlooker becomes an anonymous cutter-judge and then a voyeuristic audience, the change is very much for the worse. This realization is furthered by the film's constant undercurrent of dialogue about the connection between transcendence and immanence. The Zoe implant is a step toward technoculture's dream of isolating human consciousness and cheating death by digitizing it, and this comes through in references to the chip as if it were a living entity, even the soul of the person in which it is embedded. Hakman tells a mourner about his deceased brother's footage, for instance, "right now he's clocking in at 1 hour, 40 minutes," and the impressed client observes, staring at the plastic disk in his hand, "So this is him, huh?" A similar relocation of the self occurs when in preparing the videography of former EYE Tech executive Charles Bannister, Hakman interviews the CEO's school-age daughter. Displaying a chilling naïveté about the distinction between embodied and digitized existence, the girl asks, "Alan, are you going to fix what my daddy can remember?"

The Final Cut does not just dramatize the growing amalgamation of technology and religion, though, but self-reflexively explores cinema's potential to interrogate the relationship. Consider the architecture of the "rememory theater" where Hakman's films are viewed. On the DVD commentary, Naïm describes the room, with its glowing walls and pulpit-like projection booth, as "a cross between a church and movie theater," since "movie theaters have a very religious place in our lives" and the line is now blurring between "worshipping the visual image and worshipping a god." Indeed it is Hakman's job to serve as "a mortician or a priest or a taxidermist," in the words of his sometime-girlfriend Delila, and these roles become thoroughly convoluted. As much as Hakman attempts to satisfy his customers' straightforward narrative expectations, his own story resists that simplicity. Delila may criticize Hakman's repressive insistence that editing allows him to construct the world as he sees it—"miniature, concise, symmetrical"—but the film as a whole takes pains to display its splicing.

In fact, Delila's objection to Hakman's filmic retellings of personal history hints at the secret of *The Final Cut*, one conveyed subtly enough for most audiences to miss it entirely. Unlike the conclusion of *The Sixth Sense* (1999), here it is easy to overlook the trick ending, where in culminating a series of hints offered throughout the narrative, the film's final scene questions the reliability of its central motif, the Zoe technology itself. Earlier, Hakman prodded clients before an editing job that "there's nothing any of you can tell me that I won't know very soon," but Delila recognized that her previous boyfriend's rememory film "wasn't him, and I wanted to remember him my way." It turns out that she was not merely choosing one reality in favor of another, but laying bare the deepest weakness in the culture of "rememory." The EYE Tech system purports to reveal life as it is, free of interpretation, but the reality is that like Hollywood editors, Hakman makes numerous story decisions, and one stroke of the delete key turned a father's sexual abuse of his daughter into endearing evidence of paternal concern. What *The Final Cut* exposes, in other words, is how technology can buttress an ideology of objectivity that represses uncertainty and ambiguity and manufactures hope as if it were a purchasable commodity. As Garrett Stewart recognizes, in the features constructed from Zoe footage "we see a superficial exaggeration of how [the deceased] saw us, not what we might have meant to them, not even what they seemed or signified to themselves."[10] That is, the EYE Tech corporation's product pretends to define identity in a void, with only a forward-facing record of sights and sounds, and without any access to the emotions or previous experiences they evoked.

Building on Stewart, my further claim is that the film not only critiques the objectivist assumptions and decontextualized process inherent to the Zoe technology, but unapologetically subjectivizes the chip—and thus the film and cinema in general—as sources of historical information. Even more than *Twelve Monkeys*, the film eschews attempts at interpretive rigidity by subverting any claim to photographic neutrality. This metacinematic critique begins when the man who just viewed his brother's rememory film confronts Hakman with the bewildered observation that he had always thought their childhood fishing boat was green, not red. Rather than showing surprise, Hakman increases the man's confusion by admitting, "maybe it *was* green." The suggestion that the Zoe chip's record is not entirely trustworthy is furthered as we watch Hakman begin work on his new project, the chip removed from Charles Bannister, the former leader of EYE Tech. Seconds after Hakman inserts the implant cartridge, his computer has organized a *lifetime* of video footage into a set of discrete categories. While future computers' ability to use image matching and various algorithms to rapidly and reliably create such groups is plausible—"sleep," "eating," "personal hygiene," "wedding," and "athletics," perhaps—other classifications are far more problematic. On what basis, for instance, might artificial intelligence decide which scenes fall within or outside the boundaries of "temptation," "tragedy," or "fears"? Furthermore, perhaps the film's most poignant sequence acknowledges that "some implants have a defect: they can't differentiate between what the eye sees and what the mind sees." As we watch Hakman show Delila, implant footage is highly susceptible to individual imaginations: a girl playing on a backyard swing suddenly flies into the air above her home; marveling at gargantuan tropical fish, a couple enjoys a leisurely date underwater without scuba gear or any need for air; a herd of sheep casually enters a hotel lobby; and a woman goes diving in an evening

---

10. Stewart, "Vitagraphic Time," 178.

gown. It seems that subjectivity does play a role in the Zoe chips, and with greater regularity than Hakman's allusion to manufacturing mistakes can explain.

Like Gilliam revealing that the future scientists can surround Cole with other agents at a moment's notice, then, Naïm is purposefully undercutting the logic driving his film's climactic scenes. This becomes evident near the film's climax when Hakman decides, rather ironically, that in order to free himself from the guilt that sends him to his computer "guillotine" each day, he must attach himself to the system even more directly. Having discovered that his parents had died before telling him of his own implant, and having seen a man in Bannister's recent footage that reminds him of his boyhood friend Louis, Hakman decides to view his own boyhood footage while he is still alive, all for the purpose of finding out what "really" happened years earlier. In this "actual" memory, we gather, he attempted to save Louis from the fall, the "blood" he believed to have saturated the ground around Louis's body was really the contents of an overturned paint can, and Louis did not die. Disconnected from the computer and recovering from the shock of this cybernetic revelation, he exults, "now I remember." The problem with accepting this triumph, though, is that remembering is precisely what Hakman has *not* done. Instead, he has only traded his memory for the testimony of digitized images.

As we have seen, the film had already extensively questioned the Zoe chip's reliability; we know that one's imagination and desires are capable of affecting what the implant "sees" and "hears." While we have seen footage of a middle-aged man named Louis who cleans thick glasses in a manner akin to Hakman's long-lost friend, it hardly proves he is the boy from decades earlier. Given the phenomenon, as Stewart describes it, by which "narrative is paradoxically reframed from within, the whole recontextualized by its part,"[11] we should take seriously Naïm's DVD commentary intimation that "the implant is a false prophet." Not coincidentally, next to Louis's fallen body lies a wheel that looks much like a film reel, reminding us that Naïm is as interested in exploring cinema's self-reflective capacity as he is in critiquing technology's salvific pretensions. In fact, if one pauses the DVD to read the earlier newspaper articles about Bannister through which Hakman sorts, the first one, wittily entitled "Bannister Eyes Future," provides a nearly incontestable miniaturized confession: "Whoever wrote these headlines had as much fun as I did setting them in type and formatting them into newspaper articles. But then, this sort of headline appears in the paper regularly, so maybe we all just want to have fun. Fun: such a precious commodity

---

11. Stewart, *Between Film and Screen*, 195.

these days." Whether attributed to a set designer or Naïm himself, these lines serve as one more affirmation that the film is less committed to its fictitious biotechnology than to cinema's capacity to resist the ideology of technotranscendence.

The film's final scene, which features footage purportedly recorded by Hakman's own implant and now being edited by Fletcher, is its ultimate interrogation of technology's supposedly dispassionate vision. As Naïm's DVD commentary explains, the bathroom set we see is actually not the sink with large mirror that it seems. There is no mirror, and everything in the foreground is replicated in reverse in the background. Rather than watching an actor's reflection in a mirror, we are watching an actor facing the camera and pretending to be a reflection by matching the hand movements of a stunt double in the foreground. This is essential to understand when we watch the film's final scene, purportedly a bit of Zoe footage taken from Hakman's own implant and now being edited by Fletcher. Hakman stares at himself in his bathroom mirror, and the implant seems to work as advertised: we see as Hakman sees, his own reflection. At the last moment, however, Naïm upends the device's logic: as Hakman turns away from the mirror and walks out of the frame, the camera remains still. This is impossible since we should never be able to see Zoe footage from any perspective other than that of the person in whom the device is implanted. In effect, Naïm's last scene explicitly unveils his soundstage, providing one last hint that *The Final Cut* itself, like the video recorded by the ZOE implants, must be understood as a point of view shot, and one subject to all manner of postproduction revision.

EMBRACING THE UNKNOWN

In *Archaeologies of the Future*, Fredric Jameson celebrates the capacity of utopia to "function as a memory trace, but as a message from the future, something foreshadowed in distorted form by all the great scriptures, which give themselves as messages of otherness, but transmitted in the past."[12] One might say, then, that the dystopian films examined in this chapter operate as the negatives of such sacred documents: through their visions of possible futures in which various technologies take on religious dimensions in affording humanity a source of hope, they show us how *not* to live, where *not* to place our hope. In each case, corporate systems professing divine authority compete with flawed rebels and only half-willing messiahs who seem to believe very little, and yet in their various forms of resistance to

12. Jameson, *Archaeologies of the Future*, 99.

mechanized, prepackaged hope, powerfully evoke its poverty. Indeed these rather unheroic protagonists may be more exemplary for what they resist than what they accept: Hamilton-Wilson for his objection to the reborn game, THX for his flight from hyper-efficient cyborgification, Cole for his rebellion against technocracy, and Hakman for his sadness about the very memory revision tools to which he is himself enslaved.

This summation also reflects the gradual shift that has been occurring in recent decades. At the height of the Cold War, clear outcomes necessarily prevailed: Frankenheimer's protagonist cannot escape his unwilling sacrifice on the altar of technology, while Lucas's hero just barely does. In approaching the turn of the millennium, though, dystopian cinema becomes increasingly nuanced and self-reflective in its evaluation of new technological hopes and of religion's affinity for spectacle. In *Twelve Monkeys*, Gilliam leaves as many plot strands untied as tied, so that we have no way of knowing whether Cole has suffered in vain. The female scientist who arrives in the airplane seat next to the bioterrorist may succeed in saving the future, or she may not—and even if she does, it is doubtful how much that future will improve upon the one Cole abandons. Likewise, in *The Final Cut*, Naïm replaces Hakman as suffering servant with a new cutter who promises to render the victim's death meaningful, but whose supposed "final cut" on-screen incorporates a view of the filmic soundstage that is inaccessible to the technology it purportedly utilizes. Hope remains in these films, but one that insists on embracing doubt and the unknown rather than fleeing them. This is the paradox increasingly evident—if not always fully grasped on a first viewing—at the contemporary cineplex, especially as it imagines dystopian futures: hope and lament are less often warring opposites than partners in a still evolving dance.

BIBLIOGRAPHY

Del Rio, Elena. "The Remaking of *La Jetée*'s Time-Travel Narrative: *Twelve Monkeys* and the Rhetoric of Absolute Visibility." *Science Fiction Studies* 28/3 (November 2001) 383–98.

The Final Cut. Dir. Omar Naïm. Perf. Robin Williams, Mira Sorvino, and Jim Caviezel. Lions Gate, 2004.

Fry, Carrol, and J. Robert Craig. "A Carnival of Apes: A Bakhtinian Perspective on *Twelve Monkeys*." *Journal of the Fantastic in the Arts* 13/1 (2002) 3–12.

Jameson, Fredric. *Archaeologies of the Future: The Desire Called Utopia and Other Science Fictions*. New York: Verso, 2005.

Kaufmann, Michael W. "The Religious, the Secular, and Literary Studies." *New Literary History* 38/4 (Autumn 2007) 607–27.

Lashmet, David. "'The Future Is History': *Twelve Monkeys* and the origin of AIDS." *Mosaic* 33/4 (December 2000) 55–72.

McCabe, Bob. *Dark Knights and Holy Fools: The Art and Films of Terry Gilliam*. New York: Universe, 1999.

Seconds. Dir. John Frankenheimer. Perf. Rock Hudson. Paramount, 1966. DVD.

Stewart, Garrett. *Between Film and Screen: Modernism's Photo Synthesis*. Chicago: University of Chicago, 2000.

———. "Vitagraphic Time." *Biography* 29/1 (Winter 2006) 159–92.

THX-1138. Dir. George Lucas. Perf. Robert Duvall. Warner Bros., 1971.

Twelve Monkeys. Dir. Terry Gilliam. Perf. Bruce Willis, Madeleine Stowe, and Brad Pitt. Universal, 1995.

Ward, Graham. *True Religion*. Malden, MA: Blackwell, 2003.

Part 3

The Hope for Atheism as a Religious Utopia

9

Who We Are Is God's Dying
The Real Presence of God's Absence in Bonhoeffer's Prison Poems

—Steven Schroeder

Many times the same dream visited me in my past life, appearing in different forms but saying the same thing. "Socrates," it said, "get to work and make music. At the time, I took this to mean what I was doing already and assumed the dream was encouraging and urging me on—the way people cheer for members of their own team—to make music. And, philosophy being the greatest music, I was doing that already. But now after the trial, with the religious festival delaying my execution, it occurred to me that if the dream was urging me to make popular music, I ought not disobey but do it. It seemed safer not to go without easing my conscience by making poetry and obeying the dream. So first I wrote in praise of the god of the festival. And after god, I thought a poet had to make myth, not history, to be a poet. I was no mythmaker, so I took the myths that were at hand, those we knew, those of Aesop, and made a poem of the first one that came along.[1]

---

1. Plato, *Phaedo* 60e–61b. All translations are by the author unless otherwise indicated.

Part 3: The Hope for Atheism as a Religious Utopia

1

My purpose in this essay is neither exegesis nor exposition of Dietrich Bonhoeffer's writing. Bonhoeffer wrote clearly and succinctly and does not need me to tell you what he said. Nor do you. To understand Bonhoeffer, *read* Bonhoeffer.

But reading is active, not passive, a conversation, not a monologue; and for a number of reasons that I will outline briefly, Bonhoeffer remains one of the most interesting and provocative conversation partners I know. Though he was murdered more than six decades ago (to say that he was executed would give those who carried out the act more legitimacy than they deserve), his work remains lively and engaging.

The clarity with which he wrote is one of the reasons I return to him time and time again. His dissertation and his *habilitationsschrift* are lucid accounts of the philosophical and theological conversation that occupied Europe (and particularly Germany) as Nazism crept into power. That alone is reason to return to his work. Early, clearly, decisively, he laid a philosophical/theological groundwork for the resistance that brought him to the attention of the second half of the twentieth century. The resistance makes a compelling story, but the groundwork is indispensable. If it is true that the first step is more than half the journey, these two early documents, and especially *Akt und Sein*, deserve particular attention. The "religionless Christianity" for which Bonhoeffer is perhaps best known (certainly among theologians) was not a sudden turn taken during his imprisonment. The Christology of his early writing is the seed from which it grows, pointing as it does to an understanding of freedom as pure act and human being as *Dasein* between transcendence and transcendence. He has been criticized for laying the problems of dialectical theology entirely at the feet of the philosophical systems dialectical theologians embraced, but I think he had good reason for doing so.[2]

For me, there are also biographical reasons to turn to Bonhoeffer. As a young scholar who grew up in a conservative Lutheran and conservative rural context and went off with a firm sense of vocation to study at a conservative Lutheran university (that later advertised itself as being just far enough from Chicago), I was delighted to discover a committed scholar whose careful reading of philosophy and theology empowered his critical engagement with the world. Like many theologians and philosophers in formation at the time (particularly outside Germany), I worked my way back from Bonhoeffer's prison correspondence to his early scholarly work.

---

2. Bonhoeffer, *Act and Being*; idem, *Sanctorum Communio*; Reuter, "Afterword," 2:162–83.

Working my way back, it never seemed to me that there was a break—and I continue to be puzzled by comments like those of the editor of the German edition of *Akt und Sein* in *Dietrich Bonhoeffer Werke*, who wrote in his "Afterword" that "the bewildered reader who takes up this book after having studied his writings of the 1940s—for example, the *Letters and Papers from Prison* or the *Ethics*—may well ask whether we are dealing with one and the same author. Indeed, this very reader, whom Bonhoeffer had impressed as the theological writer of those better known works, may well have the sense when reading *Act and Being* of visiting another planet." Perhaps it was because I suspected this text might lead me closer to a rendezvous with that for which I had been waiting since early adolescence, but I did not feel bewildered. I had the feeling that I was getting to the bottom of things that mattered with an author I had already come to respect deeply.[3]

I first encountered Bonhoeffer as I was preparing to enter a conservative Lutheran seminary—at the moment, as it happens, that the Missouri Synod was taking a decisive turn away from its history of critical scholarship and the increasingly open stance toward the world that had been evolving under the leadership of Oliver Harms in the 1960s. *Act and Being* was helpful to me personally in working my way through that series of events (which, among other things, diverted me to the University of Chicago Divinity School, where I discovered Paul Ricoeur and Anglican theology, both relevant to what I am doing here). I was (and am) drawn to Bonhoeffer for many of the same reasons I was (and am) drawn to Luther (and, among Anglican theologians, F. D. Maurice)—not as an authority from whom to receive directives or obtain answers, but as a person passionately engaged in the world, a person with whom it would be possible to have a good argument. Most helpful was Bonhoeffer's reading of Kant's epistemology as decidedly *Lutheran* and his reflection on dangers posed by various responses to transcendental philosophy, particularly the turn to verbal inspiration in Protestant thinking about the Bible. In that reflection, I believe we see most clearly the philosophical foundation on which Bonhoeffer was able to maintain the consistently *critical* stance that makes his life and work so instructive now.

And it is no small thing that the trajectory of that life and work led him to lyric poetry at the same time that it led him to imprisonment and death, all the while engaged critically in the world, reflecting on time, with God (as he put it in *Akt und Sein*) always at his back.

I confess that I can't think that image of God always behind us without seeing the shadowy figure of Jean-Paul Sartre's Zeus in *Les Mouches*, always

---

3. Bonhoeffer, *Act and Being*, 162.

lurking, thinking himself *incognito*, but unmistakable on the very edge of our field of vision. But for Bonhoeffer, God on the edge as *deus absconditus*, encountered always in Christ as boundary, is a key to maintaining a critical edge in the face of the constant temptation to be like gods. Bonhoeffer, I believe, grew to understand more and more deeply that all confront the temptation to be like god and all confront it in exactly the same way, with exactly the same immediacy and in exactly the same paradise where Eve confronts it in the myth of creation and fall, with exactly the same results When we fall, we fall in on ourselves, *cor curvum in se*, and live as though we gave rise to the world because we think we did. We cannot act our way out of this or think our way out of it. And this is why Bonhoeffer (like Socrates) turned to lyric poetry while, imprisoned, he awaited execution. It would be interesting to contemplate the coincidence of Bonhoeffer's evolving understanding of what is meant by telling the truth with his resistance and imprisonment in the light of Socrates' insistence that he was no teller of tales and so turned to the familiar fictions of Aesop—tales everybody knew—when he finally decided his daemon really might want him to try his hand at what other people thought of as poetry.

Never forget that this Socrates is a fictional invention of Plato, who has his own axe to grind in turning to Aesop (to whom Luther also turned) in the middle of a tale as common as a friend dying at the hands of the State—a tale that has become more common as history has marched on. I find it interesting that this Socrates—Plato's Socrates—insists he was not ignoring his daemon but simply going on doing what he had been doing because he assumed he was doing poetry and had been doing poetry all along. He turned to something more conventionally poetic—or so Plato has his characters say—only at the end, in case he had misunderstood and because, in prison, waiting, there was time. But I will save that for another time, simply noting now that Bonhoeffer took up fiction first in the form of drama, then in the form of prose (short stories and a novel), and finally in the form of poetry while he was in Tegel prison. And he did all this at the same time he was writing a scholarly essay on time, which he says in his correspondence was nearly finished, though it is not among the fragments that survived.

But there is a sense in which the essay is finished (and in our hands) in the same way the narrative of a life is finished and in our hands (which is to say, as long as it is living, it is not). And, as with Socrates, that means a turn to old familiar stories in the form of poetry. The Bonhoeffer we know is arrested in time, confined in space. But like a number of contemporaries and near contemporaries, Bonhoeffer sees the condition of imprisonment as characteristic of life in the twentieth century (and perhaps of human life more generally). Paradoxically, what imprisons us is also a condition for our humanity: life, like poetry, calls attention to its own form. And that is a key to critical engagement. Christ as boundary makes us what we are, makes it possible for us to live the examined life, to be conscious of what we are—sinners, in language Bonhoeffer, like Kierkegaard, took up from Luther, who took it up from Paul (a sentiment pithily expressed by William S. Burroughs and Laurie Anderson in "language is a virus from outer space" and by Martha Nussbaum in her reading of Socrates' sacrifice to Asclepius, "life is a disease for which death is the cure"). As Bonhoeffer's Christological reading of the social condition of human beings (or being human) deepened and grew more radical (working its way the way roots do to the bottom), he saw Christ (again taking up a theme of Luther's) as entirely *for* others and *in* others. God disappears entirely into humanity, and the absolute absence of God becomes the real presence that makes us conscious of who we are—word made flesh, calling attention to its own form in the form of encounter with the other, who is a *person*.[4]

With that and God behind us, I turn now to a close reading (a translation in both narrow and expansive senses of the term) of the ten poems Bonhoeffer left, in the probable order of their composition.

2

The poems—ten of them, written in a period of six months during 1944—are embedded in the correspondence, particularly in the theological letters to Bethge.[5] The theological letters to Bethge are grounded in years of resistance as part of the Confessing Church and also in the early theological work—especially *Sanctorum Communio* and *Akt und Sein*. The embeddedness of this theological work (including the poetry)—the conversational architecture of it—exemplifies how *reading* ought to be done where the word is taken as a living (and embodied) thing.

The first comes with a confession to Bethge: "I feel like a silly kid, keeping from you that I've been trying my hand at poetry here from time to time.

---

4. Anderson, *Home of the Brave*. Nussbaum, *The Fragility of Goodness*

5. The translations in this essay are mine, using the German text in *Dietrich Bonhoeffer Werke, Band 8, Widerstand und Ergebung*, edited by Christian Gremmels, Eberhard Bethge, and Renate Bethge, with Ilse Tödt, published by Chr. Kaiser/Gütersloher Verlagshaus in 1998. I have consulted the translations by Nancy Lukens in *Letters and Papers from Prison. Dietrich Bonhoeffer Works, Volume 8*, Translated by Isabel Best, Lisa E. Dahill, Reinhard Krauss, and Nancy Lukens. Edited by John W. DeGruchy, Minneapolis, 2009. Nancy Lukens is currently gathering into a single volume, *By Powers of Good: The Prison Poems of Dietrich Bonhoeffer*, forthcoming from Augsburg Fortress in 2014. I am grateful for her insights and inspiration.

I've kept it secret from everyone until now—even Maria, who would be the one it concerns most!—simply because I was embarrassed somehow and I didn't know whether she might be more shocked than pleased. You are the only one whom I can be sure of telling it to somewhat reasonably, and who I hope will pour cold water over my head if need be and tell me plainly to forget it."[6]

One of the most interesting aspects of Bonhoeffer's confession (and of the "confession" of Socrates cited at the beginning of this essay) is that it simultaneously connects poetry with inwardness and with philosophy. For Bonhoeffer, poetry is so intensely personal as to be embarrassing when shared with another. (And, as a side note, this is one of many instances in the prison correspondence where Bonhoeffer suggests that the relationship between friends is more intimate—or makes a space in which more intimate matters can be shared—than the relationship between lovers.) But it is *performative*, undertaken in the context of a conversation—and so it demands a weaving together of the personal with the social.

This is a central problem addressed by Bonhoeffer in his scholarly work beginning with his dissertation. It would be interesting to connect the form that weaving takes in a context that cuts one off from social intercourse (prison) with the form it takes (in *Life Together*) in a context that imposes a common life on an intensely private person.[7] (Though it is critical to keep in mind that prison, like the underground seminary at Finkenwalde, imposed one social life as it cut participants off from others. Bonhoeffer's prison experience was no less intensely social than his experience with the underground seminary. So the devotional text and the poetry are formed in contexts with more in common than one might initially think.)

It is instructive that Plato's Socrates sees poetry as "common" (or popular) and philosophy (which is, for Socrates, a practice, a way of life) as its most perfect form. In the telling of this tale (which tells us as much about the teller—Plato—as the told), conscience drives the practitioner of the most perfect form to make it *popular* under constraints that, paradoxically, make time and space for it—an interesting comment on the way in which time and space are related in practice to the weaving of the personal and the political. Among other things that make it interesting is the connection with *piety* which Plato's Socrates also makes with philosophy. This is very much like Bonhoeffer's focus on the pure act and his turn (at the end of *Act and Being*) to the church as "solution" to the problem posed in the relationship of act with being (which he sees as the key to the loss of

---

6. Bonhoeffer, *Letters and Papers from Prison*. #3/157, 416; cited hereafter as LPP.
7. Compare Northcott, "'Who Am I?,'" 11–29.

criticism, a loss that underwrites the rise of Nazism). It is hardly surprising that a careful reader of Luther would locate freedom in constraint (perfectly free, perfectly bound): here we have paradoxical hope entirely dependent on the temporal structure we inhabit, which depends in part on the manner of our dwelling, threatened by the ever present temptation of inward collapse in our desire to be gods. And it sheds light on the absolute *absence* of God in the incarnation and the idea of the *kenosis* of the Church (the body of Christ) that is taking form with the poetry in the second half of 1944.[8]

The first poem Bonhoeffer chose to share (which is generally taken to be the first he wrote, though we can't be certain of that) begins with an instance illustrating what Husserl calls temporal perspective:

> *You left, good fortune loved so, pain so hard to love.*
> *What shall I call you? Necessity, life, bliss,*
> *Part of myself, my heart—past?*
> *The door shut,*
> *I hear your footsteps slowly fall and fade.*
> *What's left for me? Joy, pain, desire?*
> *I know only this: you left—and all is past.*

Here he connects the past with good fortune, pain, necessity, life, and bliss by way of a description of his fiancée walking away after a visit in Tegel prison. The last line of this stanza concentrates a critical reading of Husserl into a single image in which an "I" knows (and knows only this, a note on the phenomenology of awareness, which always hinges on a distinction between this and that) as a result of a "you" acting. And in that knowing, past becomes fully present (it is all) as an absence. I say this concentrates Husserl into an image; but there is as much Augustine as Husserl here, and Bonhoeffer has been grappling with both for some time. But what is most interesting philosophically and theologically, I think, consistent with Augustine and Luther, is that the past is present in the same way God is present, on the edge, as an absence.

In the letter that accompanied the poem, Bonhoeffer writes, "For me, this confrontation with the past, this attempt to hold on to it and to get it back, and above all the fear of losing it, is almost the daily background music of my life here, which at times—especially after brief visits, which are always followed by long partings—becomes a theme with variations." The temporal space we inhabit, like our consciousness, is musical. Bonhoeffer quotes music from memory in his letters to Bethge, evidence of just how attentive he is to the aurality of being in the world—and evidence of his capacity for rendering sound visually, one dimension of a capacity for poetry.

8. Bonhoeffer, "The Church as the Unity of Act and Being," 109ff.

The experience of receding footsteps translates into an experience of space rendered in much the same way space is rendered by perspective in a drawing. And Bonhoeffer's reading of this experience is evidence of the influence of a eucharistic theology centered on real presence: the past is fully present not in the grasping of it (which it necessarily eludes, so that the grasping is always after, never of) but in the absence of another constituted by a movement from here to there coinciding with then and now: this *is* . . . do this in remembrance . . . drink it all.[9]

Consciousness of time (keeping time, which is different from getting a particular past back and far removed from the fear of losing it—which is what I think is meant by the idea of perfect love casting out fear) is a musical phenomenon, an instance of the interplay of linearity and nonlinearity that is key to the ubiquity of presence Bonhoeffer takes up from Luther. The editors of the English edition of Dietrich Bonhoeffer's Works call to mind an earlier reference to an essay on "the sense of time," which Bonhoeffer said "arose primarily out of the need to make my own past present to myself. . . . Gratitude and repentance are what keep our past always present to us." (Which calls "Simple Gifts" to mind—to turn, turn will be our delight and to keep on turning till we come down right.") In the poetry, the presence of the past is undeniable—and it is manifest in the experience of absence—walking away—characterized by the repeated demand to say good-bye, the constant rhythm of brief visits (presence always a *glimpse*) followed by long partings, one after the other, all present as the experience of past.[10]

The poem continues:

> *Do you feel, as I reach for you now,*
> *how my talons grasp you*
> *so hard it must hurt?*
> *How I wound you, tear*
> *until your blood pours out,*
> *just to be near you,*
> *your embodied, earthly, entire life?*
> *Do you suspect that I now have a dreadful desire*
> *for my own pain?*
> *That I long to see my own blood,*
> *just so all does not sink*
> *into past?*

---

9. LPP #3/157, 416–417.
10. LPP #2/73, 181.

The terror of desire, closely connected with what Virginia Woolf called "the terror of the present moment" is evident here.[11] Bonhoeffer addresses it by intensifying the rhythm of *Life Together*, in which he maintained that there can be no time together if there is no time apart, no presence without absence. The connection with pain addresses *nostalgia* (a splendid Greek concoction of home and pain worthy of Homer)—but also the often overlooked terror of real presence in the Eucharist (no one sees God and lives—nobody gets out alive). The power in the blood is a terrifying recognition that everything sinks into past as long as it is living. There is terror in that, there is pain; but that is also where we dwell, where we put down roots (sinking, for better for worse, used here in much the way Virgil used it for what Aeneas did), where we make ourselves at home. (Making a home is making a self, something Bonhoeffer returns to in "Who Am I?") We have caught a glimpse of Augustine and Husserl at our backs. Now we catch a glimpse of Heidegger and his *Sorge*, living toward death. Bonhoeffer repudiates that central theme of *Sein und Zeit* Christologically, by embracing death as the moment of resurrection, dying to be free, placing the end in the middle of time. (We see this most clearly perhaps in his early lectures on Genesis.)

Bonhoeffer goes on for several verses layering pain upon pain in parting—the *algia* of nostalgia; but he grounds it in an answer to the question he poses to life in language reminiscent of the Psalms:

> *Life, what have you done to me?*
> *Why did you come? Why did you go?*

The answer (itself in the form of a question), consistent with *Akt und Sein* and still making something of Husserl's temporal perspective, is that my past remains mine when it flies from me:

> *Past, when you fly from me, –*
> *do you not remain mine, my past?*

The "I" (here under the possessive form) is a fact that endures in the act, in the flying, not the being, a reminder that Bonhoeffer has much in common with the pragmatism of William James, who understood the "fact" as a perching, a moment in the act of flight by which James defined consciousness.[12]

The pain in parting is illuminated by a series of natural images:

> *As the sun sinks ever faster over the sea,*
> *as if it preferred darkness . . .*

---

11. Woolf, *Orlando*.
12. James, *Principles of Psychology*.

> *As the hint of warm breath*
> *dissolves in cool morning air . . .*

The terrifying desire associated with the pain is unmistakably embodied:

> *I want to breathe the scent of your being,*
> *drink it in, dwell in it,*
> *as blossoms heavy on a hot summer day*
> *invite the bees*
> *and intoxicate them;*
> *as the privet makes the hawk–moth drunk at night; –*

and unmistakably associated with the fragility of the body –

> *but a harsh wind dissolves scent and blossoms,*
> *leaves me standing like a fool*
> *before the vanished past.*

and with the futility of grasping to get back the past:

> *I feel as I would if flaming tongs*
> *tore pieces from my flesh,*
> *as you, my past life, hurry away.*
> *Furious spite and anger overcome me,*
> *I hurl wild and useless questions into the void.*
> *Why? Why? Why? I say and say again.*
> *If my senses cannot hold you,*
> *passing away, past life,*
> *I will think and think again,*
> *until I find what I lost.*
> *But I feel*
> *as if everything over me, in with under me,*
> *smiles at me, unmoved and enigmatic,*
> *at my hopeless effort,*
> *to capture the wind,*
> *to win back the past.*

Bonhoeffer told Bethge that "everything depends on the last few lines" and worries that "they turned out too short":

> *I stretch out my hands*
> *and pray –*
> *and I learn what's new:*
> *past returns to you*

> *as the most living piece of your life*
> *by thanksgiving and remorse.*
> *Grasp in the past God's forgiveness and grace,*
> *pray that God bless you today and every day after.*

The danger here, with which every poet is familiar, is that everything is resolved too easily, too neatly. Bonhoeffer's concern with these lines is evidence of a critical perspective on his own work that I suspect would have made him an excellent poet had he had the chance to continue. Whether the lines are too short, the resolution too simple, after the richly layered complexity of the pain of parting behind them is an open question. But what is clear is that Bonhoeffer locates the resolution of the problem (posed by the sinking of all into past) in forgiveness and grace. This is hardly a surprise in a Lutheran theologian. But it is important as a corrective to one form of the temptation to be gods, a reminder that every action by which we would constitute a world is a passion, *pathemata mathemata* in the language of Greek tragedy that built so brilliantly on Homer's two volume foundation myth, a war story and a *nostos* tale in which the last hero standing is largely defined by all he has learned in the way of suffering.

Bonhoeffer continues to work with the image of fortune and misfortune joined at the hip (under the influence of Greek thinking about τύχη, which may be good or bad) in a poem titled "Fortune and Misfortune" that probably dates from the same time as "Past":

> *Fortune and misfortune*
> *confront and quickly overwhelm us*
> *and are in the beginning,*
> *like the sudden touch of heat and frost,*
> *almost indistinguishably close.*

Most interesting is that Bonhoeffer sees the two as virtually indistinguishable and suggests that both—"great and terrible"—can overwhelm us. This is consistent with his *Ethics* as it has been reconstructed posthumously by a number of excellent scholars beginning with Bethge. There he integrates the heritage of Greek thinking into a philosophically Lutheran understanding of faithful action as *passion*. This poem ends with the present moment as the moment of truth, *kairos* not *chronos*, as he suggested in his New Year reflection "After Ten Years" just before he was imprisoned.[13]

From the time of *Akt und Sein*, Bonhoeffer has understood identity as pure act in the presence of God—and he has further defined righteous action in much the same way Luther came to define our righteousness as

---

13. Bonhoeffer, *Ethics*.

the righteousness of God. Pure act is God's act, a radically incarnational understanding of ethics that transforms ontology in terms of the *kenosis* Paul invoked in the great christological hymn he recorded in his epistle to the Philippians and paralleled in the image of Christ in all things ("the first born of all creation") in Colossians. Practically, this works itself out in the admonition to be Christs to one another ("little Christs," as Luther suggested) that Bonhoeffer develops in the radically social image of the Christian as entirely a person for others.[14]

That this sociological/ecclesiological approach is psychologically challenging is evidenced in Bonhoeffer's "Who am I?," written in the summer of 1944, where Bonhoeffer finds himself suspended in the tension between what "they" tell him and what he "knows."

The first two stanzas begin with the same line (and the third varies it only slightly, a parallel structure reminiscent of the Hebrew poetry Bonhoeffer knew via the Psalms): "Who am I? They often tell me . . . " The person "they" tell is "calm and serene and strong" and speaks with his captors "free and friendly and clear / as if . . . " The "as if" speaks volumes about the social self. Here it announces a reversal in which the captive speaks to his captors with authority. "They" tell a person who bears "days of misfortune / calmly, smiling and proud, / like one accustomed to winning."

But this social self, told by others, is brought up hard against the self the speaker of the poem *knows*: "Restless, longing, sick, like a bird in a cage / gasping for breath, gagging, / hungry for colors, for flowers, for birdsong, / thirsty for good words, for neighborliness, / trembling with anger over arbitrary and petty insults, / driven in expectation of great things, / trembling powerlessly for friends endlessly distant, / weary and too empty to pray, to think, to make, / weary and ready to say goodbye to it all?"

And the collision leads to a question—"This or the other?"—run through a series of changes, first in terms of time—"today," "tomorrow," "at once"—and then in terms of space—"before others," "before myself." And, in a marvelously social image, the self like "a defeated army / fleeing in disorder from a victory already won?" That image of a defeated army fleeing not from defeat but from victory is followed immediately by the assertion that God knows. Now, I am tempted to play with how "God knows" plays in English as something one usually says in exasperation (when losing one's religion, as the wonderful colloquial expression for being at a loss would have it).

14. Philippians 2:5–8.

While that would be stretching, there is something in Bonhoeffer's conclusion of snatching something from nothing when he locates his identity in God's knowledge: "Whoever I am, you know me, God, I am yours!"

Bonhoeffer's poetry is consistent in taking what Descartes' doubt resolves in an "I" and moving out to an other embodied in the presence of God, always understood as Christ. It is important to be clear here that the concept of presence from which Bonhoeffer proceeds when he gets to work and sings is drawn (as is the gospel) from the Hebrew concept of Shekinah: it is here, dwelling with us, Emmanuel. And so what "they" tell—the telling, the tale, the tellers—cannot be discounted. The question of identity is thoroughly entangled with ecclesiology, always asking what we mean by "we."[15]

That is evidenced in "Christians and Heathens," where "the people" (a potentially explosive term in the Germany of 1944) and "God" are both constituted by the going to an other in need. People go to God in their need, people go to God in God's need, and "God goes to all people in their need, / fills the body and soul with his bread, / dies for Christian and heathen crucified / and forgives then both." This is a dramatic image in which who we are is God's dying, an act that is not ours but makes us who we are—an image of God's absolute absence, God's disappearance into humanity.

The influence of the Psalms on Bonhoeffer's poems, both in terms of structure and content, has already been mentioned. Structurally, this is clear in the repetition of phrases with slight variation (as in "Who Am I?"). In terms of content, it often manifests itself in lamentation, crying from the depths, singing songs of abandonment as people who do not believe they could be abandoned do. This is nowhere clearer than in "Night Voices in Tegel," which is another instance of Bonhoeffer's ability to *hear* the world—and in hearing it to hear his own soul: "I hear my own soul swaying and trembling. / . . . I hear / voices like cries / like pleas for a plank to cling to, / waking, / dreaming companions / silent night thoughts. / I hear the creaking of restless beds, / I hear chains." In the voices of the prison Bonhoeffer hears his soul trembling. And he hears what is not here, what is in another time: "I hear happy lisping teenage boys / who feast on their childhood dreams. / I hear them tugging at their blankets / and hiding from awful nightmares." This is a reminder that soldiers are, more often than not, children. But it is also a reminder of the presence of the past in a time like dream time, the past "suspended in the future," as he said in *Act and Being*, the child growing "out of the human being of conscience." But he also hears "the sighing and weak breathing of old men, / who are quietly preparing for the great

---

15. Descartes. *Meditations on First Philosophy*.

journey. / They have seen justice and injustice come and go, / now they want to see the eternal, everlasting."[16]

What follows is one of the most beautifully lyrical passages in Bonhoeffer's poems, in which Lutheran hymnody (and particularly Paul Gerhardt) sings as surely as the Psalms:

> *Mute is the choir,*
> *wide open my ear:*
> *"We old, we young,*
> *we sons of every tongue,*
> *we strong, we weak,*
> *we sleeping, we awake,*
> *we poor, we rich,*
> *in misfortune the same,*
> *we good, we bad,*
> *what we have always been*
> *we men of many wounds,*
> *we witnesses of those who have died,*
> *we defiant and we despondent,*
> *we innocent and we much maligned,*
> *by long solitude deeply troubled,*
> *brother, we seek, we call you!*
> *Brother, do you hear me?*

In the night voices of the prison, the whole world sings. And it is hearing the whole world sing in those imprisoned voices that empowers Bonhoeffer to conclude this poem with confidence rather than despair, returning to the place from which he began—on the cot, staring at a prison wall—but seeing for the first time:

> *Stretched on my cot I stare at the gray wall.*
> *Outside a summer morning*
> *that is still not mine,*
> *rejoicing*
> *among nations.*
> *Brother, after a long night*
> *our day breaks,*
> *we stand firm!*

The challenge of standing firm when the ground beneath one's feet is crumbling is understandably on Bonhoeffer's mind as it becomes clear to him that he is unlikely to be released. But that challenge was already on his mind in his turn from being to act in *Akt und Sein*. Our lives depend not on some

---

16. Bonhoeffer, *Act and Being*, 32.

fixed ground beneath our feet but on our action in the presence of others. His "Stations on the Way to Freedom" (calling the act of devotion embodied in the stations of the cross to mind) names four moments on the way that is freedom: cultivation, action ("in the deed is freedom"), suffering ("Only for an instant did you touch the bliss of freedom,"), and death ("Freedom, we have long sought you in discipline, deed, and suffering. / Dying we now know you yourself in the face of God." This may read like traditional Christian piety, rooted especially in Pauline language—and that it is. But it is also a manifesto of ethics as formation, singing what Bonhoeffer says in what we have of what was to have been his *magnum opus*.

And it is not surprising that this manifesto, emerging as it does in conversation with Bethge under conditions of imprisonment—an impossible conversation with a distant friend—is followed by "The Friend," a defiant repudiation of the blood and soil massification of Nazism that begins with a "no" like the no of Camus' *Rebel* and moves seamlessly to yes:[17]

> *Not out of the heavy soil*
> *where blood and race and oaths*
> *are mighty and holy,*
> *where the earth itself*
> *against insanity and outrage*
> *sacred ancient orders*
> *guard and protect and avenge. –*
> *not from the heavy soil of the earth*
> *but from free pleasure*
> *and free desire of the spirit*
> *that requires neither oath nor law*
> *friend to friend is given.*

The poem ends with a similar movement from no to yes—what does not make us free, what does:

> *Not orders, not compulsory foreign commands and teachings,*
> *but advice, good and earnest,*
> *makes free,*
> *seeks the mature person*
> *from the loyalty of his friend.*
>
> *Far or near*
> *in fortune or misfortune*
> *know one another*
> *the loyal helpers*

17. Camus, *The Rebel*.

*toward freedom
and humanity.*

3

To describe a body of poetic work that spans six months as maturing may smack of exaggeration. Yet this one does, and I believe that is indicative of a long preparation for poetry that precedes the writing of it in Bonhoeffer, as it almost always does in poets worth reading. Bonhoeffer was immersed in the Psalms and hymns of the church throughout his life, and that immersion—a long, careful disciplined reading of a substantial body of work—was an excellent preparation for poetry. So the maturation evident in the ten poems Bonhoeffer published for a small circle of friends (more often than not, a circle of two) is the maturation of a lifetime.

Bonhoeffer's maturation as a poet is marked by increasingly disciplined attention to form that leads him to a remarkable series of rhymed couplets inspired by the death of Moses and, finally, two hymns. The subject matter is important (and thus the question "why Moses?" that has often come up in response to the first of these three final poems), but it is the form that is remarkable and that returns us to theological work in which Bonhoeffer was already engaged when he wrote *Sanctorum Communio*. The paradoxical hope that sustained his action in the middle of time—between resistance and submission, as Bethge emphasized—is a vision of the presence of the divine embodied in human community.

I absolutely do not believe and hope in no way to imply that "formal" verse is more mature than "free" verse. But for a poet–philosopher concerned as Bonhoeffer is with the relationship between freedom and constraint, engaging formal verse with an eye on the possibilities it contains is a mark of maturity. All of the ten poems Bonhoeffer wrote are attentive to form (as poetry, even free verse, must be). I single the last three out, however, because they appear to grow out of challenges Bonhoeffer set for his art that further his work by casting light on his marking of time.

"The Death of Moses" consists of ninety rhyming couplets that scholars following Henkys have grouped into five sections. The poem has the appearance of a narrative, taking up an old story in much the same way that Plato has his Socrates take up Aesop. Bonhoeffer does not create a new story but sets an old one to music. It begins with Moses, who glimpsed the land of promise but did not dwell on it. Rather than following the life of Moses from beginning to end, however, the poem stays on the mountaintop and moves to the point at which Moses is ready to die. The story of Moses' life is contained in the moment of his dying—on the mountaintop from which he can see the promised land but not enter it. Now, this means the past is lifted up into the future—and that is *pointing* to what was *said* in *Akt und Sein*. The act of the poem is an essay on time, and that makes a prophet in the act of seeing the perfect subject.[18]

Writing ninety rhymed couplets demands a great deal of discipline from the poet (and perhaps even more from the translator). Some would say that the best way for a translator to demonstrate his or her discipline would be to abandon rhyme no matter how tempting, particularly in English. And there is something to be said for that. On the other hand, there is, presumably, *reason* in the rhyme; and that makes it interesting to explore (in much the same way that it must have been interesting to Bonhoeffer at a difficult time in his imprisonment). A discipline like this could pass the time in a place where movement is constrained, and that could serve as a metaphor for time passing while Moses stands in place on the mountaintop, in the act of dying.

On the mountaintop, in the presence of God, in the act of dying, Moses prays: "Atop the mountain's summit / stands Moses, man of God and prophet. // At the holy land of promise / his unwavering eyes gaze. // That he might prepare him to die / the Lord appears at his old servant's side." It is interesting, particularly with the sound of the world singing in Tegel prison still in our ears, that the poem seeks a place of silence in which to see the promised future.

> *Wishing for a high place where the people are*
> *silent, a place to show him the promised future,*
>
> *he spreads before the wanderer's weary feet*
> *a homeland to quietly greet*
>
> *him, blessing him in his final breath*
> *in peace to meet death.*

It is also interesting that a contrast, reminiscent of *being* and *act*, is set up between seeing and entering:

> "From a distance you shall see salvation,
> but your feet shall not enter in!"
>
> And the old eyes see,
> distant things like dawn they see.

18. Slane, "'The Death of Moses,'" 213–41.

> *Kneaded into a sacrificial chalice*
> *by God's mighty hand—Moses prays.*

Moses sees, but he will not enter. Bonhoeffer uses the strict discipline of the rhymed couplets to great effect, playing freedom off the form and wrapping one explosive paradox after another into the lines. Among other things, it appears that Moses the seer sees that he has, in fact, been in the promised land, which (true to Bonhoeffer's theology) is a way, not a destination. But Moses, along with all the people of God, has had to struggle at every step to see that. And the struggle, of great interest to Bonhoeffer, is the burden of being chosen:

> *you forgave. Yet standing faithless before*
> *faithfulness is a burning fire.*
>
> *Your nearness and your countenance*
> *are a painful light to penitents.*
>
> *Your sorrow and your great wrath*
> *dig into my flesh like a thorn of death.*
>
> *Before the holy word—that inflamed*
> *by you I preach—I am damned.*
>
> *Those who taste the fruit of doubt*
> *are from God's table left out.*
>
> *From the holy land heavy with grapes*
> *drink only those of unwavering faith.*

Only those of unwavering faith, of course, would be no one.

The words Bonhoeffer puts in the mouth of Moses recall *Shir Hashirim*, a poetic source with which Bonhoeffer was well acquainted, and one that locates sacramental power in love.[19] The holy land is "decked out as a bride, beautiful, glorious, / virgin in a bright wedding gown," its "bridal jewelry costly grace." It is "God's vineyard" moist with fresh dew, filled with heavy grapes glistening in bright sun, a garden of swelling fruit with springs from which "clear water gushes." A long sequence of couplets sings an apocalyptic vision of a hoped for utopia in which "God's rest" comes "as a great festival comes."

---

19. Bloch and Bloch, *The Song of Songs*.

> *And quiet people in simple satisfaction*
> *will plant vines and plow the fields,*
>
> *and one will call the other brother.*
> *Neither pride nor jealousy will burn in their*
>
> *hearts, and fathers will teach their*
> *children to respect the old and honor*
>
> *the sacred. Young girls, beautiful and good and pure, will*
> *be good fortune and ornaments, the honor of the people.*

As in so much of Hebrew prophecy, the apocalyptic vision is a vision of present hospitality rooted in past experience, of a people who, conscious of having been strangers, welcome strangers:

> *Those who themselves once ate the bread*
> *of strangers, strangers will not leave in need.*
>
> *To the orphans and the widows and the poor*
> *the righteous will willingly show mercy.*

It is a vision of a world transformed that ends with a declaration of present freedom: "Great is the world; it widens the sky, / looks at the people raising a ruckus. // In your word that you gave us, / you show all the people the way / to life . . . "

> *. . . Return, my people,*
> *the free earth and the free air beckons and calls.*
>
> *Take possession of the mountains and the plains,*
> *blessed be the footsteps of the pious forefathers.*
>
> *Wipe from your brow the hot desert sand*
> *and breathe freedom in the promised land.*
>
> *Wake up, reach out, it is no dream, no illusion,*
> *God has done the weary heart good.*
>
> *Look at the glory of the promised land,*
> *all is yours and you are free!"*

As the past is lifted into the future, the future breaks in to the present. And that returns the poem to where it began: "Atop the mountain's summit /

stands Moses, man of God and prophet. // At the holy land of promise / his unwavering eyes gaze."

> *You have been wonderfully good to me,*
> *turned bitterness to sweetness for me,*
>
> *allowed me to see through the veil of death*
> *these, my people, go to the highest celebration.*
>
> *Sinking, God, into your eternity,*
> *I see my people stride to freedom.*
>
> *You who punish sin and gladly forgive,*
> *God,—I have loved these people.*
>
> *That I carried their shame and their burdens*
> *and have seen their salvation—that is enough.*
>
> *Take hold of me! I drop my stave,*
> *faithful God, I am ready for my grave.*

Bonhoeffer and Bethge refer to the hymns of Paul Gerhardt throughout their correspondence, and it is clear that the sacred music of the German Lutheran tradition is always present between them. Gerhardt was a poet as well as a pastor, and the influence of his lyrics on the conversation between Bethge and Bonhoeffer could serve as a subject for another essay. But I will conclude simply by pointing to the last two poems Bonhoeffer wrote, both in the form of hymns (the last being particularly successful as such). The first turns to another prophet, Jonah, who responds to God's call by going the other way. The poem picks up the story in the middle, with frightened sailors on the ship carrying Jonah struggling to keep from being swept away by the storm.

> *They screamed before death, their bodies clawing*
> *at the wet, storm–whipped ropes,*
> *and they gazed full of horror*
> *at the sea in turmoil, its powers suddenly unleashed.*
>
> *"You eternal, you good, you angry gods,*
> *help or give a sign that may tell us*
> *who offended you with a secret sin,*
> *the murderer or breaker of oaths or blasphemer*
>
> *who hides from us his evil misdeed*

> to salvage his miserable pride!"
> So they pled. And Jonah said: "It is I!
> I sinned against God. My life is forfeit.
>
> Cast me away from you! Mine is the guilt. God is very angry with me.
> The pious shall not perish with the sinner!"
> They trembled. But then with strong hands
> they cast the culprit away. There stood the sea.

The poem begins in the middle—and it ends there as well, with the sea standing, there. God's presence is undeniable, and it is not always experienced as grace. But it stands. We know the rest of the story, so it can go without saying—and the poem, like us, can take place *in medias res*.

The final poem takes up the philosophical image of *Dasein* suspended between transcendence and transcendence and wraps it in "still and good and true" powers that enfold us. It is a sort of homily on Colossians, on Christ in all and all in Christ. The poet, like Moses, is ready to die, powerless, tasting what is promised, enfolded in the power of God, a power that resides in God's dying, an act—a source of paradoxical hope—that is not ours but makes us who we are.

> By powers enfolded still and good and true
> sheltered and consoled most wonderfully –
> so I wish these days to spend with you
> and with you a bright new year to see.
>
> The old lives on our poor hearts to torment,
> and evil days still heavy weigh us down.
> Oh Lord give our frightened souls in ferment
> a taste of what you've promised is to come.
>
> And should you offer us the cup of suffering,
> with bitterness filled up to the rim,
> grateful we will take it without trembling,
> lifted in your good and loving hand.
>
> But should you wish to give us joy once more
> in a world with bright and shining sun,
> then all that's gone before we will remember
> and know to you all our lives belong.
>
> Now let the bright warm candle that you brought us
> in our darkness flame up again today,

> *and if it can be done together lead us,*
> *all your children singing your high praise.*
>
> *By powers of good most wonderfully enfolded*
> *with joy we wait hopeful come what may.*
> *Each morning till the day is ended,*
> *God is with us every dawning day.*

It is worth noting again that Bonhoeffer's earliest scholarly work, *Sanctorum Communio*, is an exercise in ecclesiology and that his second major scholarly work, *Akt und Sein*, is a prequel to the first, reading Hegel critically with Heidegger and Husserl in mind to point to the community called "church" as solution to the problem posed by encounter with being. Encounter with being takes place in *human* being as an encounter from outside in revelation, which is an encounter with human existence.[20]

God's disappearance into humanity—God's absolute absence—is nowhere more evident than this. Bonhoeffer's ecclesiology is radically incarnational, and that means it is fully human, human without remainder. There is no place but this to meet God, and that, as Bonhoeffer sees it, is the heart of the gospel.

BIBLIOGRAPHY

Anderson, Laurie, dir. *Home of the Brave*. Warner Brothers, 1986.
Bloch, Ariel, and Chana Bloch. *The Song of Songs: A New Translation*. New York: Random House, 1995.
Bonhoeffer, Dietrich. *Act and Being* [*Akt und Sein*]. Edited by Wayne Whitson Floyd Jr. Translated by H. Martin Rumscheidt. Dietrich Bonhoeffer Works 2. Minneapolis: Fortress, 1996.
———. *Ethics*. Edited by Clifford J. Green. Translated by Reinhard Krauss, Charles C. West, and Douglas W. Stott. Dietrich Bonhoeffer Works 6. Minneapolis: Fortress, 2005.
———. *Letters and Papers from Prison*. Edited by John W. DeGruchy. Translated by Isabel Best, Lisa E. Dahill, Reinhard Krauss, and Nancy Lukens. Dietrich Bonhoeffer Works 8. Minneapolis: Fortress, 2009.

---

20. Bonhoeffer, *Act and Being*, 109. Bonhoeffer's reading anticipates Paul Ricoeur's reading of similar material in "Religion, Atheism, and Faith." It also has much in common with Jan Patočka's phenomenology, outlined in *Body, Community, Language, World*. More generally, the parallels and echoes between Bonhoeffer's radically incarnational ecclesiology and the concepts of "parallel polis" and "second culture" (associated with Patočka and the circle that included Ivan Martin Jirous, Václav Benda, and Václav Havel) are mutually illuminating and worthy of further consideration.

———. *Sanctorum Communio*. Edited by Clifford J. Green. Translated by Reinhard Krauss and Nancy Lukens. Dietrich Bonhoeffer Works 1. Minneapolis: Fortress, 1998.

Camus, Albert. *The Rebel*. Translated by Anthony Bower. New York: Vintage, 1992.

Descartes, René. *Meditations on First Philosophy: with Selections from the Objections and Replies*. Translated by Michael Moriarty. Oxford: Oxford University Press, 2008.

James, William. *The Principles of Psychology*. New York: Dover, 2006.

Northcott, Michael. "'Who Am I?' Human Identity and the Spiritual Disciplines in the Witness of Dietrich Bonhoeffer." In *Who Am I? Bonhoeffer's Theology through His Poetry*, edited by Bernd Wannenwetsch, 11–29. New York: Continuum, 2009.

Nussbaum, Martha C. *The Fragility of Goodness: Luck and Ethics in Greek Tragedy and Philosophy*. Cambridge: Cambridge University Press, 1986.

Patočka, Jan. *Body, Community, Language, World*. Edited by James Dodd. Translated by Erazim Kohák. Chicago: Open Court, 1998.

Reuter, Hans-Richard. "Afterword." In *Act and Being* by Dietrich Bonhoeffer, edited by Wayne Whitson Floyd Jr., 2:162–83. Translated by H. Martin Rumscheidt. Minneapolis: Fortress, 1996.

Ricoeur, Paul. "Religion, Atheism, and Faith." In *The Conflict of Interpretations: Essays in Hermeneutics*, edited by Don Ihde, 440–67. Translated by Charles Freilich. Evanston, IL: Northwestern University Press, 1974.

Slane, Craig J. "'The Death of Moses': Why Moses?" In *Who Am I? Bonhoeffer's Theology through His Poetry*, edited by Bernd Wannenwetsch, 213–41. New York: Continuum, 2009.

Woolf, Virginia. *Orlando: A Biography*. New York: Houghton Mifflin Harcourt, 2006.

10

TechnoTopia
The Convergence of Art and Technology in the Twentieth Century and Beyond

—*J. Sage Elwell*

In her book *The Concept of Utopia*, Ruth Levitas writes that utopia is "the expression of desire for a better way of living and being."[1] Accepting her formulation as a starting point, the question I raise here is: what informs that "desire for a better way of living and being"? That is, what are the grounding principles that shape a desire for a better way of living and being? In this chapter, I address this question to three artists who self-consciously envisioned an aesthetic and cultural utopia in light of the defining technologies of the twentieth century. At a time when technology was redefining the nature of civilization and the human experience itself these artists cast a vision of where they believed the convergence of art and technology would take humanity.

The three artists I consider are the Italian Futurist F.T. Marinetti, the British computer-artist pioneer Roy Ascott, and the Australian posthumanist artist Stelarc. Each offers a unique vision of this aesthetic and cultural ideal—their version of technotopia—in light of revolutions in industry, information technology, and the human-computer interface. And although the voice and vision of each artist is different, they each implicitly affirm what I call an aesthetic of technological atheism in place of a theological

---

1. Levitas, *The Concept of Utopia*, 91.

aesthetic of transcendence as both an artistic and cultural ideal. And it is precisely because these artists regarded the technological revolutions of their day as displacing transcendence that I have selected have selected them for consideration. My aim is to understand how these forward-looking artists who embraced the technological changes of the twentieth century believed that that technology would (or should) reshape the face of culture. As we move further into the twenty-first century and encounter increasingly radical technological revolutions, understanding this trajectory is imperative for any appreciation of the assorted technotopian ideals that lay ahead.

I unpack these ideas in three brief sections. Section one introduces the artists and the particular essay from each that is the subject of what follows. I have also incorporated into this section a cursory defense of my selection of these artists, following which, I discuss each essay in greater detail, lifting from each the common, yet distinctly formulated, usurpation of transcendence by technology as a defining principle of their respective visions of an aesthetic and cultural utopia. The second section pulls their three different articulations of this displacement together in a configuration of their respective visions of industry, information, and interface as constitutive of a technotopian ideal. The third section then offers a response to these authors and the dilemma of proposing an aesthetic or cultural utopia according to the ideals of theology or technology.

However, to preface these three sections I will clarify what I mean by transcendence and technological atheism. Transcendence has become something of a circumlocution for those who are uncomfortable with the implicit confidence of words like God, divinity, or even the holy. The language of transcendence has an almost geographical feel to it, as though it referred to a small town in rural New Mexico and not the principle and defining nature of the Absolute. In short, it is theology in philosophical clothing.

After the Renaissance, the idea that the arts were simply the handmaid of religion lost almost all credibility as faith and morality were increasingly regarded as private affairs and the arts flourished independent of their ideological service. During the eighteenth and the nineteenth centuries philosophers like Schelling, Schleiermacher, Hegel, Kierkegaard, and later, Walter Pater, saw the arts as propaedutic to religion *qua* abstract civic morality rooted in the heart's supposed innate love for the beautiful and the transcendent. At roughly the same time, Romantic poets and artists like Novalis, the Schlegel brothers, Casper David Friedrich, Gericault in France, and Ruskin in England began to formalize a vision of the arts as the mysterious work of genius in its longing for the transcendence that was the true heart of religion.

Transcendence and the language of the spiritual took the place of institutional religion and theology as the essential *topos* of the aesthetic and *telos* of culture. The philosophical construction of transcendence lacked the historical particularity that made organized religion unsavory and offered instead the universal abstracted core that purportedly animated all *true* religion. Transcendence conjures Otto's *mysterium*, Schleiermacher's feeling of absolute dependence, Novalis' *Liebesreligion*, Casper David Friedrich's infinitude, and even Kandinsky's "soul of the epoch of the great spiritual."[2] And for nearly two centuries it has served as the intellectual currency of modern theology without the burden of sacraments or dogma—and it is in full acknowledgment of this that I employ the term here.

Conversely, by technological atheism I intend the absence of belief in transcendence as the concomitant yet inverse of belief in a technological ideal. This technological ideal need not correspond to any particular technological artifact, but rather, in the spirit of Heidegger's "The Question Concerning Technology," it reflects an overall approach to life that "challenges-forth" calculative ends from a world of "disposable" "standing reserves."[3]

The essence of technological atheism is thus objectification pursuant to potential utility according to a wholly immanent teleology. Within this schema nothing supersedes what Heidegger called "calculative thinking" in "the triumph . . . [whereby] what possesses real worth, what should orient actions and social relations, is the extension of human power to shape and create realities."[4] The guiding principle of this shaping and creating is power and progress itself, even when it comes into conflict with the being of the human being whom this progress would ostensibly serve.

SECTION I

F. T. Marinetti wrote the founding manifesto of Futurism in 1909. Roy Ascott wrote "The Cybernetic Stance: My Process and Purpose" in 1968. And Stelarc wrote his "Postevolutionary Strategies" in 1991. In these three artists we have representatives from across the globe—Italy, Britain, and Australia—and spanning the twentieth century. That being said, this is an admittedly select group and is by no means intended to stand-in for all of the artists thinking through the convergence of art and technology during the twentieth century. Nonetheless, I focus my attention on these three because each in their own way made their project as an artist the task of envisioning

---

2. Kandinsky, *Complete Writings on Art*, 219.
3. Heidegger, "The Question Concerning Technology".
4. Klemm and Schweiker, *Religion and the Human Future*, 14.

an artistic and cultural utopia in light of the defining technologies of their day. For each, technology was not only an element of their artistic process or product. Rather, each person's entire artistic project orbited about the ideal advancement of the intersection of art, technology, and culture. Additionally, they share a uniquely optimistic strand of thought around the aesthetic and cultural possibilities for a coming technotopia. Considered together, they present a three-fold creative lineage of thinking and making around the question of the future of art and culture in the wake of three key technological revolutions.

This artistic and intellectual genealogy is tethered to three different technological innovations: the industrial machine, networked information technologies, and revolutions in the human-computer interface (HCI). Marinetti's writing reflects a violent embrace of industrial age technologies as the future not just of the arts, but of human civilization. Ascott's prophetic vision of what he called a Cybernetic Art Matrix foresaw, in his words, a "world brain [in] which instant-information technology"[5] would revolutionize how we create, communicate, and collaborate. Lastly, Stelarc's declaration of "postevolutionary strategies" recognized that this information matrix was rapidly being internalized and that the body itself was becoming the very interface for a networked instant-information technotopia.

Marinetti

Marinetti was principally a poet, thus his inclusion here is perhaps a bit odd. However, I include him for two reasons. First, his 1909 essay which I consider here effectively founded the Futurist movement as the first movement in the visual arts explicitly aligned with the aesthetics and culture of modern technology. Second, a year later in 1910 Marinetti published "Futurist Painting: a Technical Manifesto" wherein he articulated, among other things, 13 principles of painting all of which orbit about his admonition that artists express the "whirling life of steel, or pride, or fever, and of speed."[6] Thus Marinetti's writing defined an arena of the visual arts even if he himself was predominately a writer.

"The Founding and Manifesto of Futurism" was written at a time when Italy was largely being left out of the industrial revolution of the early twentieth century. The *Manifesto* was thus in part a statement on how Italy and, by implication, influential Italian artists were going to (or should) address the revolutionary technologies of the industrial age. Marinetti's *Manifesto*

---

5. Ascott,"The Cybernetic Stance," 111.
6. Marinetti, "Futurist Painting," 534.

declared that the arts should neither be overrun nor fearful of the new technologies of steel and speed, but instead should embrace them, indeed celebrate them, and thereby make them a centerpiece of the aesthetic and cultural identity of the new age.

The *Manifesto* begins by declaring, "We're about to see the Centaur's birth."[7] This centaur is what Hal Foster describes as the first twentieth century "technological subject, as the Futurists emerge as . . . half men, half machines."[8] Indeed, in his *Manifesto* Marinetti describes his own resurrection after a car crash as his body, which he likens to the automobile itself, is pulled from a ditch. He writes, "When I came up—torn, filthy, and stinking, from under the capsized car, I felt the white-hot iron of joy deliciously pass through my heart."[9] And thus the artist and the arts themselves are reborn in a glorious technological embrace that merges man and machine.

Marinetti continues, "Let's Go! Mythology and the Mystic Ideal are defeated at last . . . We must shake at the gates of life, test the bolts and hinges. Let's go!"[10] With the dawning of the new millennium Marinetti foresaw the fall of mystic ideals as the old gods of mythology were displaced by the aggressive "beauty of speed." As such, aggressive and uncompromising technological progress would be the watchwords of the technotopia of the future and thus the artistic movement that bore the future's name.

For Marinetti, the industrial machine *par excellance* was the then-revolutionary automobile which he celebrated in the race car with its "hood adorned with great pipes, like serpents of explosive breath . . ."[11] For Marinetti, machines of all types, but cars in particular, were extensions of the human subject's own powers and amplifications of our own impulses.

For Marinetti, and those who followed after him, the tired cultural aesthetic of subtle transcendent beauty housed in the secular sanctuaries of museums was being displaced by the militant march of the machine. Marinetti writes that, "We already live in the absolute, because we have created eternal, omnipresent speed."[12] The absolute, absent the removed aspect of the divine (transcendence), is re-envisioned as the industrial epoch of "arsenals and shipyards . . . greedy railway stations . . . factories hung on clouds . . . bridges that stride the rivers . . . adventurous steamers . . . deep-chested

---

7. Ibid., 19.
8. Foster, "Prosthetic Gods," 11
9. Marinetti, "The Founding and Manifesto of Futurism," 19.
10. Ibid., 19.
11. Ibid., 20.
12. Ibid., 22.

locomotives ... and the sleek flight of planes ..."[13] Industry and its machines were the perfection and protraction of humanity, extending their power into the future and displacing the disguised theological ideal of transcendence with the brute and pragmatic potency of technology.

Ascott

Digital computing was the most culturally significant technological invention in the sixty years between Marinetti's Futurist manifesto and Roy Ascott's "Cybernetic Stance." At the heart of this digital revolution was the realization that everything from the Bible to Beethoven's 5th could be transformed into computable bits of data; a string of ones and zeros.

Ascott has been working at the intersection of technology and the arts for over fifty years. He began incorporating the earliest digital computing devices and paradigms into his art practice in the 1960s. By 1968, when he wrote "Cybernetic Stance: My Process and Purpose," information technology was already a cornerstone of his art practice. Ascott continues to chart new territory in new media art as Professor of Technoetic Arts at Plymouth University in the UK.

In his 1968 statement on his "Process and Purpose" Ascott begins, like Marinetti, by acknowledging that his is an essentially forward-looking art practice. He writes, "The paradox we face as artists writing about our work is that the future is all that interests us, and that is precisely the part of our activity which must remain necessarily unpredictable."[14] Nonetheless, looking to the future Ascott saw an information revolution ushered in by new computing technologies; a culture defined by data. The major implication for the arts would be, as he saw it, the rise of what he called "process-oriented" art.[15] That is, art that will build on the transferability of information and the possibilities afforded to artistic practice when the limitations of space are eliminated.

In particular, Ascott suggested that as our cultural value is increasingly figured on the basis of calculable information, who we are and what we produce will be less and less important. Rather, attention will turn to the systems and processes we create and participate in at the level of measurable behavior, which can be refigured as documentable information. As he says, "Today [1968] we are concerned less with the essence of things as with their behavior; not with what they are but what they do. This unified tendency

13. Ibid.
14. Ascott, "The Cybernetic Stance," 105.
15. Ibid.

is evidently behavioural, and we can see how the vision of our time is ultimately cybernetic."[16] Here, Ascott forecasts, as did Marinetti, the substitution of some absolute, yet ineffable transcendent essence for the tangible, and ultimately quantifiable, bits of information technologies. To that end, Ascott called for a Cybernetic Art Matrix (CAM).

As Ascott envisioned it, the Cybernetic Art Matrix would be an ongoing "process for generating processes, a self-organizing system, a learning organism." He explains that, "This self-creating artform, in which human beings are their own media (properly extended and amplified with technology and bio-chemical hardware), constitutes a cybernetic art process, capable of growth and change."[17] Thus, whereas Marinetti saw the machine technologies of the industrial revolution as bodily extensions transforming the speed of walking into the speed of a racecar, Ascott reverses this formula by proposing the computing technologies of the information revolution as the model for refiguring, for reimagining, the analog body. That is, rather than considering a race car an expansion and extension of limited human speed, Ascott goes the other way round by using the paradigm of quantifiable information as the model by which we might understand embodied identity in the new digital age. Consequently, an extension of the self and its activities is an extension of and as information.

It is not simply that technology amplifies the embodied self. Rather, the embodied self is conceptually rendered as information—it becomes the technology—and only then is it extended; again, as information. Thus for Ascott, the future of art and, as he would later argue, the future of digital culture, is one where information technologies constitute the final paradigm for any mode of self-world or self-other engagement. And although he was writing almost a decade before the release of the first personal computer, in many ways he was right.[18]

Consider, for instance, the extent to which we today must comport ourselves to our digital technologies in order to engage with others or with our world at large. By way of simple and admittedly anecdotal evidence, if your cell phone rings, do you feel like you have answer it? Or if you get a text message, do you feel you must glance at the screen? If so, who is in charge in that relationship, you or the technology? Or, perhaps more plainly, consider the extent to which our relationships with people and things alike are mediated through digital technology and the Internet, which Ascott,

---

16. Ibid., 106.

17. Ibid., 111.

18. This assumes the Commodore PET, released in 1977, and the Apple II, also released in 1977, to be the first successful release of a personal computer.

some twenty years before the World Wide Web, presciently called the "world-brain." This world-brain runs on information and to engage it we must become information.

Unlike Marinetti's industrial model that saw the technologies of industry as monumental extensions of human power, Ascott saw the coming digital revolution as an informationalization of human power, knowledge, and identity pursuant to a self-perpetuating cybernetic utopia constituted and animated exclusively through the hive-like processes of informational interactions.

Ascott anticipated that as digital technology and the information it feeds on and produces became the dominant cultural paradigm, those works of art engaged at the intersection of technology and culture would mirror this data-processing orientation as process assumed the place of artistic product. The aesthetics of transcendence, and any latent theology that supported it, will be (and has been) displaced by a technological determinism that only recognizes the processes of its own algorithmic commands. The self-perpetuating informational art and culture he envisioned has neither need nor room for extrinsic justification or motivation. It is a closed, information only system. Thus what I am calling technological atheism comes in the form of digital progress itself, displacing any *telos* (theological or otherwise) that does not accord with the cybernetic matrix and the demands of the informational platform that ultimately supports it.[19]

Stelarc

Where Ascott saw the coming transformation of embodied identity into protracted information systems and processes as part of a networked Cybernetic Art Matrix, Stelarc went a step further, transforming the embodied self into the very interface of the digital and the analog—information as flesh and flesh as information—existing in as an ever-permeable human-computer interface.

In the late 70s Stelarc, who was born Stelios Arcadiou, staged of series of hook suspensions where he hung his body from gallery ceilings from large steel hooks that pierced his back, arms, and legs. Throughout the 80's he continued to use his body as a canvas for artistic experimentation,

---

19. It should be noted that although Ascott did see the displacement of the transcendent as an aesthetic *telos*, he nonetheless argued that by pursuing a radically progressive technological agenda in the arts, we might realize the transcendent, or what he simply called, the spiritual, in the very metaphysical nature of the being of human being, if not in human civilization at large.

increasingly incorporating technological elements. For instance, in the mid 90's he staged a series of performances collectively know as *Ping Body* where he wired his naked body to electrodes whose voltage and frequency were controlled by random "pings" scattered throughout the Internet. The result was a peculiar puppet dance animated by electrical shocks triggered by unknown and anonymous digital puppet-masters.

In a brief article written in 1991 for the art, science, and technology journal *Leonardo*, Stelarc set out his vision for the technological future of the arts, and by implication, for technosociety more generally. In the spirit of Marinetti's bold *Manifesto* style, Stelarc opens his statement by provocatively declaring that, "It is time to question whether a bipedal, breating body with binocular vision and 1,400cc brain is an adequate biological form."[20] Indeed, he goes on to claim, in all-caps, that "THE BODY IS OBSOLETE."[21]

In this piece and in later writings, Stelarc proposes that not only is technology an extension of the embodied self (as did Marinetti), or that the embodied self can be translated into information bits (as did Ascott), but that *the body is itself the fleshy interface of Marinetti's machine and Ascott's information*. Stelarc writes that, "Technology is not only attached but is also implanted. Once a container, technology now becomes a component of the body . . . We are at the end of philosophy and human physiology."[22] The machines that once extended the body and the information that was once the extrapolated modality of selfhood and its physical form, converge in the flesh as the mechanistic body and informational mind blur into an informational machine and become an always on, always connected, undifferentiated human-computer interface.

For Stelarc, the body itself is the place where the technological displacement of any pretense to transcendence occurs. Indeed, the theological and aesthetic machinations of transcendence are usurped through the extropian perfections made possible through technology. The artistic product is nothing other than the flesh itself as it is transformed into a technotopia where technology merges with the body in a seamless interface of the digital and the analog.

SECTION II:

The preceding discussion attended only to three artists, and even then to only a single short writing by each. Each artist has written substantially more,

---

20. Stelarc, "Prosthetics, Robotics, and Remote Existence," 591.
21. Ibid., 595.
22. Ibid.

variously expressing their views in manifestos, scholarly articles, books, and blogs. Nonetheless, the artists I selected and the pieces I attended to are representative of each artist's thought and work, and more importantly, they are representative of a general trend in the utopian aesthetics at the intersection of art, technology, and culture during the twentieth century; that trend being an progressive conceptualization of self and society as industrial machine, computer network, and digital interface.

The objectification of resources and people pursuant to their potential utility according to an immanent teleology has superseded the eighteenth and nineteenth-century aesthetic ideal of transcendence. Over the course of the twentieth-century technological atheism has largely displaced any notion of transcendence as the overarching vision of an artistic and cultural ideal. As visions of utopia—artistic and otherwise—increasingly descended from heavenly ideals to earthly realities, technology has come to be seen as the mode of its realization. In the words of Marinetti, "Mythology and the Mystical Ideal are defeated at last. We're about to see the Centaur's birth . . ."[23]

I began this chapter by quoting Ruth Levitas, who wrote that utopia is "the expression of desire for a better way of living and being,"[24] asking what should inform this desire. I suggested that the aesthetics of technological atheism as particularly expressed in the writings of Marinetti, Ascott, and Stelac, effectively displaced the metaphysical aesthetics of transcendence of the eighteenth and nineteenth centuries. Thus I implicitly suggested the transcendence of theology and the immanence of technology serve as two different guides that might inform this "desire for a better way of living and being." However, I conclude by arguing that both are flawed.

The problem with the technotopian vision proffered by Marinetti, Ascott, and Stelarc—as well as comparable visions articulated by others not cited here—is that they represent an acceptance of the dominant top-down mode of technological innovation while lacking the criticality of bottom-up subversions of technoculture. As such, they are implicitly defined and hemmed in by the techno-logic that forms the dominant cultural modality of the day. They represent an acquiescence of the analog body and mind to the industrial, informational, and interfacial technological systems of the age.

This approach neglects the political and cultural ideologies that are built into the technologies themselves. Consequently, the technology determines the utopia as opposed to a utopian vision determining technological

---

23. Marinetti, "Manifesto of Futurism," 19.
24. Levitas, *The Concept of Utopia*, 91.

development and deployment. Moreover, inasmuch as the dominant technologies of a culture tend to be aligned with (or become aligned with) established social, economic, and political power structures, the utopian impulse should be informed by a desire to disrupt and destabilize the technologies that define the cultural order; a utopian ideal that sets about fracturing, dismantling, and dis-ordering the technological order, not advancing on it.

Abandoning flimsy theology and hackneyed ideals was, as Marinetti suggested, long overdue and in fact necessary for the furtherance of the artistic project in general. But to release one false idol only to embrace another is only to trade the god of nineteenth-century humanist theology for the god of twentieth-century atheistic technology. Both share a vision of the ideal that is predicated on the illusion of perfection.

For the transcendental theism of the nineteenth-century Romantics and their intellectual progeny, the beautiful entices the soul away from the material trappings of the sensuous world through an aesthetic appeal that paradoxically aims to transcend the aesthetic. Conversely, for the technological atheism latent in Marinetti, Ascott, and Stelarc, the body is a fleshy prison calling for technological transformation pursuant to the unacknowledged ideals and ideologies instantiated in those technologies; the industrial ideals of speed, strength, and endurance, the informational ideals of quantification, efficiency, and exchange, and the interfacial ideals of convergence, identity, and extension. In both instances, the imprecise analog body with its inarticulate desires and impulses, with its grotesque fluids and inconvenient needs is colonized by a rational system; the utopias of theology or technology.

SECTION III:

What, then, are the desires that should inform a utopian vision in a technological age? There are, I believe, three core values that should determine this impulse "for a better way of living and being" in today's techno-culture. First, the reality of embodiment must be recognized and valued. Second, the frailty of the body must be recognized and valued as concomitant with the reality of embodiment. Third, and finally, the appropriation of technology pursuant to any ideal norm, whether individual or social, should entail the recognition and valuing of the finite nature of embodied existence.

When we imagine, manifesto-style, a future aesthetic—and future culture—the fragile and frightening body must be prized as the foundation of subversion and resistance, undermining the totalizing tendencies of both theology and technology with gestures of fallibility. This would be an artistic and cultural project that takes the flawed and fallible being of the human being as its normative origins so as to disrupt the technological and theological pretentions to perfection that, during the nineteenth, twentieth, and twenty-first centuries respectively, determined the dominant value structures of the societies where theologies of transcendence or technological atheism were embraced or imposed. We must not begin with far off visions of abstract ideals, but rather with the humble fact of our fragile and finite embodied existence.

There is only one perspective that we will ever have, and that is the perspective of a human being—and the being of the human being is bound up with its embodiment. Thus, the reality of our embodiment is foundational to the essence and existence of our being, and to overlook or shun it in favor of either theologies of transcendence or atheistic technological ideals is to begin from a mistaken premise. Our very ideas of transcendence, be they theological or technological, presuppose the reality of our frailty and finitude as some broad, ugly ditch to leap across. This, however, mistakes the situation. Our embodiment is not something to leap across, but is rather the very mode by which we might imagine such a leap in the first place. It is at once the condition of the possibility of imagining otherwise and the deficit that makes realizing such imaginings impossible.

Likewise, it is our frailty, the body's tendency towards decay, that encourages us to cast our vision of utopia not in an idealized future, whether a heavenly beyond or future technotopia, but in the rusty present. In this, Merleau-Ponty rightly framed perception and subjectivity in terms of their corporeality.[25] But the condition of the corporeal subject is one that is both faulty and ultimately finite. And it is both the body's limitations and the promise of its final demise that makes embodied subjective experience existentially valuable and meaningful. The *telos* that forms and informs this value and meaning is not extracted from embodied experience itself. Rather, it is found within embodied experience and the limiting factors of embodied experience that lend value and meaning to that experience.

Moreover, these limiting factors—the frailty and finitude of embodiment—suggest, again borrowing from Merleau-Ponty, an "ontology of the flesh"[26] that need not appeal to either the transcendence of theology or the rootless immanence of technological atheism. The flesh itself is the ontological ground of experience and the normative foundation of meaning and value and this meaning and value is itself contingent upon the body's very finitude.

25. Merleau-Ponty, *The Phenomenology of Perception*.
26. Ibid.

The fact of finitude secures a terminal end to our projects thereby providing the impetus to pursue and realize them. The fact of our fallibility, our tilting toward failure, makes those projects meaningful. The possibility, even likelihood, of failure is what makes our endeavors meaningful. Absent finitude, the horizon for our endeavors extends indefinitely and diminishes the impulse to realize them. Absent our frailty and the prospect of failure, our projects—the project of being human itself—likewise loses its existential, and even ultimate, meaning.

For all of human history the technologies we devised, from the spear to the telephone, had to function in a world designed for humanity. As such, those technologies had to offer a repertoire of functions that most suited the human user and his or her world. However, for the first time in human history we are creating a technological culture where we must comport ourselves to a world designed by and for our technologies; where our thoughts and behaviors must accord with the repertoire of expectations and functions of technology—and today's digital technology knows nothing of finitude or failure.

Considerations of technology's impact on artistic and cultural visions of utopia should therefore begin from and preserve these essential and defining features of our being, our finitude and frailty, rather than seeking to overcome them in a technotopia of machines and speed, computers and networks, or interfaces and exchanges.

To be clear, this is not a rejection of technology; this is not a Luddite position. Technology can and should be embraced by the arts, especially as artists envision and shape the future of culture. It has always fallen to the artists—the creators—to cast a cultural vision of the future, and technology must be a part of that vision as well as its realization. In his book *Always On*, Brian Chen compares technology (the Internet in particular) to food, noting that "Attempting to generalize 'the Internet' as good or bad is like saying 'food' is good or bad; however, different types of food can be healthy or unhealthy depending on the amount one consumes."[27] As Chen rightly observes, technology is neither wholly good nor wholly bad. However, artists and culture creators must recognize that different technologies—like different theologies—carry with them their own socio-cultural implications. That is, technology carries with it as much built-in ideology as theology, even if the ideologies of theology are more obvious.

Looking forward then to the technotopias of the future arising from the nexus of technology and the arts, we must be as bold as we are cautious; weighing both technology and theology on the scales of humanity.

27. Chen, *Always On*, 135–36.

We are (for the time being) above all defined by the frailty and finitude of our embodied being. As such, our being-toward-failure is the quintessential character of our existence and must be therefore be preserved as the programmatic source of any ultimate meaning we might derive from it.

BIBLIOGRAPHY:

Ascott, Roy. "The Cybernetic Stance: My Process and Purpose." *Leonardo* 1/2 (April 1968) 105–12.

Chen, Brian X. *Always On: How the iPhone Unlocked the Anything-Anytime-Anywhere Future—And Locked Us In*. New York: Da Capo, 2011.

Foster, Hal. "Prosthetic Gods." *Modernism/Modernity* 4/2 (1997) 5–38.

Heidegger, Martin. "The Question Concerning Technology." In *Martin Heidegger: Basic Writings*, edited by David Farrell Krell, 307–342. New York: HarperCollins, 1993.

Kandinsky, Wassily. *Complete Writings on Art*. Edited by Kenneth C. Lindsay and Peter Vergo. New York: Da Capo, 1994.

Levitas, Ruth. *The Concept of Utopia*. Bern: Peter Lang, 2010.

Marinetti, F. T. "The Founding and Manifesto of Futurism." In *Futurist Manifestos: Documents of 20th Century Art*, edited by Umbro Apollonio, 19–24. New York: Viking, 1973.

———. "Futurist Painting: Technical Manifesto." In *Art and Its Significance: An Anthology of Aesthetic Theory*, edited by Stephen David Ross, 656–60. Albany: State University of New York Press, 1984.

Merleau-Ponty, Maurice. *The Phenomenology of Perception*. Translated by Kegan Paul. New York: Routledge, 2003.

Stelarc. "Prosthetics, Robotics, and Remote Existence: Postevolutionary Strategies." *Leonardo* 24/5 (1991) 591–95.

11

The Coming Community
Agamben, Benjamin, and the Hope for a Materialist-Messianic Redemption of the Present

—*W. David Hall*

> A chronicler who recites the events without distinguishing between the major and minor ones acts in accordance with the following truth: nothing that has ever happened should be regarded as lost for history. To be sure, only a redeemed mankind receives the fullness of its past — which is to say, only for a redeemed mankind has its past become citable in all its moments. Each moment it has lived becomes a *citation à l'order du jour* — and that day is Judgement Day.[1]

From the mid-sixteenth century onward, the worldview that has come to dominate in those societies that draw their heritage from Western Europe is a secular one. With figures like Thomas Hobbes and John Locke, the view of society organized around secular civil laws began to surpass previous religious understandings of society as bound by natural laws and subject to salvation history. In the nineteenth century, thinkers like Karl Marx and Max Weber postulated that the process of "secularization," i.e., the continued modernization and rationalization of society, would continue in such a way that religious viewpoints would lose all authority, leading to

---

1. Benjamin, *Illuminations*, 254.

a general "disenchantment" of society. The values that were grounded in a religious view of the world would either lose all force or would retreat into the recesses of individual conviction; in any case, they would no longer hold sway over the public mindset. A linear account of historical progress and a secular understanding of civil society would come to replace the *anciens regimes* of European civilization.

Whether the process secularization portended by the prophets of disenchantment has run its course as intended (and there is reason to believe that things are more complicated than initially postulated), it is difficult to deny that the secular view of history and society has become the dominant paradigm, at least in those societies that we have come to call "The West." While the religionists continue to decry the forces of irreligion and to hold the trenches against the onslaught of secularism, there is little doubt that secularism is, at least for the time being, winning the battle. Whether the battle is won, however, is an open question; the religious continues to infiltrate the secular in some rather unexpected places, places that will be a principle concern of this chapter.

Whether the rising dominance of secularism is a good thing is, equally, an open question. In some ways, the answer must certainly be "yes:" The emergence of civil society has forced us to recognize the reality, indeed the value, of cultural pluralism. Civil society has surely opened previously unimaginable avenues for self-expression and self-determination. But the gains come at a cost: it is hard to dispute the value of a yearning for deep bonds of community, or the human desire for transcendence over the all-to-human condition of vulnerability and mortality, or the hope for deliverance from undeniable evil, all of which were, and are, the hallmarks of the religious viewpoint. More problematic still is the question of whether the perceived gains that accompany secular society are real or illusory. Does civil society really open avenues for self-expression and self-determination, or does it constitute, instead, a more pernicious form of power/knowledge and biopolitical manipulation precisely because it institutes itself under cover of social gains, as Michel Foucault would have us believe?[2] While I am inclined to see the gains of civil society as real, contemporary existence in the United States in the era of the "war on terror" forces me to question the degree to which these gains do indeed have a dark underside and the degree to which they are open to political manipulation. The complexities of contemporary secular society, and the possibilities for sustainable community within it, need to be addressed.

---

2. Foucault, *The Birth of Biopolitics*.

Giorgio Agamben has characterized contemporary existence as one that has reduced human existence to the condition of "bare life." The importance of this claim only comes to the surface in relation to another type of existing that Agamben calls "form-of-life:"

> A life that cannot be separated from its form is a life for which what is at stake in its way of living is living itself. . . . It defines a life—human life— in which the single ways, acts, and processes of living are never merely *facts* but always and above all *possibilities* of life, always and above all power. Each behavior and each form of human living is never prescribed by a specific biological vocation, nor is it assigned by whatever necessity; instead, no matter how customary, repeated, and socially compulsory, it always retains the character of a possibility; that is, it always puts at stake living itself. That is why human beings—as being of power who can do or not do, succeed or fail, lose themselves or find themselves—are the only beings for whom happiness is always at stake in their living, the only beings whose life is irremediably and painfully assigned to happiness. But this immediately constitutes the form-of-life as a political life.[3]

However, "Power as we know it," Agamben continues, "always founds itself — in the last instance — on the separation of a sphere of naked life from the context of forms of life."[4] In the contemporary period, i.e., that period at least since the end of World War I, the conception of existence, at least as it pertains to political existence, has been reduced to the brute facticity of biological life. In other words, those aspects of human life that we judge to be most important have become virtually inconceivable in and fundamentally dangerous to the functions of sovereign power in modern nation-states. The place where this exercise of sovereign power over bare life became most apparent, according to Agamben, was the Nazi extermination camp.[5] While the camp is the place where the reduction of human life to bare existence is manifest in its most extreme form, Agamben argues that these are, in less extreme and hence more pernicious form, the conditions in which we have come to exist.

We may take issue with the bleak, dystopic terms of Agamben's description of the contemporary political situation, but it is difficult not to recognize the seeds of truth in it in the age of the war on terror. The implacable reality of Guantanamo Bay forces us to question how far away we are

---

3. Agamben, *Means without Ends*, 3.
4. Ibid.
5. See, Agamben's *Homo Sacer* and *Remnants of Auschwitz*.

from the Nazi *Lager*. A fundamental problem for Agamben is that there is no single agency or identity that we can look to to stem the tide of sovereign infringement on life. Rather, we are faced with a state apparatus and a regime of governmentality whose very existence rests on the restriction of forms-of-life. The apparatus has taken on a life of its own such that there is no one to hold accountable.

The focus of this chapter is Walter Benjamin's materialist-messianic conception of time and the attending idea of a redeemed history. I am concerned with what this materialist-messianic ideal—as it is articulated in Benjamin's writings, and picked up in Agamben's political philosophy—might offer to possible conceptions of community. Throughout his writings, Agamben speaks of a "coming community" that will stand up to political oppression, a political community not grounded in ideals of political sovereignty. However, it is difficult to locate the contours of this community as it appears in Agamben's thought. It seems to represent a set of vague possibilities, some utopian ideal without specific form. What I hope to do here is shed some light on this coming community as it is configured through Agamben's engagement with materialist forms of messianism. Indeed, the place where the coming community appears to take on some material form is in Agamben's interpretation of the Pauline conception of the messianic community.

In exploring this coming community and the redeemed present it makes possible, I will begin by exploring Benjamin's historical materialist attack on historicism. In these writings Benjamin introduces a dimension of messianism into the historical-political project of humanity. From here, I will move to examine the political thought of Carl Schmitt, the figure with and against whom Benjamin articulates the political dimensions of his materialist messianism. Schmitt famously defined political sovereignty in terms of the exception. Schmitt's ideas became an important foil for Benjamin—and have remained so for Agamben—because, Benjamin argued, the exception had become the rule in the politics of early twentieth century Europe. After dealing with Schmitt's thought, I will move to discuss Benjamin's articulation of a "divine violence" and the materialist-messianic ideal that attends it. I will conclude by addressing the influence of Benjamin's thought on Agamben's notion of the coming community.

HISTORICISM AND THE HISTORICAL MATERIALIST ATTACK

Benjamin has typically been treated as a literary critic and theorist of aesthetics. But, as we will see, his aesthetic and literary explorations harbor powerful political views. Benjamin's sympathies with Marxism are well known, as are his acquaintances with many of the luminaries of what has come to be called "The Frankfurt School" of political philosophy. Nonetheless, political philosophers have tended to shy away from his thought. As James Martell indicates, ". . . Benjamin's work emerges as lying at the uneasy intersection between the political and the theological, between a world of action and world of faith and supernatural (or messianic) forces. In refusing to resolve that conflict (indeed, irresolution being the basis of the connection between the theological and the political), it seems that Benjamin is often seen as falling between these two stools; he's too mystical for the Marxists and too Marxist for the mystics."[6] What I hope to do in these initial sections is give some credence to the notion that Benjamin has some profound things to say to our contemporary political situation. I start by addressing his "Theses on the Philosophy of History."

Advocating a materialist dialectical account of history, Walter Benjamin criticized a view of history that he designated "historicism." The historicist understanding views history as a sequence of epic events stretched across a homogenous, empty time bound by forces of cause and effect. For Benjamin, this view was deeply troubling because it codified a process of violence and "barbarism" that found its most profound realization in Fascism. The historicist's view of history is one that empathizes with the victors and, as such, one that legitimizes a history of "progress" that comes at the expense of the defeated. The historical materialist's job is to "blow apart" this conception of history in the interest of a revolutionary awakening.[7] He "dissociates himself from it as far as possible. He regards it as his task to brush history against the grain."[8]

Blowing apart the historicist's viewpoint reveals that history is not a string of events stretched across homogeneous time, but a structure within which the materialist, from time to time, can come to occupy moments that lend perspective on the structure itself: "History is the subject of a structure whose site is not homogeneous, empty time, but time filled by the presence

---

6. Martell, "Taking Benjamin Seriously as a Political Thinker," 298.
7. Benjamin, *Selected Writings, Volume 4*.
8. Benjamin, *Illuminations*, 256–57.

of the now [*Jetztziet*]."⁹ In coming to occupy this *Jetztzeit*, this monadic "time of the now," the materialist comes to recognize history, not as the overpowering unfolding of fate, but as a set of possibilities for acting: "A historian who takes this as his point of departure stops telling the sequence of events like the beads of a rosary. Instead, he grasps the constellation which his own era has formed with a definite earlier one. Thus, he establishes a conception of the present as the 'time of the now' which is shot through with chips of Messianic time."¹⁰

This introduction of the messianic into an ostensibly Marxist-materialist account of history is jarring to say the least. In some sense, Benjamin's thought travels along two trajectories, a historical-political one informed by Marxism and a theological one informed by Jewish messianism. These two trajectories are difficult to reconcile, which has led to endless debate over Benjamin's project. Warren S. Goldstein has chronicled the debate over the compatibility of Marxism and messianism in Benjamin's work indicating two basic positions: One side argues that Marxism and messianism are incompatible; as such, Benjamin's project is doomed to failure because it is contradictory or simply incoherent. The other side argues that the two are not necessarily incompatible, that Marxism and messianism function as mutual correctives in Benjamin's thought. Goldstein argues that this debate "poses the wrong question. What is important is not whether Messianism and Marxism are compatible but the relationship between two interrelated but opposed philosophies of history."¹¹ Goldstein argues that the participants in the debate do not take time to recognize the theoretical context for the work of Marxism and messianism in Benjamin's thought: secularism. Tracing the intellectual connections between Benjamin and Ernst Bloch, Goldstein argues that both offer a sort of inverse dialectic between the sacred and the profane: "The messianic and profane move dialectically in two opposite directions. Both forces through acting increase the intensity of the one moving in the opposite direction. While they are opposed, they are mutually reinforcing; the profane assists in the coming of the Messianic kingdom. The messianic and profane have a contradictory relation, the resolution of which is the kingdom of heaven on earth."¹² Moving in inverse directions, Marxism and messianism aim for the restoration of a lost Eden: the restoration of paradise before the expulsion (messianism) and the reestablishment of a primordial communism (Marxism). Both are alterna-

---

9. Ibid., 261.
10. Benjamin, *Illuminations*, 263.
11. Goldstein, "Messianism and Marxism," 247.
12. Ibid., 248.

tive, and opposing, visions of a heaven on earth, one representing the culmination of the historical process (Marxism), the other its consummation (messianism). In this sense, Marxism represents a secularized version of messianism, but one that remains forever opposed to it.

Goldstein argues that for both Benjamin and Bloch, the dialectic remains tensive and unresolved. In this sense, the inverse dialectical account of secularization highlights the contradictory nature of secularization itself.[13] I will argue that this inverse, unresolved dialectic is key to understanding the role that messianism plays for Benjamin in the political-historical realm, and it becomes a marker for locating the coming community in Agamben. For now, however, it is necessary to move from the realm of history to the realm of politics.

THE EXCEPTION AND THE RULE

"Sovereign is he who decides on the exception."[14] With these words, Carl Schmitt begins his *Political Theology*. To understand the significance of Schmitt's definition of sovereignty, it is necessary to parse out what this sentence means, beginning with the idea of the exception. "The exception," Schmitt argues, "which is not codified in the existing legal order, can at best be characterized as a case of extreme peril, a danger to the existence of the state, or the like. But it cannot be circumscribed factually and made to conform to a preformed law."[15] The state of exception is, therefore, represented in the decision to suspend the legal order in light of a situation of emergency that threatens the continued existence of the state. As such, the state of exception exists as an ambiguous state, a suspension of the legal order—the legislature, the judiciary, the constitution—in the interests of preserving it.

This account of the exception suggests that it is dependent on the legal order for its existence, but Schmitt argues precisely the opposite: "The rule proves nothing: the exception proves everything: It confirms not only the

---

13. "The contradictions of secularization are expressed in the dialectical relationship between the sacred and the profane realm—between Messianism and Marxism. One is the secularization of the other; they are dependent on each other but opposed to each other. The dialectical theory of secularization hopes in a resolution of this dialectical conflict. However the dialectic remains unresolved and therefore the contradictions need to be expressed. Benjamin and Bloch were not fusing Messianism and Marxism but expressing this contradictory relationship" (Goldstein, "Messianism and Marxism," 248–49).

14. Schmitt, *Political Theology*, 5.

15. Ibid., 6.

rule but also its existence, which derives only from the exception."[16] The rule of law is unable to encompass the state of exception because of its unpredictability; rather the exception proves the rule by presenting its boundary and limit. Indeed, the attempt to make the rule the criterion for the exception precisely undermines the possibility for an adequate understanding of political sovereignty. I quote Schmitt at length:

> It is precisely the exception that makes relevant the subject of sovereignty, that is the whole question of sovereignty. The precise details of an emergency cannot be anticipated, nor can one spell out what may take place in such a case, especially when it is truly a matter of an extreme emergency and of how it is to be eliminated. The precondition as well as the content of jurisdictional competence in such a case must necessarily be unlimited. From the liberal constitutional point of view, there would be no jurisdictional competence at all. The most guidance the constitution can provide is to indicate who can act in such a case. If such action is not subject to controls, if it is not hampered in some way by checks and balances, as in a liberal constitution, then it is clear who the sovereign is. He decides whether there is an extreme emergency as well as what must be done to eliminate it. Although he stands outside the normally valid legal system, he nevertheless belongs to it, for it is he who must decide whether the constitution needs to be suspended in its entirety. All tendencies of modern constitutional development point toward eliminating the sovereign in this sense.[17]

Thus, Schmitt's account of political sovereignty is one that defines it entirely against liberal constitutional government; the attempt to define the state within the bounds of the rule of law undermines the very possibility of an account of sovereign political action.[18]

Schmitt argues, "All significant concepts of the modern theory of the state are secularized theological concepts not only because of their historical development—in which they were transferred from theology to the theory of state, whereby, for example, the omnipotent God became the omnipotent lawgiver—but also because of their systematic structure, the recognition of which is necessary for a sociological consideration of these concepts."[19] Hence, his philosophy of sovereignty is a "political theology." Within the po-

---

16. *Ibid.*, 13.
17. *Ibid.*, 6–7.
18. See Schmitt, *The Crisis of Parliamentary Democracy*.
19. Schmitt, *Political Theology*, 36.

litical order, the exception holds a place analogous to the miracle in relation to the natural order, i.e., the suspension of the natural order upon which the entirety of creation depends. The sovereign holds a place within the political order analogous to God with respect to the natural order—upon him the entire political order depends for its very continuity. The sovereign is not bound to the political order even though he remains a part of it.[20] The whole rule of law depends on the event, the exception, that signals its suspension and on the sovereign decision concerning the exception, just as the created order depends on the miraculous intervention of the deity.

Roughly contemporary with Schmitt's *Political Theology*, Benjamin's "Critique of Violence" treats the means by which the state maintains the legal order. For Benjamin, violence, *Gewalt*, is the means for such preservation. The critique is a rich and complicated text that defies easy explanation, and I will forgo a complete examination. I will focus on those portions that foreground Benjamin's engagement with Schmitt's thought. Central here are the distinctions Benjamin draws between legitimate, or sanctioned, violence and illegitimate, or unsanctioned, violence, and between law-preserving and law-making violence.[21]

For Benjamin, violence always, or nearly always, serves as a means to accomplish certain ends. The fundamental purpose for a critique of violence then is to locate the criteria by which any violent action can be judged legitimate or illegitimate, or the conditions for the legitimacy of violence. Two possibilities present themselves: from the perspective of natural law, the means are sanctioned if the ends they seek are just. But, given that the justness of ends lies, as an absolute standard, outside the criterion of legality, the question of the legitimacy or illegitimacy of specific means is ultimately closed to natural law theory. Instead, Benjamin mounts his critique from the perspective of positive law which concerns itself specifically with the question of sanctioned means. He explains:

> [T]he central place is given to the question of the justification of certain means that constitute violence. Principles of natural

20. Ibid., 36, 46.

21. Those familiar with Benjamin's corpus will recognize that I am treating his specific works out of chronology. "Critique of Violence" is one of his very earliest essays; "Theses on the Philosophy of History" is one of his last. In this sense, justifiably or unjustifiably, I am treating the messianic somewhat isomorphically as a vector that runs across his project, however much the concept may develop over the course of it. Likewise, I am presenting his and Schmitt's political theologies as more static than is really justified. For purposes of space and focus, I have chosen to forgo a discussion of how each thinker's position developed in response to the other. For a detailed treatment of this development see de Wilde, "Meeting Opposites."

> law cannot decide this question, but can only lead to bottomless casuistry. For if positive law is blind to the absoluteness of ends, natural law is equally so to the contingency of means. On the other hand, the positive theory of law is acceptable as a hypothetical basis at the outset of this study, because it undertakes a fundamental distinction between kinds of violence independently of cases of their application. This distinction is between historically acknowledged, so-called sanctioned violence, and unsanctioned violence. . . . The question that concerns us is, what light is thrown on the nature of violence by the fact that such a criterion or distinction can be applied to it at all, or in other words, what is the meaning of this distinction?[22]

From this perspective, violence is legitimate so long as it serves ends that are themselves defined by the legal order, and the ultimate end of the legal order is its own preservation.

If such is the criterion upon which a critique of violence is begun, Benjamin continues, the state must reserve for itself a monopoly on the use of legitimate violence, because violence in pursuit of purposes other than the preservation of the state is, by definition, illegitimate: "[T]he law's interest in a monopoly of violence vis-à-vis individuals is not explained by the intention of preserving legal ends but, rather, by that of preserving the law itself; that violence, when not in the hands of the law, threatens it not by the ends that it may pursue but by its mere existence outside the law."[23] In nearly all cases, therefore, the legitimate use of violence is the sole province of the state. As such, from the perspective of positive law, legitimate violence takes two principle forms: law-making violence and law-preserving violence.

Law-making violence represents that use of force that serves to initially set the legal order in place. The paramount example of this form of violence is, for Benjamin, military violence. While military violence may initially be engaged for natural, i.e., extra-legal, purposes—for example, control of territories and resources—military victory sets the conditions for a new legal order. Benjamin explains that "in primitive conditions that know hardly the beginnings of constitutional relations, and even in cases where the victor has established himself in invulnerable possession, a peace ceremony is entirely necessary. . . . This sanction consists precisely in recognizing the new conditions as a new 'law,' quite regardless of whether they need *de facto*

---

22. Benjamin, *Reflections*, 279.
23. Ibid., 281.

any guarantee of their continuation."[24] The peace treaty binds victor and vanquished alike to conditions that limit action.

Law-preserving violence is waged by the state apparatus in the maintenance of conditions that define the law. The notion that the law is preserved through non-violent means is ruled out by Benjamin. Whether conceived in terms of a mythical social contract or in terms of constitutional government, the existence of law introduces into human existence a violence that compels individuals act within the bounds of law.[25] At this point, Benjamin's critique of violence seems to echo Schmitt's concerns about the constitutional undermining of political sovereignty, and here we find opportunity to address Schmitt's decision on the exception from the angle of violence.

On Schmitt's view, the sovereign is he who holds the monopoly on the legitimate use of violence, and the decision on the exception is the most fundamental prerogative of that monopoly. The exception then represents the principle exercise of the sovereign's law-preserving violence, but an odd sort of preservation it is. In the exception, the sovereign power preserves the law by suspending it. At this point, however, it becomes difficult to distinguish law-preserving violence from law-making violence. Schmitt's theory of sovereignty comes to resemble another type of violence that Benjamin calls police violence:

> [I]n this authority the separation of lawmaking and law-preserving violence is suspended. If the first is required to prove its worth in victory, the second is subject to the restriction that it may not set itself new ends. Police violence is emancipated from both conditions. It is lawmaking, for its characteristic function is not the promulgation of the laws but the assertion of legal claims for any decree, and law-preserving, because it is at the disposal of these ends. The assertion that the ends of police violence are always identical or even connected to those of general law is entirely untrue. Rather, the 'law' of the police really marks the point at which the state, whether from impotence or because of the immanent connections within any legal system, can no

---

24. Benjamin, *Reflections*, 283.

25. "When the consciousness of the latent presence of violence in a legal institution disappears, the institution falls into decay. In our time, parliaments provide an example of this. They offer the familiar, woeful spectacle because they have not remained conscious of the revolutionary forces to which they owe their existence. Accordingly, in Germany in particular, the last manifestation of such forces bore no fruit for parliaments. They lack the sense that a lawmaking violence is represented by themselves; no wonder that they cannot achieve decrees worthy of this violence, but cultivate in compromise a supposedly nonviolent manner of dealing with political affairs" (ibid., 288).

longer guarantee through the legal system the empirical ends that it desires at any price to attain.[26]

This power becomes most ignominious, according to Benjamin, in situations where the legislative and executive authorities are united in the person of the sovereign. Thus, the sovereign power that rests most basically in the decision on the exception represents the place where the line between law-making and law-preserving is blurred, the place where the exception and the rule become indistinguishable.

This state of indistinction between exception and rule is a central concern of Agamben. Addressing specifically Schmitt's account of the sovereign exception, Agamben states:

> In our discussion of the state of exception, we have encountered numerous examples of this confusion between acts of executive power and acts of legislative power; indeed, as we have seen, such a confusion defines one of the essential characteristics of the state of exception. . . . But from a technical standpoint the specific contribution of the state of exception is less the confusion of powers . . . than it is the separation of a 'force of law' from the law. It defines a 'state of law' in which, on the one hand, the norm is in force [*vige*] but is not applied (it has no 'force' [*forza*]) and, on the other, acts that do not have the value [*valore*] of law acquire its 'force.' . . . The state of exception is an anomic space in which what is at stake is a force of law without law (which should be written as force-of-~~law~~. Such a 'force-of-~~law~~,' in which potentiality and act are radically separated, is certainly something like a mystical element, or rather a *fictio* by means of which law seeks to annex anomie itself.[27]

The threat is not just the confusion of powers, but the indistinction of norm and exception that allows it to happen. The threat is that the state of exception might, perhaps has, become the rule. Benjamin, witnessing the rise of National Socialism in Germany, believed the exception had become the rule. For Agamben, writing in the shadow of an expanding executive power, the indistinction of a rule of law and a state of exception constantly looms. This point marks the place of divergence between Schmitt's political philosophy and those of Benjamin and Agamben. While Schmitt defends the right of sovereign power, Benjamin and Agamben look for possibilities of emancipation from sovereign authority over bare existence. Here we turn

26. Ibid., 286–87.
27. Agamben, *State of Exception*, 38–39.

to Benjamin's articulation of another distinction, that between mythical violence and divine violence.

Concluding the "Critique of Violence," Benjamin shifts levels of inquiry, treating violence no longer as a means to an end, but as a manifestation of power. As a manifestation of power, Benjamin describes law-making violence, and in relation to it law-preserving power, as aspects of mythical violence. The figures to which Benjamin turns to articulate the idea of mythical violence are Niobe and Prometheus; Niobe and Prometheus are stricken by the gods, not because they have broken the law, but because they have defied fate. This defiance leads to punishment, but not punishment under the law; indeed, the punishment meted out is itself the announcement and instantiation of the law: "The legend of Niobe contains an outstanding example of this. True it might appear that the action of Apollo and Artemis is only a punishment. But their violence establishes a law far more that it punishes for the infringement of one already existing. Niobe's arrogance calls down fate upon itself not because her arrogance offends against the law but because it challenges fate—to a fight in which fate must triumph, and can bring to light a law only in its triumph."[28] In this sense, the law imposes itself as fate, in the pronouncement of a guilt that preexists law.

The law presupposes guilt and demands retribution for the offense, whether the individual recognizes the offense or not. Thus, the law, in the form of mythical violence, pronounces guilt like a fate on the human condition. But, in so doing, mythical violence misses the better part of the human; it reduces human life to mere life:

> Law condemns, not to punishment but to guilt. Fate is the guilt context of the living. It corresponds to the natural condition of the living, that illusion not yet wholly dispelled from which man is so far removed that, under its rule, he was never wholly immersed in it, but only invisible in his best part. It is not therefore really man who has fate; rather the subject of fate is indeterminable. The judge can perceive fate wherever he pleases; with every judgement he must blindly dictate fate. It is never man but only the life in him that it strikes—the part involved in natural guilt and misfortune by virtue of illusion.... The guilt context is temporal in a totally inauthentic way, very different in its kind and measure from the time of redemption, or of music, or of truth.[29]

Fate poses human existence in terms of an inexorable guilt, as a fallen existence. As such, fate is the context for the imposition of law. In this way,

28. Benjamin, *Reflections*, 294.
29. Ibid., 308.

Benjamin's critique of legal, i.e, mythical, violence meets up with his criticism of historicism. Just as the historicist conceives history as the inevitable unfolding of historical progress driven by the epic event, so law imposes guilt like a fate upon human existence. Indeed, law becomes the avenue for historical progress, the means to the end of progress; law is the political face of historical progress. Benjamin defines a more authentic human temporality, in opposition to fate, in terms of "character."

If fate represents the imposition of an external order on human time and action, character preserves the active dimension of human life and temporality: "No definition of the external world can disregard the limits set by the concept of the active man. Between the active man and the external world all is interaction, their spheres of action interpenetrate; no matter how different their conceptions may be, their concepts are inseparable."[30] Character expresses the possibility of a redeemed existence, a human life not bound by guilt and law. This possibility of redeemed existence lead Benjamin to posit, in "Critique of Violence," the notion of a divine violence in opposition to mythical violence.

> Far from inaugurating a purer sphere, the mythical manifestation of immediate violence shows itself fundamentally identical with all legal violence, and turns suspicion concerning the latter into certainty of the perniciousness of its historical function, the destruction of which thus becomes obligatory. This very task of destruction poses again, in the last resort, the question of a pure immediate violence that might be able to call a halt to mythical violence. Just as in all spheres God opposes myth, mythical violence is confronted by the divine. And the latter constitutes its antithesis in all respects. If mythical violence is lawmaking, divine violence is law-destroying; if the former sets boundaries, the latter boundlessly destroys them; if mythical violence brings at once guilt and retribution, divine power only expiates; if the former is bloody, the latter is lethal without spilling blood. . . . Mythical violence is bloody power over mere life for its own sake, divine violence pure power over all life for the sake of the living. The first demands sacrifice, the second accepts it.[31]

These passages are notoriously difficult to interpret. Placed in the context of the distinction between fate and character, we might suggest that divine violence strikes at the forces that reduce human existence to an object of fate. If character designates authentic human existence, that aspect of

30. Ibid., 305.
31. Ibid., 296–97.

human action and interaction that seeks to affect the external order, mythical violence reduces human life to passivity in the face of the external order. As Judith Butler indicates, "Divine violence does not strike at the body or the organic life of the individual, but at the subject who is formed by law. It purifies the guilty, not of guilt, but of its immersion in law and thus dissolves the bonds of accountability that follow from the rule of law itself."[32] If the law dictates fate, divine power is the force that crushes fate "for the sake of the living," i.e., that active human life preserved in character. Mythical violence inaugurates the imposition of fate and law; divine violence is the immediate destruction of law that inaugurates the possibility of a redeemed history and a redeemed humanity. This interpretation seems to be confirmed by Benjamin's desire to distinguish between "Man" and "mere life."[33] Human existence is not defined by its mere existence, but by a dimension of transcendence, a capacity to rise above brute facticity via self-determination and transformation of the forces of the external order on it. I think it paramount to recognize this distinction as a precursor to Agamben's distinction between form-of-life and bare life.

The context within which Benjamin introduces the distinction between mythical and divine violence is his discussion of Georges Sorel's analysis of the proletarian general strike. Unlike the political general strike, which strikes in the interest of changing existing working and living conditions but not the political order itself, the general strike, Benjamin argues, "takes place not in readiness to resume work following external concessions and this or that modification to working conditions, but in the determination to resume only a wholly transformed work, no longer enforced by the state, an upheaval that this kind of strike not so much causes as consummates. For this reason, the first of these undertakings [the political strike] is lawmaking but the second is anarchistic."[34] The proletarian strike seeks the dissolution of the entire existing legal order; it is anarchic.

Does Benjamin then see the proletarian general strike as a manifestation of divine violence? Butler seems to suggest so. Benjamin indexes divine violence to the commandment not to kill.[35] As such, we may be inclined

---

32. Butler, "Critique, Coercion, and Sacred Life,'" 211.

33. "Man cannot, at any price, be said to coincide with the mere life in him, no more than with any other of his conditions and qualities, not even with the uniqueness of his bodily person. However sacred man is (or the life in him that is identically present in earthly life, death, and afterlife), there is no sacredness in his condition, in his bodily life vulnerable to injury by his fellow men" (Benjamin, *Reflections*, 299).

34. Benjamin, *Reflections*, 291–92.

35. "The premise of such an extension of pure or divine power is sure to provoke, particularly today, the most violent reactions, and to be countered by the argument that

to see the general strike as the genesis of divine destruction of the legal order. The strike lives up to its bloodless nature so long as it attends to the commandment. Butler concludes:

> For Benjamin, violence outside of positive law is figured as at once revolutionary and divine—it is, in his terms pure, immediate, unalloyed. It borrows from the language in which Benjamin describes the general strike, the strike that brings an entire legal system to its knees. . . . In this sense, destruction is at once anarchistic moment in which the appropriation of the commandment takes place *and* the strike against the political legal system that shackles its subjects in lifeless guilt. It is also *messianic* in a rather precise sense.[36]

If I understand her argument correctly, Butler poses divine messianic power as the undercurrent that drives the revolutionary general strike; anarchistic striving and messianic power coalesce in the revolutionary act. But, I think this is too easy a reading.

In "Theologico-Political Fragment," Benjamin claims, "Only the Messiah himself consummates all history, in the sense that he alone redeems, completes, creates all relation to the Messianic. For this reason nothing historical can relate itself on its own account to anything Messianic. . . . From the standpoint of history it is not the goal but the end."[37] To the extent that the general strike remains an historical revolutionary act with the goal of a new history, therefore, it cannot itself *be* messianic, at least not in a pure sense. Recall Goldstein's idea that the sacred and the profane exist in an unresolved, inverse dialectical relation in Benjamin's thought. If such is the case, then the revolutionary strike and messianic consummation are both related and opposed to each other. While the strike is informed by latent messianic aspiration, it points in a different direction than the messianic, at the culmination of the historical process in the advent of the communist state, not the final redemption of humanity in the consummation of history. The strike is revolutionary, not redemptive; the proletariat is the revolutionary community, par excellence, but not the messianic community. What then would such a redeemed community look like?

---

taken to its logical conclusion it confers on men even lethal power against one another. This, however, cannot be conceded. For the question 'May I kill?' meets its irreducible answer in the commandment 'Thou shalt not kill.' this commandment precedes the deed, just as God was 'preventing' the deed" (ibid., 298).

36. Butler, "Critique, Coercion, and Sacred Life," 214–15 (original emphasis).
37. Benjamin, *Reflections*, 312.

THE "NOW OF RECOGNIZABILITY" AND THE REMNANT

Nothing historical can relate itself directly to anything Messianic. As such, no historical revolutionary action can achieve the final redemption toward which it aims; it will always fall short. Yet, Benjamin asserts: "The past carries with it a temporal index by which it is referred to redemption. . . . Like every generation that preceded us, we have been endowed with a *weak* Messianic power, a power to which the past has a claim."[38] While history remains forever separated from the messianic age, a weak messianic power touches history such that it is empowered with possibilities. This weak messianic potential is what the historical materialist seeks to uncover. Benjamin explains:

> Materialistic historiography . . . is based on a constructive principle. . . . The historical materialist approaches a historical subject only where he encounters it as a monad. In this structure he recognizes the sign of a Messianic cessation of happening, or, put differently, a revolutionary chance in the fight for the oppressed past. He takes cognizance of it in order to blast a specific era out of the homogenous course of history—blasting a specific life out of the era or a specific work out of the lifework. . . . The present, which, as a model of Messianic time, comprises the entire history of mankind in an enormous abridgment, coincides exactly with the stature which the history of mankind has in the universe.[39]

In this sense, weak messianic potential is tied to Benjamin's notion of *Jetztziet*, the time-of-the-now we encountered at the beginning of this chapter. Focusing on the affinity of this notion with another of Benjamin's, the idea of the dialectical image, which he articulates in *The Arcades Project*,[40] Samuel McCormick argues that the time-of-the-now presents a "passage out of time," a time out of time that shocks the historical materialist and her community with a momentary recognition of the past freed of its ideological baggage.[41] This momentary "now of recognizability" provides an image, a dialectical image, that provokes the community to relate itself dialectically to its own era, unleashing a "revolutionary chance." The risk, however, is that the moment may pass without reaching its potential. "Thus, if the

---

38. Benjamin, *Illuminations*, 254.
39. Ibid., 262–63.
40. Benjamin, *The Arcades Project*.
41. McCormick, "Neighbors and Citizens," 435.

historian has the task of wresting dialectical images from the continuum of history, the present has the responsibility to prevent them from returning to this continuum, disappearing irretrievability.... When the dialectical image slips through our grasp, retuning to a state of oblivion or advancing to a state of enshrinement, it always becomes a tool of *conformism*, reinstating the ideology of progress from which its sudden appearance once promised to redeem us."[42] It must be asserted, however, that for Benjamin, this revolutionary potential is a *weak* messianism. David Ferris explains: "What Benjamin offers is a messianic concept of history into which no Messiah steps ... Only the messianic is present and only then in a fragmentary form. With this distinction, Benjamin refuses a theological solution to a history because it would have neither political nor historical meaning. Where redemption of the past occurs, it must occur within history in order to have political significance."[43]

In *The Time that Remains*, Agamben argues that the secret figure at work behind Benjamin's writings on the messianic, especially those reflections in "Theses on the Philosophy of History," is St. Paul. The persuasiveness of this argument is a matter of debate, but my interest here is not to defend Agamben's argument; rather, I want to work in the opposite direction to show the influence of Benjamin's ideas on Agamben's own retrieval of Paul.[44] Indeed, Agamben presents the Pauline account of the messianic age in terms precisely parallel to Benjamin's *Jetztzeit*. He argues that positions that equate Paul's articulation of the messianic era with the end-times have missed the significance of the type of temporality at play in Paul's writings. "How should this time be represented?" Agamben asks.

> On first glance, things seem simple. First you have secular time, which Paul usually refers to as *chronos*, which spans from creation to the messianic event (for Paul, this is not the birth of Jesus, but his resurrection). Here, time contracts itself and begins to end. But this contracted time, which Paul refers to with the expression *ho nyn kairos*, "the time of the now," lasts until

42. Ibid., 439–40.
43. Ferris, *The Cambridge Introduction to Walter Benjamin*, 134.
44. Biblical scholars will surely chafe at much of Agamben's treatment of the Pauline corpus. Surely, it can be debated whether Paul is the theorist of time that Agamben makes him out to be. Certainly, Agamben wrests Paul's letters out of their historical context, so important for understanding what is going on in Paul's rhetoric. However, my interest is not whether Agamben offers an adequate treatment of the Pauline corpus; instead, I am concerned to show the importance of this treatment for Agamben's own political thought, particularly as it pertains to the notion of a "coming community." Thus, I will refrain from criticizing any possible unjustified liberties he takes in his analysis.

> the *parousia*, the full presence of the Messiah. The latter coincides with the Day of Wrath and the end of time (but remains indeterminate, even if it is imminent). Time explodes here; or rather, it implodes into the other eon, into eternity.... Messianic time is that part of secular time which undergoes an entirely transformative contraction.... In this schema, messianic time is presented as a part of the secular eon that constitutively exceeds *chronos* and as a part of eternity that exceeds the future eon, while being situated in the position of a remainder [*resto*] with regard to the division between the two eons.[45]

On Agamben's reading, Paul articulates a dimension of time outside of secular time, a temporal dimension where history bumps up against the *parousia* while remaining short of it. This temporality enacts a transformative effect on the members of the community that occupies this "time of the now," and this transformation locates, for Agamben, the truly messianic character of Paul's opposition to the law, particularly as this appears in the Letter to the Romans.

Recall that Paul's concern with the law of the covenant in Romans is the manner in which it serves to divide Jew from Gentile. In a series of complex moves, he attempts to show that righteousness is judged, not by conformity to law, but by the faith shown by Abraham and reinstituted by the death and resurrection of Jesus Christ. Important in this string of arguments is Paul's articulation of what constitutes a true Jew: "For a person is not a Jew who is one outwardly, nor is true circumcision something external. Rather, a person is a Jew who is one inwardly, and real circumcision is a matter of the heart—it is spiritual and not literal" (Rom. 2: 28–29). This distinction between outward and inward is instrumental in Paul's declaration that faith, not law, justifies; it is the same inward disposition of faith "in Christ" that redeems both Jew and Gentile. On Agamben's reading, Paul constructs a third category out of what appear to be logically exhaustive categories of Jew and non-Jew. Within the category of Jew, he enacts a further division: Jew according to the flesh, i.e., the one who is a Jew only outwardly, and Jew according to the spirit, the true Jew. Likewise, Paul divides the category of non-Jew: non-Jew according to the spirit, i.e., the non-Jew who lives by faith, and non-Jew according to the flesh, the true non-Jew. As such, according to Agamben, Paul, through a sort of "Apelles cut," creates a third category, a remnant, the "non-non-Jew:" "He who dwells in the law of the Messiah is the non-non-Jew.... What is significant in this 'division of divisions?' Why do I think that the Pauline aphorism is so important? First and

---

45. Agamben, *The Time that Remains*, 63–64.

foremost, because it forces us to think about the question of universal and particular in a completely new way, not only in logic, but also in ontology and politics."[46]

For Agamben, the dawning of messianic time institutes a new ontological-political condition operationalized through the messianic call. Recall Paul's assertion, in 1 Corinthians 7:24, that one called to Christ is to remain in the condition in which he was called. For Agamben the *kleisis*, the messianic vocation, performs a sort of double movement in the life of the one called. The call does not erase the factical condition of the one called: "For Paul, the *ekklesia*, the messianic community, is literally all *kleseis*, all messianic vocations. The messianic vocation does not, however, have any specific content; it is nothing but the repetition of these same factical or juridical conditions *in which* or *as which* we are called."[47] At the same time, however, the messianic vocation is the revocation of every existing vocation: "To be messianic, to live in the Messiah, signifies the expropriation of each and every juridical-factical property (circumcised/uncircumcised; free/slave; man/woman) under the form of the *as not*. This expropriation does not, however, found a new identity; the 'new creature' is none other than the use and messianic vocation of the old."[48] To occupy the "time of the now," to be called to the messianic vocation, is, for all intents and purposes, to occupy the same factical conditions one did before, but in such a way that those conditions have been made "inoperative," i.e., in such a way that they are no longer the ontological qualifiers, or at any rate not the only ones, that define one's existence. At this point, Agamben's retrieval of Paul comes exceedingly near to the coming community.

THE COMING COMMUNITY AND THE COMING POLITICS

Recall Carl Schmitt's claim that all significant political concepts are secularized theological concepts. At the end of this long itinerary, I am in a position to make the claim that Agamben's "coming community" is a secularized vision of the Pauline messianic community as he understands it. To some degree, Agamben points us in this direction himself: "If I had to mark out a political legacy in Paul's letters that was immediately traceable, I believe that the concept of the remnant would have to play a part. More specifically, it allows for a new perspective that dislodges our antiquated notions of a

46. Ibid., 51.
47. Ibid., 22–23.
48. Ibid., 26.

people, a democracy, however impossible it may be to completely renounce them. . . . This remnant is the figure, or the substantiality assumed by a people in a decisive moment, and as such is the only real political subject."[49] The coming community is, I would suggest, a remnant community, a community that refuses to be reduced to the qualities of the individuals that compose it.[50] Such a reduction is tantamount to the reduction of form-of-life to bare life in Agamben's parlance. As such, the coming community is opened to the potentialities that crystallize in the moment of recognizability.

At stake here is the recovery of a distinct type of being, "singularity," defined by a distinct ontological mode, *quodlibet* or "whatever:"

> The Whatever in question here relates to singularity not in its indifference with respect to a common property (to a concept, for example: being red, being French, being Muslim), but only in its being *such as it is*. Singularity is thus freed from the false dilemma that obliges knowledge to choose between the ineffability of the individual and the intelligibility of the universal. The intelligible, according to a beautiful expression of Levi ben Gershon (Gersonides), is neither a universal nor an individual included in a series, but rather 'singularity insofar as it is whatever singularity.' In this conception, such-and-such being is reclaimed from its having this or that property, which identifies it as belonging to this or that set, to this or that class (the reds, the French, the Muslims)—and it is reclaimed not for another class nor for the simple generic absence of any belonging, but for its being-*such*, for belonging itself. Thus being-*such*, which remains constantly hidden in the condition of belonging ('there is an *x* such that it belongs to *y*') and which is in no way a real predicate, comes to light. . . .[51]

Agamben argues that the orientation within which singularity comes most profoundly to light is love. The lover loves the beloved not for this or that quality it possesses, but precisely as the being that it is. Love does not cancel out those qualities, rather it recognizes the qualities as belonging to the beloved. But the lover does not love this or that quality; "The lover wants the loved one *with all its predicates*, its being such as it is. The lover

---

49. Ibid., 57.

50. Jessica Whyte has indicated the connections that exist between Agamben's *The Time that Remains* and his *Coming Community*. However, she has not detailed the structural relation between the Pauline remnant and the coming community I am attempting to highlight. See Whyte, "'A New Use of the Self.'"

51. Agamben, *The Coming Community*, 1–2.

desires the *as* only as it is *such*—this is the lover's particular fetishism."[52] The lover does not reduce the beloved to its qualities, rather the lover loves the beloved *as such*, with all its qualities. To focus on the qualities is to miss the being of the beloved.

The recovery of the "whatever-mode" of singularity opens the individual to potentiality. If specific qualities can be viewed as limiting aspects of existence, then the capacity of the being to *be* beyond, or above, or perhaps even in spite of those qualities, signals a capacity to be open to unforeseen potentialities; it is a life that cannot be separated from its form-of-life. "The passage from potentiality to act, from language to the word, from the common to the proper, comes about every time as a shuttling in both directions along a line of sparkling alternation on which common nature and singularity, potentiality and act change roles and interpenetrate. The being that is engendered on this line is whatever being, and the manner in which it passes from the common to the proper and from the proper to the common is called usage—or rather *ethos*."[53] Whatever being then resembles a political version of the Pauline messianic vocation. (Agamben's claim that love is what recognizes whatever singularity is further confirmation of this fact.) The one who is called remains in her station, qualified by the juridical-historical conditions that define her, but in such a way that those conditions are no longer decisive. Recall that, under that messianic call, those conditions are opened for a new, messianic use. The "new being" exists within yet outside the historical-juridical condition.

The coming community, then, is a community composed of singularities, beings who coalesce around a pure belonging without identifiable qualities. As such, on Agamben's view, the coming community exists fundamentally in opposition to the exercise of sovereign power over it. Recall that, for Agamben, sovereign power is posited on the reduction of human life to bare existence. The State is capable of conceiving individuals only as bodies, as objects to be manipulated and controlled. The recovery of singularity works against this drift, aiming to protect life in its form-of-life. Agamben concludes *The Coming Community* with the following statements:

> In the final instance, the State can recognize any claim for identity—even that of a State identity within the State (the recent history of relations between the State and terrorism is an eloquent confirmation of this fact). What the State cannot tolerate in any way, however, is that singularities form a community without affirming an identity, that humans co-belong without

52. Ibid., 2.
53. Ibid., 19.

> any representable condition of belonging (even in the form of a simple presupposition). . . . A being radically devoid of any representable identity would be absolutely irrelevant to the State. This is what, in our culture, the hypocritical dogma of the sacredness of life and the vacuous declarations of human rights are meant to hide. . . . Whatever singularity, which wants to appropriate belonging itself . . . and thus rejects all identity and every condition of belonging, is the principal enemy of the State. Wherever these singularities peacefully demonstrate their being in common there will be a Tiananmen, and, sooner or later, the tanks will appear.[54]

The coming community is a revolutionary community that defines itself dialectically against the historical forces in which it finds itself. It seeks the bloodless destruction of the force of law that threatens to reduce human life to bare existence.

That Benjamin exerts a profound influence on Agamben's thought is not a controversial claim; Agamben was the editor of the Italian translation of Benjamin's works, and his many references to Benjamin are ample evidence of the deep consonance between the two. That St. Paul is an influence is, perhaps, a more interesting finding. (Or, perhaps not, given the resurgence of interest in the apostle to the Gentiles among the continental philosophers.)

I have argued that Agamben's coming community represents a secularized version of the Pauline community as he understands it. On the face of it, this seems to suggest that Agamben moved from Paul to articulate a new kind of politics. In fact, the reverse is the case: ten years separate the publication of *La comunità che viene* and *Il tempo che resta*, the original Italian texts of *The Coming Community* and *The Time that Remains*. Given this chronology, we might suggest that Paul represents for Agamben a sort of dialectical image, a now of recognizability, against which the coming community breaks into view and receives some determinate form. As such, Pauline messianism represents for Agamben a moment of awakening that crystallizes a relation between a definite past as it appears to a specific present. The moment unleashes a weak messianic potential, a revolutionary chance for a coming politics and a hoped for redemption of the time in which we live.

---

54. Ibid., 85–86.

BIBLIOGRAPHY

Agamben, G. *The Coming Community*. Translated by M. Hardt. Minneapolis: University of Minnesota Press, 1993.

———. *Homo Sacer: Sovereign Power and Bare Life*. Translated by D. Heller-Roazen. Stanford: Stanford University Press, 1998.

———. *Means without Ends: Notes on Politics*. Translated by V. Benetti and C. Casarino. Minneapolis: University of Minnesota Press, 2000.

———. *Remnants of Auschwitz: The Witness and the Archive*. Translated by D. Heller-Roazen. New York: Zone, 1999.

———. *State of Exception*. Translated by Kevin Attell. Chicago: University of Chicago, 2005.

———. *The Time that Remains: A Commentary on the Letter to the Romans*. Translated by P. Dailey. Stanford: Stanford University Press, 2005.

Benjamin, W. *The Arcades Project*. Translated by H. Eiland and K. McLaughlin. Cambridge, MA: Harvard University Press, 1999.

———. *Illuminations*. Edited by H. Arendt. Translated by H. Zohn. New York: Schocken, 1969.

———. *Reflections: Essays, Aphorisms, Autobiographical Writings*. Edited by P. Demetz. Translated by E. Jephcott. New York: Harcourt Brace Jovanovich, 1978.

———. *Selected Writings, Volume 4, 1938–1940*. Edited by Howard Eiland and Michael W. Jennings. Translated by Edmund Jephcott et al. Cambridge, MA: Harvard University Press, 2003.

Butler, J. "Critique, Coercion, and Sacred Life in Benjamin's 'Critique of Violence.'" In *Political Theologies: Public Religions in a Post-Secular World*, edited by H. de Vries and L. E. Sullivan, 201–19. New York: Fordham University Press, 2006.

de Wilde, M. "Meeting Opposites: The Political Theologies of Walter Benjamin and Carl Schmitt." *Philosophy and Rhetoric* 44/4 (2011) 363–81.

Ferris, D. *The Cambridge Introduction to Walter Benjamin*. Cambridge: Cambrige University Press, 2008.

Foucault, M. *The Birth of Biopolitics: Lectures at the College de France, 1978–1979*. Edited by M. Senellart. Translated by G. Burchell. New York: Picador, 2008.

Goldstein, W. S. "Messianism and Marxism: Walter Benjamin and Ernst Bloch's Dialectical Theories of Secularism." *Critical Sociology* 27/2 (March 2001) 246–81.

Martell, J. "Taking Benjamin Seriously as a Political Thinker." *Philosophy and Rhetoric* 44/4 (2011) 297–308.

McCormick, S. "Neighbors and Citizens: Local Speakers in the Now of Their Recognizability." *Philosophy and Rhetoric* 44/4 (2011) 424–45.

Schmitt, C. *The Crisis of Parliamentary Democracy*. Translated by E. Kennedy. Studies in Contemporary German Social Thought. Cambridge, MA: MIT Press, 1985.

———. *Political Theology: Four Chapters on the Concept of Sovereignty*. Translated by G. Schwab. Studies in Contemporary German Social Thought. Chicago: University of Chicago Press, 2005.

Whyte, J. "'A New Use of the Self': Giorgio Agamben on the Coming Community." *Theory and Event* 13/1 (2010) 1–19.

12

No-Places for Sacred Communities
Hope and the Failure of *Fight Club*

—Daniel Boscaljon

In David Fincher's 1998 cult classic *Fight Club*, based on Chuck Palahniuk's 2005 novel, Edward Norton plays an anonymous protagonist lured away from a corporate life of khakis and power points by the charismatic proclamations of Brad Pitt's Tyler Durden. Durden's message responds to social conditions in the late twentieth and early twenty-first century, unmasking the twinned ideological frameworks supporting America: consumerism and religion. I base this assessment on Paul Ricoeur's discussion of the conservative nature of ideology, which "conserves, in the sense of making firm the human order that could be shattered by natural or historical forces, by external or internal disturbances."[1] The work of conservation occurs on three levels—integration, dissimulation, and domination—that maintains the originary spirit of a collective. Ricoeur writes, it is necessary "for a social group to give itself an image of itself, to represent and to realize itself. . . ."[2] This movement toward realization means that ideology "is always more than a *reflection*, it is always also a *justification* and *project*"[3] that eventually "operates behind our backs rather than appearing as a theme before our eyes."[4]

---

1. Ricoeur, *From Text to Action*, 318.
2. Ibid., 249.
3. Ibid., 250.
4. Ibid., 251.

The conservative form of union offered by ideologies emerges through the appearance of *dissimulation* and *domination* as modes that ensure that an initial moment of integrative unity is perpetuated into the future.[5]

Fight Club reveals how merely unmasking the dissimulations of the current dominant group without thinking through alternative models for social integration inadequately corrects the conservative function ideologies play, leading to new forms of dissimulation and domination instead of new possibilities for authentic living. Thus, in the story, Tyler Durden forms fight clubs—underground boxing groups—as an alternative to the religious and corporate culture he sees poisoning America. Members of fight clubs embrace their new collective identities, fed by pithy maxims that embrace criticisms of a society steeped in consumerist fantasies. Ultimately, both novel and movie reveal the inadequacy of Durden's group, as the "army" that emerges uses a corporate structure that undermines the group's explicit anarchist goals, ensnared by a desire to conserve its authentic original impulse. Focusing on how ideologies were concretized (dissimulation and domination), instead of on the conservative impulse that corrupts the positive possibilities of ideology, transformed Durden's army into a different version of the same.

Fight Club successfully and accurately denounces what is false and broken in society: more importantly, it illustrates how the work of ideologies obscures the possibility of finding community (not society) in the intimacy of shared pain instead of the transcendence of spiritual healing, a community that resists external influences (God, money, anarchy). In addition, both the book and its relatively faithful adaptation disclose how living in simple, unilateral opposition undermines the successful unworking of an ideological world. These components invite a theological reading that discloses how communities can more successfully create and perpetuate a non-symbolically mediated form of community capable of resisting the allure of society and ideology. In order to perform this work, I begin by discussing the dangers of grounding society on ideology, and the limitations of a hermeneutic of suspicion in confronting this danger. Building on *Fight Club*, I discuss the advantages of valuing *community* (based in a moment of shared finitude) over *society* (grounded on the illusion that finitude can be overcome), concluding this section by describing how hope permits communities to expand without becoming anchored in external mediating influences. I finally turn to describe the specific hopes available to the perpetuation of non-symbolically mediated communities before defining how making utopias, no-places, becomes the path to accomplishing the hope of

---

5. Ibid., 252–55.

more widespread communities capable of undermining the domination of ideology.

THE NATURE OF IDEOLOGY

Participation in a positive union with others, feeling that we are a part of a larger whole, is vital for human flourishing. Society meets this need by providing us with ways to see ourselves in terms of a dynamic collective: most social groupings operate through a principle of minimal exclusion, maximizing the number of those who can (or desire to) identify with a society. The standards for inclusion are moderated by those in a position of power: ideologies secretly supply the right for those in power to enforce their particular standards. As Ricoeur puts it, ideology bridges "the credibility gap of every system of authority" by supplying "a kind of overvalue or surplus value to the belief in the validity of authority such that the system of power may implement its claim to legitimacy."[6] Put otherwise, ideologies perform an invisible marriage of a particular value system with respect for an authority who guarantees the perpetuation of that ideology's illusion of givenness within the society. Those who desire inclusion into a society also implicitly accept the power structure that maintains that society. This shortcut, however, eliminates the option to believe: while ideology thereby ensures continuity within the social order, it does so by obviating the importance of faith. What is contingent is presented as absolute, relative values are transformed into normative goods. As a result of their conservative impulse, ideologies erase alternatives, including the option of believing in an alternative vision of the sacred that emerges within and grounds authentic community. As a result, ideologies erase the option of believing in another that grounds authentic community, perverting this moment of trust into a self-deceived mode of bad faith.

Ideologies clearly benefit society: assenting to an overarching ideology allows societies to become more than the sum of their parts, making a society more than a merely geographically proximate set of beings. Ideologies knit societies together by identifying and projecting similarities among individuals, offering a shared symbolic network and legitimizing the use of force (military or otherwise) to uphold the worth of this set of symbols. Ideologies remain anchored to the history of the society, and originate as a means of conserving its particular combination of values and goods, prescribing how right and wrong are defined and defended. Societies recognize themselves as participating with their progenitors through the intervention

6. Ibid., 320.

of ideology, even if social particularities differ radically from its origin point. These qualities are not bad in themselves, nor is it intrinsically wrong to unite with others through the addition of a third, symbolic entity: ideologies become problematic only through the conservative bent that seeks to prolong and universalize what was once local, particular, and personal.

Despite the advantages gained by generating a feeling of participation with a larger whole, the sacrifice of the moment of faith in community renders human connections within the social world shallow, empty, and fleeting. As *Fight Club* capably depicts through its protagonist, a man who gradually realizes that purchasing trendy goods does not generate satisfaction, eliminating authentic human connections results in despair. Alienated, dissatisfied with an upwardly mobile existence, the protagonist (an American version of the abstracted center of Tolstoy's Ivan Ilych) finds the fissures and flaws in a world that had appeared solid and whole. Feeling abandoned, he searches for those who suffer, hoping that pain will reveal meaning in life. His existential crisis discloses the credibility gap Ricoeur described: the protagonist no longer trusts the authorities who equate consumption with happiness. The protagonist experiences how suffering is more real, more true than the deceptive harmony promoted by ideology. *Fight Club* introduces audiences to despair as it reveals how hopes tied to ideologies are false, illusions instead of futures. The connections formed by seeking pain in a violent embrace of finitude feel more valid, both to the protagonist and to the audience: problematically, because faith still has no place, the characters are vulnerable to Durden's anarchic ideology, no better than what they had rejected. No matter what its content, ideologies mask the true foundation of authentic human relationships, and the resulting despair primes us to return to the false solace offered by ideology and society.

Beyond replacing the fragile difficulty of authentic human connection with an illusory assumption that we can appropriate identical identities as provided by the social matrix, ideologies also weaken authentic participation by promoting a drive toward knowledge, certainty and domination. We accept what societies manufacture as something given, as something "natural," and allow this shared sensibility to speak louder than the mysterious, awesome experiences of realizing (after the fact) that one has been united with a larger whole, a feeling of loss that lingers when witnesses of a moment of horror or participants in a work of beauty suddenly are returned to their individual lives from a prolonged moment of union. The corporate identity offered through the mediation of ideology is effective, but only by convincing humans to understand themselves as nothing more than abstracted quantities, interchangeable and functional. Enframed (to build on Heidegger's term), humans sink to the level of objects, able to be studied and manipulated without concern: such is the *telos* of a technoscientific or posthumanist utopia. This end produces claustrophobia: depriving reality of its unknowns results in a closed world that imprisons the members of the society who dwell within it.

Two of the major ideologies that have continued to structure and orient American society into the twenty-first century are capitalism and Christianity. Each takes a turn parading as "nationalism," circumscribing the choices that politicians make and justifying the use of power to reinforce the importance of each in establishing the historical social order. Problematically, using dissimulation and domination to conserve an originary moment allows those in power to use means or pursue ends that are contrary to the given values that they ostensibly preserve. Thus, the drive to profit led Wall Street to undermine the viability of the market and create widespread economic devastation, while the message of love preached by Christ becomes redacted into various validations of "traditional" beliefs. Even when they result in actions consistent with stated values, ideologies fail to acknowledge their incomplete nature—even when they operate in tandem with another ideology, each sees itself as independently sufficient to the creation of a social world. The illusion of totality provides a necessary buttress to the work of legitimation ideologies perform, a conservation of commonalities that promote the perpetuation of a certain social order, one that rests on the implicit exclusion of other differences.

Humans remain capable of identifying the actual spaces of the Real that infest the illusory completeness of ideological realms, witnessing and attending to occurrences of dissonance. Systematically discovering such spaces requires a hermeneutic of suspicion, although this stance of suspicion sunders us from the surrounding world, leading to a feeling of isolation that makes us especially susceptible to an ideology's insidious summons. Ricoeur argues that a hermeneutics of suspicion, following and building upon the nineteenth-century work of Marx, Nietzsche and Freud, plays an important role in unmasking the fraudulent pretense of ideologies and thereby opening the possibility of justice. Recognizing the human tendency to unmask one ideology only to replace it with another, Ricoeur adds that those undertaking this hermeneutical work must remain self-critical. *Fight Club* also discloses this danger, as the conclusion of the story shows how easily men, enlightened to the failings of Christianity and capitalism, embrace lives that look astonishingly similar to the corporate monotony they had "left behind."

Even if successful, a prolonged lifestyle predicated on undermining a particular ideology does not offer great benefits. Alienated from both the certainty and community that ideologies support, such extreme skepticism severs people from an ability to work jobs, pay taxes, or donate goods: lacking the solace provided by participating in a larger whole, such individuals are prone to despair. In other words, the space of absolute suspicion produces a lack of faith, and results in damage equivalent to what ideology creates. This manifestation of despair differs because it is created through circumstances generated by the desire for a more authentic truth than the impossible wholes and perfected totalities offered by ideologies. Absent an ideological structure, those who persevere in their resistance to ideological worlds might, at most, find others similarly dispossessed. Such gatherings, however, would be limited to a negative work that eschewed the promise of a positive union—a short lived solution, for false companionship feels better than enforced isolation. Participation in a positive union with others is necessary for true human flourishing.

THE SACRED DEPTHS OF ATHEIST RELIGIOUS COMMUNITIES

Fight Club has two parts: the first depicts the creation of fight clubs, where embracing pain allows men to accept the death of God. The second half focuses on "Project Mayhem," which attempts to destroy symbols of consumerism. The first part shows the development of community, forged in shared pain, sweat, and sacrifice: the second part shows the evolution of society, as members of "Project Mayhem" are melded with an ideological role that obeys the assignments of Tyler Durden. Having discussed why this anti-ideological stance falters, I turn now to discuss the value and shortcomings of the community discussed in the first portion of the story, emphasizing how the occurrence in a fight between the participants (and even, perhaps, the observers) grasps a sacred mediated neither by symbol nor by ideology.

This immediate sense of the sacred, gathered into shared finitude, preexists ideological or doctrinal discussions that ground communities centered on symbols—this quality makes possible thinking of an atheist religious community. Unlike post-religious communities whose antagonism ties them to tired symbolic forms, and unlike post-secular communities that desire to appropriate new symbols capable of reenchanting the world, an atheist religious community emerges immanently and in terms of an absolute sacred (making it religious) that operates indirectly, without symbolic mediation. My decision to refer to these groups as communities follows Jean-Luc Nancy's essay "The Inoperable Community," which distinguishes between the societies that rely on ideologies and the communities that do not. While a *society* requires an ideological structure (and work that reinforces and builds upon this structure), *communities* are born through the failure of this work. Communities emerge in a mutual acceptance of finitude, while societies sacrifice this promise of community by offering the hope that we can transcend our isolated natures through participation.[7] We *commune* at our limits, in our pain, through a speechless and unquantifiable event in which I, broken, am shared. Societies sustain us in the absence of this type of community, using ideologies to bridge over the gap that a lack of community forms, providing a mediated version of being-with others. The function of the mediation is to allow individuals to meet in a symbolic center instead of blurring the lines of their own individualities.

The occurrence of community requires that ideologies be interrupted through an absence of intentionality; similarly, the absolute, anonymous sacred emerges in a moment of sharing found in merging weakness, when we linger with our limitations. Nancy writes, "Community is the sacred . . . but the sacred stripped of the sacred. For the sacred—the separated, the set apart—no longer proves to be the haunting idea of an unattainable communion, but is rather made up of nothing other than the sharing of community."[8] We never truly lose this sacred, just as we never are fully rid of community, although these foundational moments are sublated and usurped by ideologies, which do not require us to exist at the raw edge of vulnerability. The sacrality of communities in *Fight Club* emerges through the shared passion and ecstatic sufferings of those fighting and bleeding, quivering and crying. Unlike the symbolically mediated experience of the sacred, where an escape from experiences of pain, loss, or despair is translated through words, the immanent sacred of community occurs in the communication of wounds. The direct and non-mediated presentation of the sacred in community occurs for the two in the center of the ring, and perhaps for those watching whose racing pulses makes the blood flow more swiftly from their recent wounds.

Experiences of existing within ecstatic communities of shared passion resemble, in some ways, that of dwelling within the silent spaces formed in the negation of ideological worlds. Both short-lived groups exist only for the moment intense enough to achieve the interruption of my singularity,

---

7. Nancy, *The Inoperative Community*. I prefer Nancy's account to that of *communitas* offered by Victor Turner (although I appreciate Turner's description of the fleeting nature of the event, and agree with his account of community as more primordial than society), because, with Nancy, I share a hope for human gatherings that come through the interruption of singularity at the point of finitude, not through a mediating external force outside. See Turner, *The Ritual Process*, 96–97.

8. Nancy, *The Inoperative Community*, 35.

of my self-consciousness.[9] Shaken after an experience of community, I come back to my senses, return to myself, recall the duties and obligations made meaningful by the social ideology that guides my self-understanding. Both liminal spaces require disrupting ideology and society, and rejecting the solace of transcendent promises: both emerge at the limits of finitude.

Although similar, the event of community differs from the experience of rejecting ideological worlds in a number of important ways. First, rejecting ideologies comprises an intentional choice (although it may arise from our despair when we grasp the illusory nature of social promises), while the experience of community grasps us intimately, without our consent: the first is active, the latter passive. Because rejecting ideologies requires intentionality, doing so permits me to retain a memory of the past and anticipation of the future—the intense experience of community leaves no remainder, thrusting me wholly into the immediacy of a prolonged moment. Second, rejecting ideologies tends to exacerbate our feeling of individuality and loneliness: we lose the goals and values offered by society without gaining a replacement. On the contrary, community is an unintended, momentary breach in singularity that wholly eliminates our individuality and sense of separateness, violating our assumptions about everyday possibilities. Rejecting society overcomes our vulnerability to ideological deceptions, while community exists through the communication of vulnerabilities in the experience of mingled finitude. In the isolated space between ideological worlds, all is certain because I have only myself: in community, nothing is certain because I cannot tell myself from another. In this way, communities maintain the advantages of distance from ideology and simultaneously reject the despair of loneliness, gathering the sacred into its presents.

HOPE AND THE PROMULGATION OF COMMUNITY

Relative to the desired good of human fulfillment, the only advantage that rejecting ideologies has over community is the possibility for intentionality and a sense of futurity. My goal is to demonstrate how *hope* allows community to retain its potency while gaining both intentionality and futurity as desirable qualities. According to Aquinas, hope is a good that is futural, arduous and possible. Within a social imaginary, hope manifests in utopic visions, through what Ricoeur refers to as the hermeneutics of affirmation (the complement of the skeptical hermeneutics that unmask ideologies). The self-consciously literary stylings of utopia generate vibrant social imaginaries by outlining the possibility of future goods within reach of the

---

9. Ibid., 19.

society—though difficult to attain.[10] Because the event of community lacks a symbolic grounding or self-conscious intentionality, it would seem that the hope of a community could not extend beyond simple repetition—where those who enjoy the dissolution of singularity desire its reoccurrence. Intentional in nature, hope would manifest between occurrences of community, an intentionality lost during times of community that one rediscovers only after-the-fact.

But other hopes remain possible, even though they, too, exist in the times between moments of community. First, I can hope for more endurance as I experience community, hope that I become more comfortable with community's temporary suspension of identity and society, hope to relish these moments as necessary goods instead of searching for swift escapes. This intentionality focuses on my own internal expectations, producing a positive work that nonetheless remains distant from social ideology. Seeking a comfort with community, I enable myself to enjoy and anticipate its reoccurrence, finding it possible to welcome that form of subjective dissolution. Although this is arduous, I know that community is both good and possible, and therefore I embrace it as a hope.

Second, I can hope that I become more able to share my vulnerabilities openly, more ready to embrace my finitude, more capable of interrupting the singularity of others, more prone to generating moments of community without focusing on the destruction of society. This hope allows me to intentionally promote spaces of community with those around me: familiar with myself, I can touch the world with the hope of piercing the barriers of flesh and history that seemingly separate me from others. I no longer attend to ideological illusions or promises; instead, I embrace my future in my embodied finitude and seek to share this miracle with others. Although *Fight Club* discusses this possibility as emerging through pain, and culture reduces intentional modes of sharing to the ecstasy of sexual experiences, I acknowledge the physical roots of each of my feelings and appropriate the potentialities of the range of my emotional palate.

Third, and most powerfully, I can hope that individuals within my society begin to value community, increasing its potential manifestations. This is the most arduous hope, depending on a shift among strangers that I will never meet, desiring an outcome that, finite, I cannot conceive of causing. Because societies remain supported by ideologies, it is neither likely that a society would desire the types of interruptions that community provokes, nor that an ideology would seek its own undoing. Nonetheless, I can hope that my work (within myself and among those I know) becomes replicated

---

10. Ricoeur, *From Text to Action*, 318–24.

beyond myself, as the society becomes increasingly able to appropriate its own finite foundation.

Although I cannot conceive of this hope becoming the foundation for an ideology, it remains possible for me to weave the social emphasis on experiencing community into a utopic narrative. Emphasizing confrontations with weakness would promote widespread social changes capable of altering the points at which people feel vulnerable. In other words, such a society would no longer accept the presence of poverty, homelessness, starvation, illness or physical abuse: instead, we would work to alleviate the systemic deprivation of these goods so that communities would emerge as shared loves or shared hopes. The finite bond that becomes obliterated in my being-with another through the occurrence of the immanent sacred would no longer occur at the level of subsistence (being hungry, sick, impoverished) but at the level of the struggle for shared values (definitions of justice, ethics, autonomy). Such ecstatic unions, born out of a shared struggle for a particular vision of the good, would yield communities that would still interrupt the singularity of my being in an unworking inoperativity, but the tenor of this community would be rooted in joy instead of terror. Although still disconcerting, such moments of shared joy are more enticing than encounters generated by raw suffering.

In *Fight Club*, a vision of a society freed from idle talk and corporate values led to the proliferation of a masculine community grounded in shared moments of pain, suffering and violence. Rightly suspicious of the consumerism and Christianity driving American ideology, these men transformed their community into a society whose rival ideology violently attacked symbolic targets representing the credit card industry. My utopic vision, sketched briefly here as a fragile hope, follows *Fight Club*'s suspicions. I recognize as perverse the versions of Christianity used to promote American ideology: its publicized manifestations promote xenophobia, self-righteousness and an intolerance toward differences. Additionally, I condemn ideologies that invite consumerism without considering the damage done to other humans and the environment. Methodologically, however, I take seriously Ricoeur's warning (echoed in *Fight Club*'s conclusion) that mere skepticism is inadequate to produce the changes that I desire. In discussing communities and hope, my goal is to provide a third way of allowing change, a change open to the recognition of a sacred that refuses to play an ideological role (going so far as to interrupt ideologies), and one that perpetuates communities that attend to and prioritize the needs and pains of others.

UTOPIA AS THE WORK OF HOPE FOR ATHEIST COMMUNITIES

Having identified how hope for a certain utopic vision might allow for the extension of community in terms of frequency and length and also how this vision would provide a resource for undermining the pernicious effect of ideology and society, I now turn to discuss how this vision might become localized and enacted in our world. In working toward this hope, in enacting utopia, I desire the proliferation of communities that provide the experience of a deep participation, inviting those involved to better resist the allure of a new ideology. Because communities are inevitably limited—occurring in new places, with different participants and for varying reasons—this utopia would never "exist" as a totalized or static whole. Instead, this utopic vision guarantees the incorporation of limitation, finitude and impermanence within a larger communal structure. I begin this section with a brief discussion of the spaces in *Fight Club* before turning to varieties of no-places, or utopias, that flourish in our world in contrast to what I advocate. I conclude by articulating one way to think through how the sacred uniquely manifests in this latter form of utopia.

The Spaces in Fight Club

Fight Club provides an instructive glance at two kinds of spaces and two different ways that the narrator frames these spaces for the audience. I understand *space* as an anonymous, dehumanized cultural creation conforming to reductionist modes of organization (valuing grids, efficiency), and *place* as an appropriated domain of personalized dwelling. In both the book and the movie, readers are introduced to the story through an abstract space (a skyscraper), whose symbolic importance for the society makes it a target for Tyler Durden's project of violent transformation. Both versions of the story move quickly from this initial scene to a flashback that takes place within the basement of a church, occupied for a few hours by a support group. Palahniuk provides duplicate examples of these kinds of spaces throughout the book: together, they reveal how the temporary transformation of ideologically conscripted spaces by communities provide a more authentic and satisfying moment of participation than a violent transformation of social space through the demolition of symbolic social structures.

The first and third chapters of the novel, and corresponding initial moments of the movie, locate readers within the abstract spaces that dominate late twentieth- and early twenty-first-century Western societies. The first scene is located in a socially significant symbolic space—the book calls it the Parker-Morris building, the tallest building in the world, while the movie refers to it as "1888 Century Park East," the center of a group of bank and credit card headquarter buildings whose destruction Durden believes will bring "economic collapse. One step closer to global equilibrium."[11] The movie's alteration of the book expands and clarifies Durden's hope for the destruction of space: creating the end of the world as we know it, feeling fine. Although the movie alters the book, framing the bombings as successful, this change confirms the irrelevance of such spaces: whether or not these spaces are destroyed, the audience understands that our society continues to be anchored in a variety of other less flashy, inconspicuous spaces. Spending time in unremarkable, banal spaces—not those with symbolic importance—frame, structure, and increase our willingness to participate in society.

These mundane spaces—airports and cubicles—recur throughout the story, and the movie provides an excellent visualization of Palahniuk's invocation of them. In Chapter Three, Palahniuk provides a series of place names that most Americans recognize: Air Harbor International, O'Hare, LaGuardia, Logan. These spaces are always the site of awakenings, "You wake up at Dulles . . . You wake up at Love Field . . . You wake up at SeaTac,"[12] but it performs a repetitive mantra that serves as a lullaby, emphasizing the similarity of all such spaces. The movie replicates this effect by having Edward Norton (who plays the protagonist) intone these proper names as a mantra: the audience sees him jolting awake in an airplane seat, and running through corridors filled with plastic chairs and fluorescent lights. This scene visually reproduces the protagonist describing insomnia in terms of distance, where everything is "a copy of a copy of a copy": in the movie, Fincher uses Uhls' script to show as "Other people make copies, all with Starbucks cups, sipping."[13] The point of both is to reveal how people become reduced to the functionality of their spaces, becoming mere duplicates. Palahniuk's novel emphasizes "switching" to disclose how this occurs, mixing a description of the series of abstract spaces (proper names without details) with descriptions of the job of a film projectionist, whose role is to switch from one particular roll of film to the next without the audience noticing, producing continuity. This is Tyler Durden's part-time job, thanks to a union that calls him when another worker is ill. On the space of a page, Palahniuk orchestrates a series of abstract spaces (airports, movie screens) and parts within these spaces (workers, frames of film), demonstrating how our ideological

11. Http://www.imsdb.com/scripts/Fight-Club.html.
12. Palahniuk, *Fight Club*, 26.
13. Http://www.imsdb.com/scripts/Fight-Club.html.

drive toward efficiency has created a world filled with indistinguishable and interchangeable elements: spaces, tools, humans. Our ideological engine produces this as a way of fulfilling its utopic vision, a series of interlocking, replaceable and duplicatable parts that work within equally interlocking, replaceable and duplicatable wholes.

The protagonist initially understands his prolonged exposure to such spaces as insomnia: his lack of particularity generates the feeling that nothing is real. Appropriating the utopic desire for banal identity, sharing in and reproducing it, works to undermine one's own sense of individuation: one loses one's self, and thus the ability to participate in a larger whole *as* one's self. The story targets such spaces with corresponding acts of violence with two implied goals. The first goal is an interruption of the relentless drive toward abstraction (the precondition for interchangeability) through the incorporation of the human body. Thus, Tyler incorporates single frames of pornography (depictions of the naked human body) into the interchangeable films that he screens, marking and particularizing them. In his job as a hotel caterer, Tyler urinates into the bland, mass produced meals (an echo of the single serving airplane food the narrator notes at the beginning) and thereby returns something particular and human into a process that has anonymous food prepared and delivered by anonymous hands to anonymous faces: *this* meal no longer is a copy of a copy. It is no longer indistinguishable from other meals. It has been made personal. Each of these actions particularizes social space and materials with the presence of what is finite, particular and embodied—with what is human.

Eventually, as the beginning of the story intimates, the resistance to such spaces becomes violent as Tyler replicates the logic of the ideology he set out to destroy. This begins as Durden uses the tools and models of the office industry as a way to promote fight club and Project Mayhem, as evidenced by an original that the protagonist leaves on the copy machine and the file folders that organize the targets Durden selects. The shaved heads and black suits of the "space monkeys" who participate in Project Mayhem becomes another variation of the corporate aesthetic (in which the semblance of difference emerges in a tie of a different color). Rather than encouraging particularization and individuation in opposition to an increasingly abstracted society, Durden duplicates the ideological drive toward organization and efficiency. The goal of Project Mayhem becomes another version of an abstract utopia in which no space can be distinguished from any other—the sole difference is Durden's desire to destroy current spaces, transforming the landscape into unproductive rubble. Although Durden may desire "global equilibrium," he achieves it only by eliminating hopes and forcing humanity to primitive levels of naked survival.

The only positive possibilities promised by this method occur in the attack on the narrator's home—a condominium filled with condiments and Swedish furniture that the movie shows as though it were still in a catalog, with the Dust Brothers supplying a version of the music one hears when on hold, or in an elevator. The explosion of the apartment and the destruction of the abstracted goods he had gathered therein push the narrator to call Tyler Durden and become his housemate, liberating the protagonist from an unfulfilling life that pursued one particular utopic vision. The implication that the movie toys with—but ultimately rejects—is that such a liberation could occur on a large scale order: the destruction of all abstract spaces would require that those humans comfortable with conforming to the demands of interchangeability find new homes in particular places. The movie undermines the viability of this solution by showing how the new "home" lacks the community that the narrator had hoped to find, as it is corrupted by an anarchic permutation of an abstracted and undifferentiated utopia. Thus, even though violence potentially interrupts ideological arcs by reminding us of our finitude and limitations, momentarily individuating us, it also runs the risk of replicating the situation of abstraction from which we would be "rescued." Further, the brute destruction of places or property seems an ill-suited strategy for restructuring society: because ideologies are reflected in their spaces on a vast level, undermining specific locations does little to create change. Ultimately, *Fight Club* points to the inadequacy of violence to alter society in a meaningful way.

Palahniuk provides an alternative model for understanding the transformation of society and the subversion of ideology, depicting groups who repurpose ideologically demarcated places for specific moments that allow particular communities to emerge and dissipate without remainder. After the initial scene that allows the story to be understood as a flashback, *Fight Club* begins in the interior spaces of churches (Trinity Episcopal and First Eucharist are the two names mentioned), but these spaces have been repurposed during those moments for support groups intended for those dealing with potentially fatal illnesses. The narrator embraces these groups, finding that "losing all hope was freedom," encountering a series of deaths and resurrections mediated through those experiences of community.[14] Although Christian churches frequently foreground the theme of death and resurrection, the narrator's experience of these themes arrives differently—it does not partake of the overarching ideology, but instead translates it into his body through the physical embrace of suffering flesh. The sacred power that provides the experience of death and rebirth is not *sacred* and does not

---

14. Palahniuk, *Fight Club*, 22.

emerge through a symbolic moment—although the symbols of death and resurrection are used to translate this sacred in a repurposed and atheistic sense.

Another example of this repurposed space is a bar whose basement hosts the fight clubs that the narrator starts with Tyler Durden. Palahniuk uses the same language of community, suffering and the sacred to illustrate what occurs within these basements: the scale of these spaces accumulates the longings of the fighters whose pugilism strikes the sacred. Once again, the narrator makes recourse to language familiar through Christian ideology, claiming "You aren't alive anywhere like you're alive at fight club . . . There's grunting and noise at fight club like at the gym, but fight club isn't about looking good. There's hysterical shouting in tongues like at church, and when you wake up Sunday afternoon you feel saved."[15] Both forms of community—the support groups and the fight clubs—allow individuals to partake of moments that interrupt their singularity, a suspension that allows for the inbreaking of a non-symbolically mediated sacred. Both erupt within social spaces that serve as anchors of Western ideologies—Christianity and consumerism—ideologies that are ignored or twisted in the experience of community.

The story of *Fight Club* demonstrates the ease with which the wrong lesson can be gleaned from a positive experience and turned to tragic ends. The experience of finitude found in the community of those forced to face death in particular moments of intimacy led to an active form of community, fight clubs, also designed to instill an experience of community by incarnating an awareness of physical frailty. This permutation installed the sacred in a place created within an ideologically determined zone, and improved upon the former group by being opened to the healthy and fit. The final expansion of this type of community sublated the intentionality that the fight clubs added, but neglected the necessity of the personal and particular. Although the avowed inclinations of Project Mayhem—equality and the subversion of ideologies of consumption—are perhaps laudable, the choice of violence indicates the sublation of what was accidental and not essential to the community caused by fight clubs.

The Varieties of No-Places

At this point, I want to deviate from the path that Palahniuk points toward, meditating on how to sustain community, avoiding the pitfalls revealed by Durden's reliance on violence. My goal is to sublate the successful

15. Ibid., 51.

incorporation of communities that exist at the co-mingled point of human frailty that emerged in the support groups with the notion of intentionality that comprised fight clubs, allowing such communities to emerge as emplaced possibilities, interrupting the singularity of others without negating their well-being through the violence caused by weapons or abstraction. My hope is that envisioning utopia as a series of no-places capable of interrupting ideological narratives will provide instances where I can produce communities in an edifying way, undermining the influence of ideology and expanding access to the non-symbolically mediated sacred that rests at the depth of human interactions.

My preference for community causes me to depart from Ricoeur's perspective, which was satisfied in allowing ideology and utopia to balance each other in mutual critique. Problematically, this tension allows societies to flourish at the expense of community. Therefore, as a conclusion, I will focus on how understanding utopia as the generation of no-places can serve as the work of hope for communities without promoting ideology or society. Sartre's discussion of the unique ways that humans produce small pockets of negativity—through an expectation that is disappointed—provides the theoretical foundation for my account. In *Being and Nothingness*, Sartre argues that pools of non-being are produced when we expect to see a friend in a café—but see *nobody* instead; similarly, I would like to argue that anticipating a confirmation of the actualization of ideology will reveal its failures, its fractures, the fallibility at its seams, creating pools of nothingness—no-places—in the ideological world around us.

Before clarifying what I mean by the production of no-places and how they might promote communities without generating a new ideology, I wish to discuss other permutations of no-spaces that flourish in our world today. In order to provide a schema that delineates the similarities and differences relative to their treatments of utopia, I will describe how they integrate the real with the imaginary. The first example of a no-place promotes the real at the expense of the imaginary, sacrificing all hope of the possibility of an ideal, stripping away illusion. Two types of inhabitants populate these no-places: those who enter into the place to preserve it from a position of power, and those who are taken into this place without clear explanation or justification and imprisoned. Such no-places have been given names: Auschwitz, Guantanamo Bay. Within these spaces, as Agamben has discussed, humans are stripped of their humanity and are transformed into bare life. Constructed without the possibility of hope, and without the pretext of law, these no-places actualize (in the most horrifying way) the utopic *telos* of a certain reductionist, calculating attitude toward power.[16]

The opposed type of no-place at odds with my vision is the site of absolute fantasy, the idealistic vision of a functional technotopia with everything in the right place. The inhabitants of this world occupy the impossibly perfect future and thus remain blind to geographical abominations like Detroit, the ruined wasteland that the implementation of a capitalist ideology (first Ford, then the housing collapse) leaves in its wake. True believers, these individuals rid themselves of hope as their understanding of the world reveals its plentitude. Put in terms of the concentration camp example, these individuals live as though they were the guards, but in actuality are the prisoners: ridding themselves of hope and access to the real world, they deprive themselves of the possibility of creating actual change in broken spaces that require healing.

A third type of space occurs as a paradoxical blend of the real and the imaginary through a successful incorporation of local geography into a purely ideological space. Such spaces are no-places as they abstract all particular features from the space, negating them in favor of an abstract, universal, ideological utopia. Fantasies like *Fight Club* focus on such spaces, as the blend of reality and fantasy found in retail spots is suited for fictional accounts. We willingly enter into such no-places: the stripmall with the fast food business, the friendly coffee chain and fashionable male clothing store. This negation of local particularity generated by conforming to ideological standards creates a departicularized space, a space that becomes no place and all places simultaneously. Each space is designed to offer the benefits of the universal, but the price of admission is a sacrifice of all particularity. We lose ourselves in order to enjoy ourselves within its confines.

In contrast to each of these spaces, I wish to offer a vision of utopia, of no-place, that rejects both real and ideological modalities in an embrace of hope through finitude. Gaining access to these spaces requires approaching space in a mode of skeptical expectation. In other words, rather than engaging in a hermeneutics of suspicion which would reject what appears in a desire to unmask it from terms outside of itself, a hermeneutics of skeptical expectation pushes into the space on its own terms to locate the limits of its success. Willing this perspective, one generates a pool of nothingness based on unmet expectations[17] and simultaneously finds within this space of nothingness, this no-place, a reservoir of hope. Put practically, instead

---

16. See Agamben, *State of Exception* and *Homo Sacer*, for a more robust explanation of this account.

17. See Sartre, *Being and Nothingness*, 53.

of either accepting the doctrines of the Christian Church as a given truth or rejecting them as antiquated myth, I appropriate this perspective to find spaces where Chistendom seems least successful, no-places overlooked both by those who immediately reject religion and by those who embrace it as already enacted. My perspective would hearken to dissenting voices within the tradition, ones that desire that the Church address the needs of the poor, the hungry, and the unjustly persecuted. These voices are often silenced in places and spaces, and thus only resonate in a no-place that I create. Accepting the viability of an ideology only in order to remain attuned to the limitations of its success, I locate new sources of hope that are neither real nor imaginary: they are possibilities that, for now, can only exist in this utopia.

Embracing this no-space, I locate places around me that serve as real anchors—even if they are merely transitory. I hearken to the confessions of finitude revealed to me at the margins of the real and the ideological, and reach out in community with those that I thereby identify. The event of this community, its occurrence, transforms the space around me into a new kind of place—much as the support groups transformed the space of the church into a community grounded on a different variety of the sacred. I perpetuate this no-space about me, welcoming others into its silence (which remains more comforting than the noisy babble of empty praise). I generate utopia in its most humble and finite sense, particularizing a no-place here and now—in this space, for these moments—and allow it to disappear without clinging to it.

The modern landscape provides individuals with frequent opportunities to practice dwelling utopically. For example, urban residents are often confronted with the sight of an artificially flattened landscape covered in black asphalt, illuminated with fluorescent bulbs that shine from aluminum poles onto the rainbows of automotive inhabitants. The first mode of utopian would be concerned with the *realpolitiks* necessary to perpetuate these conditions: indifferent to the networks of property value, I might speculate on exploiting an illegal workforce to construct such sites. The second mode of utopian would remain blissfully unaware of this setting, mediating this experience through technolgical marvels that make space magical: music flows from a digital device into a six surrounding speakers as I gaze at news from friends made instantly available to me on a tablet computer. The third mode of utopian would understand this space as familiar and comfortable, the harbinger of good products at low prices: parking lots are part of this world, making it convenient for me to enter into other familiar spaces—the bookstore, the restaurant, the coffee shop whose aisles (like the parking lot) are reproduced throughout the country: such spaces provide a homecoming to my departicularized self.

The type of utopia I promote looks to the not-real in a way that honors the topography of the place that was: I notice the sloped land beyond the flat asphalt reminiscent of what had once been a valley between rolling hills, I attend to grass occurring through gaps in asphalt, I notice the movement of water that longs to find its displaced bed. I find joy in native flowers that root themselves in the ditches surrounding spaces ideologies prefer. These remnants, these ghosts of the place that used to occur at this site, are neither imaginary (I can touch and smell them) nor wholly real (the place where they had dominion has been lost). These items are not symbols, for they do not participate in a whole that was, is, or is to come: instead, I with them form a community in a moment when my own fragile immanence is grasped and held in a new localization that has little to do with the centers of money and power. These are not symbols, for they do not point beyond themselves to something immaterial: they point only to the event of their growing, the ability to localize and concretize a new center, a new dance, a new movement, a new community.

This vision of utopia as a no-place produced within the failures of ideological spaces taken on their own terms is at odds with both a Foucauldian heterotopia and the habits of a Deleuzian nomadology.[18] I share the desire to transform spaces into sites that resist dominant powers, but wish to locate these spaces as new centers that interrupt and trouble the dominant flows of space *within* them instead of outside of them. Instead of travelling through a region, I remain emplaced within a community at that moment, lingering instead of wandering. Pausing allows me to enjoy the utopian community that emerges in my perception and attunement in response to my longing. Anchored in this hope, producing communities in no-places, I transform the world for moments at a time and offer those nearby me the gift of interrupting their singularities, perhaps momentarily reparticularizing them. I embrace the importance of finitude in my projection of these communities but do not resort to the violent subversions of Project Mayhem: instead, I offer my own self-aware admission of finitude, failure and physicality as an open gift that conjoins others as an entity greater than the sum of our parts—but existing in a no-place where the function of a mediating ideological or symbolic matrix has been obviated.

---

18. See Foucault, "Heterotopia"; Deleuze and Guattari, *A Thousand Plateaus*; and Casey, *The Fate of Place*.

The Sacred Depths of No-Places

Some view a secularized world, constructed after the death of God, as a place finally rid of the weight of childish traditions. Some view this same world as false, a veneer through which the living God continues to shine. Both of these views filter different experiences of the world as enabling different varieties of utopia—one anticipates the coming of the kingdom of technology and rationality, the other clings to the hopes of an arriving Messiah. Both of these views of God are powerful enough to provide an approximation of a universalized mode of symbolically mediated and fulfilling participation.

A third point of view neither embraces nor denies the death of God: instead, those with this perspective welcome the possibilities opened by embracing the presence of this death. They might explore the limits of this death, pushing beyond questions of factuality (did it happen?) to haptic facticity (where can I touch this death?), longing to feel where the infinite loss takes finite roots. Accepting that we no longer can question "what is God" or "who is God," I contentedly ask "where is God?" in anticipation of finding fragments of the sacred. Even mortal deaths leave echoes and traces of a past life that resonate long after the flesh has become reintegrated into the surrounding environment: so, too, might traces of God resonate after an announced demise. Instead of interpreting these traces as proof of life, or ignoring them as impossible given God's death, one embraces these fragments as reminders of our need to remain undeceived.

Toward the end of his essay "Of Divine Places," Jean-Luc Nancy argues that communities are crucial for maintaining the attitude that humans once had toward gods, the measure of mortality that reminds us of our limits. An experience of the infinite mediated by a transcendent, divine symbol has the power to awaken an awareness of our limitations, weaknesses, finitude, fallibility. We understand this most fully in the context of the presence of that which lacks these elements—the perfect divine being of a monotheistic religion. At the level of human experience, however, Nancy finds that—in communities—we are "exposed to each other in the same way as we could, together, be exposed to the gods. It is the same mode of presence, without the presence of the gods."[19] In a secularized world, it is paramount that we seek out places for community, for it is within these experiences (whether gathered around god's presence or god's absence) that we might find ourselves measured as we truly are. In other words, just as violence was unnecessary to the formation of community in *Fight Club*, so also is the presence of God unnecessary to the experience of the sacred within com-

---

19. Nancy, *The Inoperative Community*, 143.

munity. It is for this reason that Nancy commends us to "lead community toward this disappearance of the gods, which founds it and divides it from itself."[20] Communities allow a mode of exposure that reflects what occurred in the presence of the gods, although these gods now are absent: communities jointly perform this work of exposure.

Ideologies displace God, and provide humans with a larger version of themselves—augmented with the technological marvels of digital prosthetics, buttressed with the accumulated weight of revealed traditions. Finding a home in neither one nor the other of them, one might freely wander the world in search of places where communities might be gathered in the no-places of brokenness, a brokenness that provides a hope that lingers in a world where everything pretends to perfection.

As I walk, looking for a place where I might abide—if only for a moment, or collection of moments—in community with another, I pray. I do not pray to the community, and I do not pray to god. I pray instead at the place where I am. I do not need to know *who* God is, or *what* God is because these are questions for historical theologians. I only seek to know *where* God might be found—or, if not found, then where a remnant of God might still summon and found a fragile community. In this mode of praying, God becomes equivalent to the no-place where God still exists, the sum of the weaknesses that interrupt my singularity for an eternal moment. I pray to know God in no-place, through no-place, protecting God from the idols where ideologies incarcerate the divine.

As I walk, I pray with the protagonist of *Fight Club*, although not to Tyler. I pray:

> "May I never be complete.
> May I never be content.
> May I never be perfect."

Acknowledging my limitations, my imperfections, my incomplete nature, I pray that my singularity be removed from me and that the sacred be restored to the world from the no-places where it hides. And I pray that this be done within the secular world, now, here, nowhere, separated out from it in the hopes that one never completely erases the other.

BIBLIOGRAPHY

Agamben, Giorgio. *Homo Sacer*. Translated by Daniel Heller-Roazen. Stanford: Stanford University Press, 1998.

---

20. Ibid.

———. *State of Exception*. Translated by K. Attell. Chicago: University of Chicago, 2005.
Aquinas, Thomas. *The Summa Theologica*. Translated by the Fathers of the English Dominican Province. Chicago: Encyclopaedia Britannica, 1955.
Casey, Edward S. *The Fate of Place: A Philosophical History*. Berkeley: University of California Press, 1997.
Deleuze, Gilles, and Félix Guattari. *A Thousand Plateaus: Capitalism and Schizophrenia*. Translated by Brian Massumi. Minneapolis: University of Minnesota Press, 1987.
Fight Club. Dir. David Fincher. Perf. Brad Pitt, Edward Norton. Twentieth Century Fox Home Entertainment, 2002. DVD.
Foucault, Michel. "Of Other Spaces: Utopias and Heterotopias." Translated by Jay Miskowiec. http://web.mit.edu/allanmc/www/foucault1.pdf.
Heidegger, Martin. *The Question Concerning Technology, and Other Essays*. Translated by Albert Hofstadter. New York: Harper & Row, 1977.
Nancy, Jean-Luc. *The Inoperative Community*. Translated by Peter Connor et al. Minneapolis: University of Minnesota Press, 1991.
Palahniuk, Chuck. *Fight Club*. New York: W. W. Norton, 1996.
Ricœur, Paul. *From Text to Action: Essays in Hermeneutics, II*. Translated by Kathleen Blamey and John B. Thompson. Evanston, IL: Northwestern University Press, 1991.
Sartre, Jean-Paul. *Being and Nothingness: An Essay on Phenomenological Ontology*. Translated by Hazel Barnes. New York: Philosophical Library, 1956.
Turner, Victor. *The Ritual Process*. Ithaca, NY: Cornell University Press, 1977.

www.ingramcontent.com/pod-product-compliance
Lightning Source LLC
Chambersburg PA
CBHW050438240426
43661CB00055B/2436